Psychological Assessment of the Elderly

MEDICINE IN OLD AGE

Psychological Assessment of the Elderly

EDITED BY

John P. Wattis
MB ChB DPM MRCPsych
Senior Lecturer and Consultant in the
Psychiatry of Old Age, St James's
University Hospital, Leeds, UK

Ian Hindmarch
BSc PhD FBPsS
Head of Human Psychopharmacology
Research Unit,
Department of Psychology
University of Leeds, UK

CHURCHILL LIVINGSTONE
EDINBURGH LONDON MELBOURNE AND NEW YORK 1988

CHURCHILL LIVINGSTONE
Medical Division of Longman Group UK Limited

Distributed in the United States of America by
Churchill Livingstone Inc., 1560 Broadway, New
York, N.Y. 10036, and by associated companies,
branches and representatives throughout the world.

First published 1988

ISBN 0-443-03320-X

ISSN 0264-5602

British Library Cataloguing in Publication Data

Psychological assessment of the elderly. —
    (Medicine in the old age, ISSN 0264-5602).
    1. Geriatric psychiatry
    I. Wattis, John   II. Hindmarch, I.
    III. Series
    618.97'689   RC451.4.A5

Library of Congress Cataloging in Publication Data

Psychological assessment of the elderly.
    (Medicine in old age, ISSN 0264-5602)
    1. Aged — Psychology. 2. Aged — Testing.
I. Wattis, John, 1949-   . II. Hindmarch, I. (Ian),
1944–   .   III. Series. [DNLM: 1. Aged — psychology.
2. Psychological Tests — in old age.   WT 150 P9736]
HQ1061.P79   1988   155.67   87-22399

Produced by Longman Singapore Publishers (Pte) Ltd.
Printed in Singapore

Contributors

Stig Berg PhD
Professor of the Psychology of Ageing, Department of Geriatric Medicine and Longterm Care, Vasa Hospital, University of Gothenburg, S-411 Gothenburg, Sweden

Michael A Church BSc (Ord) BSc (Hons) MPhil
Top Grade Clinical Psychologist, Leicestershire Health Authority, Towers Hospital, Humberstone, Leicester LE5 OTD

Martin G Cole MD FRCP(C)
Director of Psychogeriatrics, St Mary's Hospital, 3830 Avenue Lacombe, Montreal, Quebec H3T 1MS, Canada; Associate Professor of Psychiatry, McGill University, Canada

John R M Copeland MA MD FRCP FRCPsych DPM
Professor and Head of Department of Psychiatry, University of Liverpool, PO Box 147, Liverpool L69 3BX; Director of Institute of Human Ageing, University of Liverpool

Jim T Eccles MB ChB MRCP
Consultant Physician in Medicine of the Elderly, St James's University Hospital, Beckett Street, Leeds LS9 7TF

Robert Golden PhD
Associate Professor, Center for Geriatrics and Gerontology, Columbia University, Faculty of Medicine, 100 Haven Avenue, 3–29F, New York, NY 10032, USA

Barry J Gurland MD
Director and John E Borne Professor of Clinical Psychiatry, Center for Geriatrics and Gerontology, Columbia University, Faculty of Medicine, 100 Haven Avenue, 3–29F, New York, NY 10032, USA

Roni Gurland DBO
Research Scientist, Center for Geriatrics and Gerontology, Columbia University, Faculty of Medicine, 100 Haven Avenue, 3–29F, New York, NY 10032, USA

Ian Hindmarch BSc PhD FBPsS
Head of Department, Human Psychopharmacology Research Unit, University of Leeds, Leeds LS2 9JT

Stuart A Montgomery BSc MD FRCPsych
Reader in Psychiatry, St Mary's Hospital Medical School, Praed Street, London W2 1NY

Christopher Q Mountjoy FRCPsych
Consultant Psychiatrist, St Andrew's Hospital, Northampton NN1 5DG; Honorary Senior Research Associate, Department of Psychiatry, University of Cambridge Clinical School, Cambridge

Lars Nilsson MD PhD
Physician-in-Chief, Department of Psychiatry, Vasa Hospital, University of Gothenburg, S-411 33 Gothenburg, Sweden

Anne H Pattie MA MSc DPhil
District Clinical Psychologist, York District Health Authority, Clifton Hospital, Clifton, York Y03 6RD

Alvar Svanborg MD PhD
Professor and Chairman, Department of Geriatric Medicine and Longterm Care, Vasa Hospital, University of Gothenburg, S-411 33 Gothenburg, Sweden

Jeanne A Teresi EdD PhD
Research Scientist, Center for Geriatrics and Gerontology, Columbia University, Faculty of Medicine, 100 Haven Avenue, 3–29F, New York, NY 10032, USA

John P Wattis MB ChB DPM MRCPsych
Senior Lecturer and Consultant in the Psychiatry of Old Age, St James's University Hospital, Beckett Street, Leeds LS9 7TF

David E Wilder PhD
Deputy Director, Center for Geriatrics and Gerontology, Columbia University, Faculty of Medicine, 100 Haven Avenue 3–29F, New York, NY 10032, USA

Contents

Introduction

One of the major social phenomena of the end of this century and the beginning of the next is the ageing of the population of the developed nations. The North Western European countries have led this increase, but other countries such as Australia and the USA are only a decade or two behind. The developing countries will face a similar challenge somewhere quite early in the next century. Grundy (1983) has described these world-wide demographic trends in some detail. In addition to the increasing number of old people the aged societies in North-western Europe face the ageing of the elderly population itself, with an increasing proportion of very old people. Further, the number of people in the middle-aged groups who provide most of the care is declining relative to the very elderly population (Wells 1979) and very old people have an especially high prevalence of disabling disorders, including dementia. They also often live alone in substandard accommodation and relative poverty. The challenge presented to all of us is enormous.

In the UK and the USA there has been a great deal of concern recently about the cost of our health and social services. One way of helping limit this cost would be to involve more fit old people in looking after their unwell peers. Within the existing medical and social services where, even in the UK with some degree of centralised planning and control, developments have been random and chaotic (Wattis et al 1981, Wattis & Arie 1984), there is a need for better planning and efficiency. There is also a need to evaluate the various new treatment strategies for mental illness in old age, especially the dementias, to ensure the best value for money. It is necessary to be able to describe and measure the needs of the population as well as to evaluate the quality of the services and the efficiency of the treatment. It is with the task of describing and measuring diseases, disabilities and the needs of old people that this book is largely concerned.

Measurement is fundamental to scientific endeavour. It is the means by which we compare one thing with another. In medicine, it helps us to test hypotheses about the classification of diseases, their outcome and the effects of treatment. The process of abstraction involved in standardised instruments inevitably results in some loss of information, but it is none the less essential if results are to be compared. In order to ensure the widest applicability of research findings, it is essential that workers, as far as possible, use a common language. A recent compilation of assessment instruments for old people (Israel et al 1984) lists over a hundred and twenty different scales, and briefly describes them, for the first time providing a relevant 'dictionary' of research language. In this book we have taken a more selective approach, aiming for a collection of original and authoritative essays by some of those at the frontiers of knowledge in this area. We have also included contributions on three major methodological issues: what is 'normal' in old age, the place of longitudinal (as against cross-sectional) studies, and the correlation between clinical ratings and pathology. The fundamental aim of all our endeavour is to help patients, and to ground this work in the clinical situation, we have included a chapter on psychological approaches to treatment.

USES OF INSTRUMENTS

Scales are often devised for relatively specific purposes. Despite this, if they prove serviceable, their use is frequently extended into overlapping fields. This seems desirable, since the comparison between different areas of work is then made more readily. At least three different fields of use for scales can be distinguished (Table 1.1).

Table 1.1　Uses of measuring instruments

Clinical	Differential diagnosis
	Placement of patients
	Identifying problems
	Measuring severity
	Quantifying response
Administrative	Measuring the burden of care
	Reallocating patients and resources
	Planning services and manpower
Research	Diagnostic practices
	Patterns of disease and outcome
	Behaviour-environment interaction
	Changing conditions of care
	Clinical trials
	Testing hypotheses about nature of disease.

Clinically scales can be used in several different ways, though a note of caution has been sounded against being too arrogant in our assumptions about the objectivity of our assessment (Muir Gray 1985). They may, like Hachinski's (1975) ischaemic scale, be used to assist in decisions about differential diagnosis. Hachinski's scale mixes historical data (for example, history of hypertension) with observations of current neurological and neuropsychiatric status to arrive at a score. A high score carries a probability of multi-infarct dementia, and a lower score carries a probability of

Alzheimer's-type dementia. This scoring system, initially verified on studies of regional cerebral blood flow, has subsequently been confirmed and modified by neuropathological studies (Rosen et al 1980). A diagnostic scale in the sphere of depressive illness is the Newcastle scale (Carney et al 1965). This also depends on a mixture of historical and cross-sectional data and is weakened by the considerable subjective element in scoring some of the data. Both these scales illustrate a dilemma in scales used to help differential diagnosis. It is easiest to ensure validity on observational data and hardest when dealing with historical data. The process of clinical diagnosis however depends heavily on historical data and so these factors must be taken into account when designing diagnostic scales. Validity in terms of reflecting 'real-life' diagnostic processes is thus at variance with the reliability of scoring. This discrepancy can be reduced by carefully defining historical data but this in turn may make the scale too cumbersome and time-consuming for regular use.

Some scales contribute to decisions as to where patients should be placed. The Clifton Assessment Procedure for the Elderly (CAPE, see Ch. 5) and the Crichton Royal Behavioural Rating Scale (Robinson 1961) are often used in this way. These scales, designed to be completed by nursing staff or other care-givers, list various aspects of behaviour and provide the rater with a choice of responses denoting varying degrees of severity. A range of such scales has been reviewed by Hall (1980). They can help identify discrepancies between one area of functioning and another, thus focussing therapeutic endeavours. They must be interpreted with caution since they do not measure all aspects of behaviour and largely ignore the effects of environment on behaviour.

Measurement of the severity of a disease may also be undertaken clinically and the shortened memory-information scale of Hodkinson (1972) is frequently used to assess the memory loss associated with dementia. Sometimes it is also used as a 'diagnostic scale' but this use can be misleading if a simple equation between score on the scale and diagnosis is assumed without taking into account clinical confounding factors such as the presence of physical illness or severe depression. In difficult cases of depression, too, some clinicians will use a rating scale (e.g. that of Montgomery & Asberg 1979, see Ch. 9) to provide a more objective measure of patient response to treatment.

Administratively scales may be used to measure the burden of care and how it is distributed, resulting in moves to rationalise care by grouping patients with similar problems. The CAPE has been used in this way. The disability levels in different age groups can be measured and used, in conjunction with demographic data, to predict the needed provision of services for the future. Sometimes cohort effects can interfere with these predictions and this needs to be considered when interpreting data from such studies. Longitudinal as well as cross-sectional studies are necessary to allow fully for cohort effect (see Ch. 4). Ratings of disability can also be used, in conjunction with predetermined standards of care and work study methods, to predict staffing needs of various groups of patients. Wilkinson and Graham-White's (1980) Psychogeriatric Dependency Scale uses as the chief measure of dependency, the nursing time needed, and could be the basis for this kind of work. Such scales can also be abused to justify low levels of nursing staff, either by failing to set a suitable standard of care or by slipshod methodology (Wattis et al 1986).

Research into diagnostic practices, patterns of disease and outcome is facilitated by instruments like the CORE/CARE and Geriatric Mental State Schedules (GMS) (see Chs. 7, 8). The Hospital Anxiety Depression scale (HAD) (Zigmond & Snaith 1983) has been used as a measure of anxiety and depression among old people in a general practice population and its association, independent of major physical illness, with disability or a restricted life style (Rose 1985). Scales of this type enable clinical findings to be quantified. They may sometimes be too long for general clinical use, but the principles underpinning such work can also serve to improve the quality of clinical assessment. Behavioural rating scales can be used to explore the inter-relationship between environment and behaviour and for research into changing conditions of care for old people (Wilkin et al 1978). Relevant scales can be used to measure the outcome of clinical trials or the effects of psychological interventions. In this sort of usage, it is especially important that we recognise the limitations of scales. In one demented patient whom we treated we found no measurable improvement on the Crichton Royal Behavioural Rating Scale but the spouse reported a marked decrease in the frequency of previously noted episodes of evening confusion. This improvement was not within the competency of the scale and in a research study this might have been marked as a treatment 'failure', thus missing what was, to the wife, a highly significant lessening of the burden of care. Scales, especially those which selectively measure different psychological functions, may be used to evaluate hypotheses about the nature of disease, for example the relationship between alcoholic brain damage and 'premature ageing' (Shelton et al 1984).

CHARACTERISTICS OF INSTRUMENTS

Instruments can be classified in several complementary ways: purpose, derivation, specificity, content, type, duration and rater.

Purpose and applicability are the first to consider. An instrument designed for research purposes may nevertheless, in shortened form, find wide clinical applicability. Good examples of this are the survey form of the CAPE and Hodkinson's abbreviation (1972) of the Memory Information and Orientation Scale of Blessed and his colleagues (1968). Although scales can often be used for purposes other than those for which they were originally designed, caution must be exercised in such translocations. The problems of using severity scales as if they were diagnostic scales must again be stressed. Blessed, Tomlinson and Roth's scale was never intended to be used diagnostically. Unfortunately, Hodkinson's modification has tended to be so used. Other scales which often fall victim to this perversion of purpose are those designed to measure severity of depression.

Historical derivation is an important consideration. Most scales are built on the foundation and modification of earlier work. Sometimes this modification is intended to make a scale more applicable in a different language or culture. This may simply mean the substitution of an alternative word for 'blue' meaning 'sad' in English versions of American scales such as the Zung Self-Rating Depression Scale (1965) or may involve more complicated linguistic or cultural changes. Scales may be derived from other scales by shortening and other changes designed to improve their use. The behavioural rating scale of the CAPE was derived from the Stockton Geriatric Rating Scale (Meer & Baker 1966) in this way. The monumental work of Israel et al (1984) lists the derivation and inspiration of many instruments. In some cases, sophisticated statistical methods may be used to reduce the number of questions in a test (e.g. Hodkinson 1972) or increase their specificity. Cole (Ch. 7) used such methods to ensure that his battery of tests conformed to his theoretical hierarchical model.

Specificity indicates how far an instrument applies to a particular group, in our case, old people. The most specific tests are those derived especially for a target population but tests derived for a different population may still be applicable, although this needs to be tested out. Not only age but also sex, type of residence and many other factors may limit the applicability of a scale to a different population. A scale derived in hospital may, for instance, be biased towards measuring severe levels of disability and may therefore lose sensitivity in a less disabled outpatient population.

The *content* of instruments has been classified by Israel et al (1984) as mental, physical or social, or some mixture of these. Mental phenomena commonly measured in instruments used with old people are cognition, behaviour and mood. Measures of physical disability in this field are normally concerned with problems that will cause a demand on informal care-givers or services. The social dimension concerns interaction with others and cannot really be separated from behavioural aspects of mental state. Some scales have a very mixed content including, for example, mood, cognition and behaviour. Unless these can be separated from one another in analysis, such scales are not really suitable for basic research and can be misleading in other situations. The Hospital Anxiety Depression Scale (Zigmond & Snaith 1983) has attempted to avoid this trap by concentrating on the emotional aspects of anxiety and depression. It is currently being validated in an elderly population. Ideally all scales should measure only one characteristic of the target population or, if they measure more than one characteristic, the scoring system should allow these to be separated from each other. The characteristic measured should also have a clear relationship to a practical clinical or research problem.

The *type* of instrument that may be used varies from what is in effect a structured clinical interview with rules and a format for recording the outcome (GMS, Ch. 7) to a simple test which the patient has to perform (Isaacs & Akhtar 1972). Between these extremes there are check lists which allow only a single alternative answer to each question, and questionnaires with several appropriate answers. The answers to these tests are recorded on scales which may be of three types: nominal (membership or non-membership of a class), ordinal (enabling grading or ranking of severity) or interval (with equal intervals between the points on a scale). Sometimes in analysing results the mistake is made of using statistical techniques intended for interval scales in the analysis of ordinal data.

In instruments to be used directly with old people *duration* is an important variable. Tests that are too long may be biased by fatigue effects unless they are administered in parts of manageable duration. Scales that have to be completed by busy professionals are also more likely to be used properly if kept to a reasonable length. On the other hand, in specific research projects the need for depth of information may justify much longer procedures provided the staff are available to administer them.

The final variable in classification of instruments is *who is intended to use them*. Self-rating scales have an inherent attractiveness in eliminating the possible bias introduced by an external observer. However, with ill old people, they are rarely applicable. The depressed patient may not be motivated, and the demented patient may be cognitively incapable of completing a rating schedule. Rating by an observer is therefore generally preferred, though some instruments (e.g. the Beck Depression Inventory) (Beck & Beamsdorfer 1974) have been designed for both self- and observer rating and short self-report scales have been used in a research study of patients admitted to hospital with depression (Gilleard et al 1981). When an observer method is used, the degree of skill and specialist training required varies from test to test. The Montgomery & Asberg Scale (Ch. 9) and the CAPE (Ch. 5) have both been designed to be fairly robust in the hands of workers with relatively little training, whilst the GMS (Ch. 7) requires special training, ideally superimposed on basic professional training.

DESIRABLE FEATURES OF INSTRUMENTS

Validity

Perhaps the most important technical requirement of any instrument is that it should be valid: it should measure what it sets out to measure and nothing else. *Face* validity is a commonsense evaluation. Does the scale appear to correspond with everyday experience? *Construct* validity is concerned with how well the results of a scale fit in with theoretical concepts. If the originator of an instrument believes that there is a dichotomy between milder neurotic forms of depression and severer psychotic forms he will be concerned to see whether the results of his instrument support that dichotomy. The Newcastle scales (Carney et al 1965) for the assessment of depression are based on just such an assumption, though the underlying assumption has been challenged by others (Kendell 1976). The depressive element of Zigmond and Snaith's (1983) HAD scale is based on the premise that the essential feature of severe depression is loss of the capacity to experience pleasure.

Concurrent validity is concerned with correspondence between an instrument and others intended to measure the same phenomenon. One of the present authors, with his colleagues, has shown a correspondence between scores on a shortened version of the Crichton Royal Behavioural Rating Scale and the behavioural rating scale of the CAPE (unpublished work). Eastwood et al (1983) have published a comparison of three brief clinical tests for assessing dementia. There is great scope for further research work in comparing and refining different scales.

External validity is a more sophisticated version of face validity. External criteria such as a physicians' diagnosis or assessment of severity are used to check out the validity of an instrument. One early study compared the results of a battery of tests with EEG findings suggestive of dementia and selected Raven's Progressive Matrices, the Face Hand Test, Names Learning and Orientation tests as the best of the seven tests evaluated (Irving et al 1970).

Predictive validity describes an instrument's ability to predict outcome. Roth's (1955) original diagnostic criteria for different disease entities, and the CAPE (Pattie & Gilleard 1979) were validated in this way.

Reliability

This measures how reproducible the results of an instrument are. Reliability can be measured between different raters, which is important if more than one rater is to be used in a scientific study or if the results of one study are to be compared with another. It may be measured between the same rater rating the same subject, on different occasions (test–retest reliability), though here comparison can be confounded if the subject has changed. Reliability has also been tested by measuring the results on one part of an instrument against the results of another part of the instrument (internal consistency). This last method is not easily applicable to instruments which are designed to measure several different functions.

Sensitivity

Sensitivity is concerned with an instrument's ability to detect differences between two individuals or changes in an individual over time. To some extent it is in competition with test–retest reliability. The more sensitive an instrument, the more likely it is to show variation between two occasions of testing. The diagnostic clinical interview, which is usually highly sensitive, is extremely difficult to reproduce over time or between different raters, though structured interview schedules such as the GMS go some way in this direction. Some instruments have been designed with the object of maximising sensitivity whilst retaining reliability (Montgomery & Asberg 1979).

Essentially this is an unsolvable conundrum and researchers and clinicians alike have to choose those instruments which have the best balance of reliability and sensitivity for their particular purpose.

Breadth of application

This is another highly desirable feature for instruments, though it is not often noted. A highly specific instrument designed for a particular environment and purpose may be valid, reliable and sensitive. In some cases, such an instrument may be needed. However, if results are to be compared between different situations and workers, such an instrument is likely to be too inflexible. The search is therefore for instruments which retain their validity, reliability, and sensitivity whilst being sufficiently 'portable' for general application. Unfortunately such instruments are often unduly long, and again a compromise has to be made between general applicability and length. There is a need for further research comparing the validity, reliability, sensitivity, ease of use and breadth of application of the many current scales to determine their relative merits and to point the way for future developments.

SPECIAL PROBLEMS IN OLD AGE

Cultural and educational values can confound the results when cross-sections of populations in different age groups are compared at one point in time. This has been one reason for the controversy about whether intelligence declines with age. Longitudinal studies suggest that any such decline in the well elderly is much less marked than appeared from simple cross-sectional studies (Ch. 4). Also, a global concept like 'intelligence' contains many components, which may behave differently with increasing age. A concept of what is 'normal' in old age is therefore absolutely vital (Ch. 3).

Changing patterns of disease in old people sometimes make instruments designed for a younger population inapplicable. GMS data, for example, show that elderly depressives have relatively more retardation and somatic preoccupation than their younger counterparts. In addition, the frequency of physical illness amongst non-depressed people rises with increasing age. The association between mental illness and physical health has been explored by Maule et al (1984). A scale such as the Hamilton Rating Scale for Depression (Hamilton 1967), with its heavy emphasis on somatic symptoms and hypochondriacal complaints, might give a spuriously high score in the relatively mildly depressed old person. For this reason, scales such as the Montgomery Asberg and the Hospital Anxiety Depression scale may be more useful in old age.

Many tests designed initially for the well younger person prove too time-consuming for use in an ill elderly population. The Wechsler Adult Intelligence Scale (WAIS 1955, 1981), for example, has to be administered by a psychologist and requires an hour to an hour and a half to complete. This is beyond the limit of tolerance for many ill, and some well, old people, and so shortened forms for aged persons have been developed (Brittan & Savage 1966).

A problem for behavioural scales is that they assess behaviour in a context but the scores are often wrongly interpreted as absolute values. A demented old woman at home may be doubly incontinent, poorly mobile, and apparently unable to dress herself. This could produce a high score on a standard scale, suggesting that she was 'too deteriorated' for a residential home for old people. However, in a controlled environment, with regular medication for arthritis, the patient's mobility and hence her ability to dress herself and become continent may return. This phenomenon is also seen in the 'Jekyll and Hyde' syndrome (Boyd & Woodman 1978) where an elderly person admitted to hospital appears well and good tempered but at home is rendered bad-tempered and apparently severely disabled by family interactions. A patient suffering from chronic depression may be looked after by relatives and her 'role' in the family taken over. If she is restored to health, the family structure may no longer be able to accommodate this without help, and so she may be forced back into her depressed 'role' even though her depression is biochemically better (Wattis & Church 1986). Again, any rating of depression that depends on external behaviour will produce different results in the hospital and home contexts. In planning care situations by using behavioural rating scales, one of the paradoxes we have to face is that shifting a patient to a unit with a higher staff ratio can produce a significant improvement in the patient, perhaps to the extent that she is no longer judged to need such intensive care! However, remove that extra care, and the patient will revert to her previously higher level of disability. The mnemonic equation 'Behaviour = Person × Environment' will help us to remember the importance of environment.

Screening of elderly populations to detect mental illness presents special problems. Postal surveys must be followed up by personal visits to non-responders, as this group is likely to contain a higher proportion of ill people than responders. Screening instruments tend to misclassify a proportion of the 'normal' population as ill when their sensitivity is adjusted to pick out the majority of those who are genuinely ill (Savage & Britton 1967). A follow-up study using a more refined (and time-consuming) assessment, of those initially classified abnormal by such a screening instrument, is therefore usually needed.

CONCLUSION

The ideal instrument to measure the psychological state of an old person would measure a wide range of functions: cognition, mood, other aspects of mental state, and behaviour in the social context. The struture of the instrument would also allow these elements to be analysed separately. The instrument would be short, valid, reliable, sensitive and easily administered by any professional with the minimum of training. It would be robust to changes in culture, language and age group. It would yield data of equal value to the clinician, the administrator, and the researcher. It would correlate well with other, more specialised assessments. Needless to say it does not exist and probably never will. Perhaps what we can hope for, though, is a relatively small and highly selected group of tests of different derivations and application but all correlating well one with another. In this book we have concentrated on a few of the most promising candidates for such a collection and invited contributions from those who have been intimately involved in the design and evolution of these instruments.

REFERENCES

Beck A T, Beamsdorfer A 1974 Assessment of depression: the depression inventory. In: Pichot P (ed) Psychological measurements in psychopharmacology. Modern Problems in Pharmacopsychiatry 7, Karger, Basel 151–169.

Blessed G, Tomlinson B E, Roth M 1968 The association between quantitative measures of dementia and senile change in the grey matter of elderly people. British Journal of Psychiatry 114: 797–811

Boyd R V, Woodman J A 1978 The Jekyll and Hyde syndrome. Lancet 2 (8091) 671–672

Britton P G, Savage R D 1966 A short form of the WAIS for use with the aged, British Journal of Psychiatry 112: 417–418

Carney M W P, Roth M, Garside R F, 1965 The diagnosis of depressive syndromes and the prediction of ECT response. British Journal of Psychiatry 111: 659–674

Eastwood M R, Lautenschlaeger E, Corbin S 1983 A comparison of clinical methods for assessing dementia. Journal of the American Geriatric society 31: 342–347

Gilleard C J, Willmot M, Vaddadi K S 1981 Self-report measures of mood and morale in elderly depressives. British Journal of Psychiatry 138: 230–235

Grundy E, 1983 Demography and old age. Journal of the American Geriatric Society 31(6): 325–332

Hachinski V C, Illiff L D, Zilka E, Du Bonlay G H, McAllister V L, Marshall J, Russell R W R, Symon L 1975 Cerebral blood flow in dementia. Archives of Neurology 32: 632–637

Hall J N 1980 Ward rating scales for long stay patients: a review. Psychological Medicine 10: 227–288

Hamilton M 1967 Development of a rating scale for primary depressive illness. British Journal of Social and Clinical Psychology 6: 278–296

Hodkinson W H M 1972 Evaluation of a mental test score for assessment of mental impairment in the elderly. Age and Ageing 1: 233–238

Irving G, Robinson R A, McAdam W 1970 The validity of some cognitive tests in the diagnosis of dementia. British Journal of Psychiatry 117: 149–156

Isaacs B, Akhtar A J, 1972 The set test: a rapid test of mental function in old people. Age and Ageing 1: 222–226

Israel L, Kozarevic D, Sartorius N 1984 Source book of geriatric assessment (2 vols) Karger/WHO, Basel

Kendell R E 1976 The classification of depression: a review of contemporary confusion. British Journal of Psychiatry 129: 15–28

Maule M M, Milne J S, Williamson J 1984 Mental illness and physical health in older people. Age and Ageing 13: 349–356

Meer B, Baker J A 1966 The Stockton Geriatric Rating Scale. Journal of Gerontology 21: 392–403

Montgomery S A, Asberg M 1979 A new depression scale Designed to be sensitive to change. British Journal of Psychiatry 134: 382–389

Muir Gray J A, March 1 1985 The myth of objective assessment. Community Care, Business Press International, Sutton, Surrey

Pattie A H, Gilleard C J 1979 Manual of the Clifton Assessment Procedures for the Elderly (CAPE). Hodder and Stoughton, London

Robinson R A 1961 Some problems of clinical trials in elderly people. Gerontologia Clinica 3: 247–257

Rose T 1985 Mood disorder and dysfunction in the elderly. Unpublished MMedSci thesis, Leeds University.

Rosen W A, Terry R D, Fuld P A et al 1980 Pathological verification of the ischaemic score, Annals of Neurology 7: 486–488

Roth M 1955 The natural history of mental disorder in old age. Journal of Mental Science, 101: 281–301

Savage R D, Britton P G 1967 A short scale for the assessment of mental health in the community aged. British Journal of Psychiatry 113: 521–523

Shelton M D, Parsons O A, Leber W R 1984 Verbal and visuospatial performance in male alcoholics: a test of the premature ageing hypothesis. Journal of Consulting and Clinical Psychology 52: 200–206

Wattis J P, Arie T H D 1984, Further developments in psychogeriatrics in Britain. British Medical Journal 289: 778

Wattis J P, Church M 1986 Practical psychiatry of old age, Croom Helm, London, pp 59–60

Wattis J P, Wattis F E, Arie T H D 1981, Psychogeriatrics: a national survey of a new branch of psychiatry. British Medical Journal 282: 1529–1533

Wattis J P, Rix K J, Collins D 1986 How many nurses do we need? — standards or pseudo work-study. Bulletin of Royal College of Psychiatrists 10: no. 10

Wechsler D 1955 Manual for the Wechsler Adult Intelligence Scale. Psychological Corporation, New York

Wechsler D 1981 WAIS-R Manual. The Psychological Corporation, Harcourt Brace Jovanovich, New York

Wells N E J 1979 Dementia in old age. Office of Health Economics, London

Wilkin D, Jolley D. Masiah T 1978 Changes in behavioural characteristics of elderly populations in local authority homes and long stay hospital wards 1976–77. British Medical Journal 2: 1274–1276

Wilkinson I, Graham-White J 1980 Edinburgh Psychogeriatric Dependency Rating Scale. In Israel L, Kozarevic D, Sartorius N (eds) Source book of geriatric assessment Karger/WHO, Basel

Zigmond A S, Snaith R P 1983 The Hospital Anxiety and Depression Scale. Acta Psychiatrica Scandinavica 67: 361–370

Zung W W K 1965 A self-rating depression scale. Archives of General Psychiatry 12: 63–70

What is normal in the elderly?

INTELLIGENCE AND AGEING

Although there is debate about the meaning of intelligence tests, their results are widely used for comparison of individuals and groups within the population. When applied to different age groups, a 'classical ageing pattern' has emerged (Botwinick 1977). This consists of a decline in the scores of tests that measure performance or psychomotor skills, and involve speed, conceptualisation and physical manipulation. The elderly compare equally with young adults on the vocabulary parts of intelligence tests, and it is thought that verbal abilities decline relatively little with advancing age (Crandall 1980). Heron and Chown (1967) confirmed this sparing of vocabulary scores with ageing, compared with consistent and marked decline in all other areas. In their study of people aged 20 to 79 years, they found that age effects on some test performances began earlier than others. Performance on the Perceptual Mazes and Raven's Progressive Matrices began to decline by thirty, a decline which accelerated in the sixties and seventies. Digit coding declined from the fifties onwards. However, some tests including Digit Span, Memory for Designs and Trail Making showed little alteration until the sixties and seventies, when a marked decline occurred (Davies 1967, 1968).

Many other studies have shown how selective these age effects are, and how variable according to the particular test used (Davison 1974a, Rabbitt 1977, Welford 1977). There seems to be a general agreement, however, that there is a decline in motor performance skills from at least the forties, appearing very marked by the sixties (Klove 1974, Welford 1958). Age effects on learning processes are well-documented, from animal and human studies, and they demonstrate at least two areas of decline with age: 1) a need for more time to absorb the information presented to the subject with increased age; and 2) a deterioration in the 'encoding' of adequate information within the memory (Arenberg & Robertson-Tchabo 1977). It is well established that short-term memory is markedly affected by ageing. What is less well known is that long-term memory is also affected. Whether or not the short-term memory impairment is more marked than the long-term memory impairment is debatable, because of methodological problems. What is clear, however, is that older subjects are poorer than younger ones at recalling and recognizing events from the past, and that the notion that memory for remote events is unimpaired in the elderly should now be rejected. According to Craik (1977) the evidence for the idea of a well-preserved remote memory in the elderly was entirely anecdotal, and has now been contradicted by three independent investigations. The defects in the memory of the elderly are, however, overshadowed by the relatively greater impairment of reaction time (Crandall 1980) and the selective deterioration in the performances of tasks which require 'immediate adaptive intelligence' (Reed & Reitan, 1963).

PSYCHOLOGICAL EVALUATION AND AGEING

There are many methodological problems involved in studying the mental performance of the elderly on a large scale (Huppert 1982). One problem is the source of the study population, which may include volunteers (Heron & Chown 1967), members of senior citizens' clubs (Plutchik et al 1978), residents in retirement communities (Pfeffer et al 1982), residents in social services' homes for the elderly (Gilleard & Pattie 1977), hospital clinic patients and referrals from certain sections of the community (Pfeffer et al 1984) and hospital in-patients (Stonier 1974). The studies quoted have added a great deal to our knowledge of mental functioning in elderly people, but none of the groups examined are truly representative of the 'normal elderly'. An example of this is the social services' residential home, now shown to have a very high percentage of mentally impaired residents (Wilkin et al 1982). The elderly in any one geographical area will include both healthy, and also physically and mentally impaired, subjects, and the question of whether or not to separate the healthy ones to examine is difficult, as it immediately involves the investigation in the grey area of mild dementia versus the mental impairment of ageing.

Any investigator who is used to elderly hospital patients and their abilities will be surprised to discover just how mentally well-preserved the elderly are in the general population, as hospital in-patients are the most unrepresentative group of all. Studies of the elderly living at home are the most representative, even though they do not include the small minority who are in residential or hospital care. Few large-scale community-based studies of the elderly have been done in the UK, in the field of mental impairment. For the classic study of the elderly in Wolverhampton, Sheldon (1948) took a random sample from the register of ration cards then in operation, and conducted house-to-house surveys based on this sample. Of this highly representative group he classified 81.8% as mentally normal, 11.2% as slightly mentally impaired, 3.2% as eccentric but intelligent and 3.8% as mentally ill. Another large survey of the elderly at home by Hobson and

Pemberton (1955) revealed 4% of subjects to be suffering from dementia, but a remarkably high incidence of anxiety or depression (on simple questioning) of 25% of men and 50% of women. The disadvantages of cross-sectional surveys when looking for age-related changes have been pointed out by several authors (Bromley 1966, Lorge 1957, Welford 1958). Cross-sectional studies may show some differences between age strata that are not due to age alone, but may be influenced by a different level of education, a different nutritional history, and differences in culture and life experience (Huppert 1982). There are some examples of the re-testing of the mental abilities of the aged. Eisdorfer (1963) re-tested 165 aged volunteers using the WAIS test battery, and found little evidence of overall decline in performance after 3 years. Unfortunately it has not been practical for most investigators to attempt any large-scale longitudinal mental assessment of the elderly.

The elderly may perform less well in psychological testing because of reduced motivation and drive, although if these do decline with age, it may be partly because of the expectations of society (Cowdry 1939). A variety of sensory factors may affect the elderly subject's performance of psychological tests, including impairment of hearing (Corso 1977). Herbst and Humphrey (1980) found that 60% of their sample of people over 70 living at home had impaired hearing, but that an apparent association between deafness and dementia was due to age alone. Age-related changes in the central nervous processing of speech may also play a role in causing problems of impaired speech perception in the elderly, though there is still not enough evidence to be certain of this (Bergman 1980). Age-related deterioration in vision and visual perception may occur (Fozzard et al 1977) and may influence the performance of a wide variety of psychological tests. Screening tests are not as satisfactory as an ophthalmological examination for this purpose (Chamberlain 1973). The subject's general health may be a very important determinant of the performance of intelligence tests, and may be more closely related to performance than is the subject's chronological age (Anastasi 1968). A theory of 'critical loss', where a terminal decline in intelligence occurs in the elderly shortly before death, was recently questioned by Steuer et al (1981), though they did find a relationship between the presence of organic brain syndrome and subsequent mortality.

Ageing may selectively affect those aspects of intelligence situated in the non-dominant cerebral hemisphere (Klisz 1978), and this may be reflected in the impaired performance of perceptual tests with ageing (Walsh 1976). This may lead to difficulties in determining the presence of organic brain syndromes, which could mistakenly be attributed to an elderly subject if normal values obtained for younger subjects were used (Schaie & Schaie 1977). When localised organic brain damage occurs, the age at which it occurs may influence recovery (Davison, 1974b). Finally, it is also important to recognise that differences between the sexes may co-exist with age effects. For example, older subjects exhibit poorer verbal and non-verbal processing, but non-verbal processing may be less effective in women, a difference which becomes more marked in older age groups (Elias & Kinsbourne 1974).

DEMENTIA AND AGEING

The Royal College of Physicians' College Committee on Geriatrics (1981) defined dementia as the global impairment of higher cortical function including memory, the capacity to solve the problems of day-to-day living, the performance of learned perceptuo-motor skills, the correct use of social skills and control of emotional reactions, in the absence of gross clouding of consciousness. The condition is described as often irreversible and progressive. The Royal College reported the results of several cross-sectional surveys, with a prevalence of definite dementia of between 5 and 7.1% of people over 65. The prevalence rate of dementia rises from about 2% at the age of 65–70 to around 20% in those over the age of 80. Mild dementia was found to be much more vaguely defined, and estimates of its prevalence ranged from 5 to 53%. The Royal College report noted that one study of mild dementia found that only one-third progressed to definite dementia in 3 years, whereas most of those who developed dementia had previously been categorised as normal. This must raise the possibility that 'mild dementia' is capable of being confused with normal ageing processes, or with so-called 'benign senescent forgetfulness'. The pathological changes involved in the definite cases of dementia are mostly either Alzheimer's disease or multiple cerebral infarctions. Large surveys in several countries suggest that Senile Dementia, Alzheimer's Type (SDAT) is more common than 'arteriosclerotic dementia' and is more common in females.

When the physician is faced with a confused elderly patient, his most urgent task is to detect, diagnose and treat acute confusional states, which may be difficult to distinguish from dementia if no history is available. As Hodkinson (1973) reported, these acute confusional states may have some very treatable and reversible primary causes, such as pneumonia, cardiac failure and urinary infection. Depression also showed an association with toxic confusional states in Hodkinson's study. A variety of screening tests have been devised to detect mental confusion in the elderly, including the ten-question abbreviated Royal College of Physicians score (Hodkinson 1972), and the set test (Isaacs & Akhtar 1972). Some tests have attempted to assess physical and social functioning as well as mental function (Gilleard & Pattie 1977, Pfeffer et al 1981). Investigators who have worked with the elderly have made the point that some tests are more suitable for use with the elderly than others (Lloyd Evans 1976), and have suggested that simpler, shorter and less fatiguing tests which correlate well with larger, standard psychological tests would be more useful for the elderly (Denham & Jeffreys, 1972; Schaie & Schaie 1977). As an example of this, Isaacs and

Akhtar (1972) demonstrated that the set test correlated highly with standard psychological tests, including the Mill Hill Vocabulary Scale and Raven's Progressive Coloured Matrices. Isaacs and Walkey (1964) have combined a mental status questionnaire with a constructional test as an extended but still very short assessment of general mental function in the elderly.

PSYCHOLOGICAL TESTS FOR USE WITH STROKE PATIENTS

Critchley (1962) described various syndromes of higher motor and sensory impairment which may occur following stroke, and which he associated with damage to the parietal lobes of the brain. He described tactile inattention, astereognosis, constructional apraxia, impairment of body image, unilateral visual neglect and colour agnosia. Disorders of higher perception, such as tactile inattention, unilateral neglect and impaired body image, have been associated with a poorer prognosis for recovery and with increased difficulty in rehabilitation (Adams & Hurwitz 1963, Knapp 1959). It has therefore become possible to determine prognosis by the use of neuropsychological tests with stroke patients (Meier & Resch 1967), and even quite simple tests such as the pen/key test for visual inattention and the shape sorting box have proved valuable for this purpose (Isaacs & Marks 1973)* Agnosia and apraxia detected by such tests have correlated with difficulties in performing actual activities of daily living in occupational therapy sessions following stroke (Fox 1969). Andrews et al (1980) have shown that poor performance of picture drawing tests can be impressively associated with increased mortality, morbidity, confusion, depression, hemianopia, incontinence, immobility and pressure sores following stroke.

The side of the cerebral lesion is relevant, since perceptual problems are more pronounced in non-dominant (usually right) hemisphere lesions. As Andersen (1951) put it: patients with dominant hemisphere damage forget what to do, but patients with non-dominant hemisphere damage forget how to do. These laterality differences are therefore reflected in the prognosis, with a relatively more impaired recovery from left hemiparesis (Adams & Merrett, 1961). In patients with agnosia, as demonstrated by simple tests such as drawing, or the construction of a felt body, the localisation of lesions in the right occipito-parietal cortex has been demonstrated by arteriography, neurosurgery and at post-mortem examination (McFie et al 1950). It has also been demonstrated by electrical stimulation (Fried et al 1982).

One of the great founders of neuropsychology, Aleksandre Luria (1970, 1973), has described the sensory processes situated in cortical areas of primary, secondary and tertiary perception. Andrews (1978) described these

---

* The pen/key test examines the ability to follow an object into an area of hemianopia; the shape sorting box test involves selecting and placing 3-dimensional shapes into matching slots.

three sensory areas with the example of a pencil held in the hand: the primary area recognises a sensation of touch, the secondary area recognises the shape and texture sensation as that of a pencil, and the tertiary area correlates the information with information from other areas and recognises it as the pencil which belongs to a friend. Areas of primary, secondary and tertiary perception exist for tactile sensation, sight and hearing. The consideration of sensation at these three levels shows that higher sensory deficits should not be diagnosed if primary sensory function has not been carefully examined first. In the elderly, a variety of mental and physical factors may affect the performance of perceptual tests (Benton & Van Allen 1972, McMenamin 1976). An example of this is the impairment of vision and hearing commonly found in the elderly (Williamson et al 1964). Ageing itself may appear to be associated with impaired performance of perceptual tests (Hertzog et al 1976). Sex differences are also seen in the results of perceptual tests (Cohen et al 1977). Several investigators have made the case for simple perceptual tests for use with the elderly (Andrews et al 1980, Cohen et al 1977). In their excellent guide to perceptual tests for use with stroke patients, Siev and Freishtat (1976) advise the use of a mental status questionnaire when considering the usefulness of perceptual testing, and suggest that a score of less than 20 out of 40 for the set test indicates that perceptual test results may not be valid, because of the degree of general mental impairment. They pointed out that very few of the objective perceptual tests have been standardised for adult populations.

A STUDY OF NEUROPSYCHOLOGICAL TESTS FOR USE OVER THE AGE OF 65

The aims of this study were: 1) to standardise commonly used perceptual tests; 2) to standardise two commonly used mental status questionnaires; 3) to determine whether age and various physical and mental factors influence the performance of perceptual tests; 4) to examine the randomly selected group of subjects over 65 for other details of interest, e.g. medication; 5) to use the results of the study to formulate advice on the use of perceptual tests over the of 65.

The sample was taken from all patients over 65 on the age–sex register of a large urban general practice in Manchester. The total number of patients over 65 was 2700, and details of the age strata within this group

Table 2.1 Sampling frame. Total population over 65 in the practice

Age	Men	Women	Total
85 and over	55	182	237
75–84	303	658	961
65–74	609	897	1506
Total	967	1737	2704

are given in Table 2.1. From these patients 190 were selected by stratified random sampling (Williamson & Milne 1978, Heron & Chown 1967). The six strata chosen were: female, 65–75, 75–84 and 85 plus; male, 65–74, 75–84 and 85 plus. There were 30 patients in each of the four youngest strata in the original sample, and 35 in the two oldest strata, to weight the sample for the higher number of deaths and moves expected in the older strata. The final sample, after 39 deaths and moves since the register was compiled, 25 refusals and 10 miscellaneous withdrawals is shown in Table 2.2. The percentage that each stratum of the sample represented of each stratum of the sampling frame was used to correct each of the final results (where given as percentages) so that they represent the expected results in the sample population.

Table 2.2 Final stratified sample

Age	Men	Women	Total
85 and over	12 (21.8%)	19 (10.4%)	31
75–84	23 (7.6%)	16 (2.4%)	39
65–74	24 (3.9%)	22 (2.5%)	46
Total	59	57	116

In brackets: the sample of that stratum of the sampling frame expressed as percentage

The perceptual tests were largely chosen from a survey of the tests used on patients over 65 with strokes, in the occupational therapy (OT) departments of seven local geriatric units. The most commonly used tests were: right/left orientation, stereognosis, texture perception, formboards, shape post-box, felt body, cube designs, and drawing a house, a man and a clock. These tests are used in the OT departments to diagnose disorders of higher perception after stroke, and then the disorder is related to difficulties which may occur in activities of daily living. Before using these tests, it is common practice to use the abbreviated mental test (Hodkinson 1972; Qureshi & Hodkinson 1974) to screen for dementia.

Each patient was questioned personally by me in their home situation (Fig. 2.1). In most cases details of activities of daily living and medication were verified by relatives and the patient's general practitioner respectively. The mean time for completion of the questionnaire was 46 minutes. (The questionnaire, with scoring details, is available from the author on request.)

Predictor variables

The actual perceptual tests were preceded by a very extensive examination of possible predictor variables, i.e. a variety of tests of physical and mental factors which might influence the performance of the perceptual tests. The predictor variables included age, sex, residential state and the following factors.

Fig 2.1 Personal questioning in the patient's home.

Medical history: neurological symptoms, stroke, incontinence, chronic chest disease, limb fractures or amputation, mobility, handedness and details of present medication.

Activities of daily living (Meyrick & Cox 1969) were assessed in some detail, though only by questioning. Difficulty with such activities has been related to the performance of mental status questionnaires (Wilson et al 1973) and has been associated with unilateral neglect of the hemiplegic side in stroke (Denny-Brown et al 1952).

Physical examination: dyspnoea, tremor, pulse, blood pressure, hearing and examination of the vision. Vision was examined for blindness, hemianopia or visual inattention. The pen/key test was used to detect unilateral visual neglect, as after stroke (Andrews 1979, 1982). The eye movements were examined. Visual acuity was tested with a near-vision testing booklet, as the most appropriate distance of vision to examine was that involved in the perceptual tests, i.e. eyes to table (approx. 60 cm). Power in both arms was tested from fingers to shoulder, and muscle tone. Sensation to light touch was examined in the hands. Proprioception was examined using the thumb-finding test (Chalmers 1980), since increased age itself may be related to impaired proprioception (Levin & Benton 1973).

Mental status questionnaires. Two commonly used questionnaires were employed — the abbreviated (10-question) mental test score (Hodkinson 1972; Qureshi & Hodkinson 1974), and the set test (Isaacs & Akhtar 1972). The set test has been recommended by Siev and Freishtat (1976) as a screening test for general mental impairment prior to attempting to use perceptual tests. The usefulness of short mental status questionnaires is well established in the domiciliary assessment of the elderly (Wilson & Brass 1973), though it is probably enhanced by adding the examiner's own opinion of the presence or absence of mental confusion (Silver 1978).

Language assessment. A 16-question language test was used, the questions having been inspired by a much more extensive assessment described by Strub and Black (1977). The observer's diagnosis of speech impairment was also used.

Apraxia test. Six tasks were used involving face, hand and arm to detect obvious apraxia (if power preserved), and were again derived from a more comprehensive set (Strub & Black, 1977).

Perceptual tests

The 'perceptual tests' used were in fact a wide variety of simple tests of secondary and tertiary perception, constructional ability and body image, mostly derived from the previously described survey of tests used with stroke patients. The equipment used for the tests is shown in Fig. 2.2. Many of the tests involve the use of children's toys or equivalent equipment. Adams (1974) had reservations about the validity of using this type of toy test until the tests had been standardised with large numbers of elderly people, as this study is attempting to do to some extent.

The perceptual tests used included:-

Right/left orientation. Three questions involving the discrimination between right and left limbs, derived from longer assessments (Strub & Black 1977, Walsh 1978).

Stereognosis. Four objects — a comb, pencil, key and spoon — were to be identified by touch alone in a cloth bag, with each hand separately. This tests an important type of tactile perception, and visual clues must not be included (Denny-Brown et al 1952, Gregory & Aitken 1971).

Weight perception. Tested by distinguishing between visually identical matchboxes of different weights, in each hand separately and then between left and right (Denny-Brown et al 1952, Andrews 1982).

Texture perception. Four different texture were to be identified by touch alone, each from a choice of the four with eyes open (Denny-Brown et al 1952, Gregory & Aitken 1971).

Size perception (visual). Five square cards were to be arranged in order of size (McMenamin 1977).

Colour perception. Ageing processes may affect colour discrimination (Corso 1971, Mashiah 1978), which was tested by sorting 12 square cards of four colours (McMenamin 1977). Colour vision may be impaired by cerebral infarction, most dramatically by infarction of the occipital lobes (Whiteley & Warrington 1977).

Formboard. This was a pegboard (Fig. 2.2) with a variable number of holes, to be fitted over pegs on a small board (Adams & Hurwitz 1963, Adams 1974). It has been used in many units to diagnose spatial impairment due to stroke.

Shape posting box. The plastic shape posting box used (see Fig. 2.2) is a widely available toy which has six different shapes, and has been previously used to asses mental ability in the elderly (Isaacs 1963, Morgan 1972).

Felt body. This has been used in the past to demonstrate impaired body image after stroke (McFie et al 1950), but has only been standardised as a test with children (Reynell 1970). It is demonstrated in Fig. 2.2.

Matchstick tests. A variety of matchstick designs has been used to detect agnosia and constructional apraxia (Mayer-Gross 1935, Warrington 1970). The designs assessed in my questionnaire were a triangle, a 5-match zig-zag design and a matchstich star (Ettlinger et al 1957).

Cube construction tests. This type of test has been used to detect constructional apraxia (Gregory & Aitken 1971). Simple step designs of three, six and then ten cubes were used in this questionnaire, and those designs have been standardised on children (Lezak 1976). The final cube design which was used is a more complex design, of two 3-cube bridges joined by a final central bridging cube (7-cube bridge design) (Lezak 1976). This last test has been shown to be very difficult for patients with severe visuo-constructive disability due to right parietal lesions (Lesak 1976).

Fig 2.2 Materials used in the 'perceptual tests'.

Figs 2.3–2.12 Mixed pictures. For explanation see text.

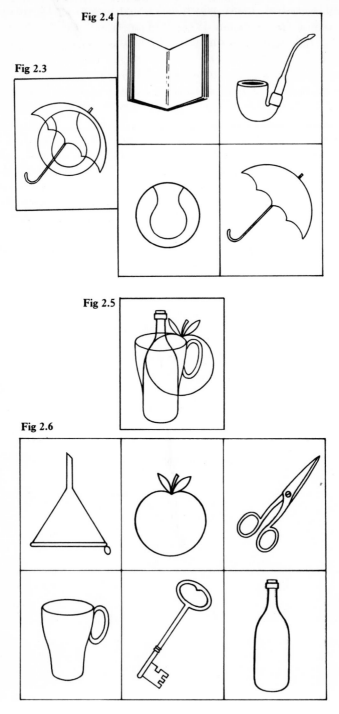

Picture drawing tests. The patient is requested to copy the picture of a house, and to draw pictures of a clock and a man. The clock is expected to have hands, a face and twelve figures; the man to have a head, body and 4 limbs. Such drawings have been used to assess stroke patients, and the results may relate to the side of the lesion (Walsh 1978) and the prognosis for recovery (Andrews et al 1980) which is worse in patients who perform these tests badly. Results of the drawing tests have also been compared with mental test scores (Moore 1981). Piercy et al (1960) noted that patients with left cerebral hemisphere lesions tend to be helped to draw by the provision of an original drawing to copy, whereas patients with right hemisphere lesions found the copying no easier than drawing from memory.

Mixed pictures. Overlapping line drawings of more than one object were devised, and the constituent objects had to be selected from a choice of individual drawings — two mixed pictures from a choice of four (Figs 2.3 and 2.4), three mixed pictures from a choice of six (Figs 2.5 and 2.6), and four mixed pictures from a choice of eight (Figs 2.7 and 2.8). Mixed pictures have been used to assess higher visual perception (Milner & Teuber 1968) and have already been standardised in children (Ghent 1956).

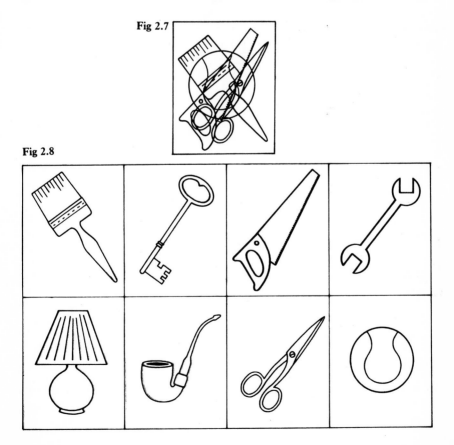

Fig 2.7

Fig 2.8

Incomplete pictures. Identification of these shaded drawings with sections erased is impaired in agnosia (Lezak 1976, Milner & Teuber 1968), but although two of the drawings were easily recognised by many fit elderly subjects (the vacuum cleaner and wheelbarrow — Figs 2.9 and 2.10), the telephone and camera (Figs 2.11 and 2.12) proved to be more difficult.

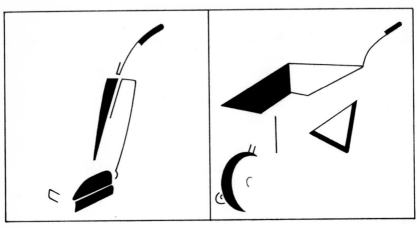

Fig 2.9   **Fig 2.10**

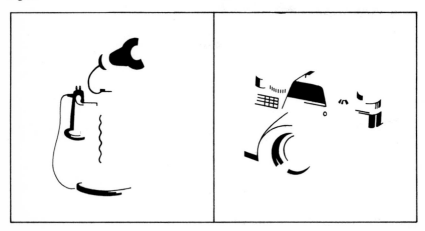

Fig 2.11   **Fig 2.12**

RESULTS OF THE STUDY

All percentage figures have been adjusted to take account of the stratified sampling fractions, and therefore represent the expected results for the sample population of people over 65 on the register in that practice.

Predictor variables

Age. The age range of the patients studied was 65 to 95 and the breakdown of the patient group into age strata has been outlined in Table 2.1.

Residential state. 44% lived alone, 55% lived with others (mainly relatives) in their own or their relatives' home, and 1% lived in hospital. The sample had not included anyone living in residential homes. All the residential homes in the practice catchment area were therefore visited to look for patients whose care had been transferred to another practice when they entered the residential home. The small group of such patients that I discovered amounted to less than 1% of the practice population of over 65-year-olds.

Incontinence. 7% admitted to urinary incontinence on direct questioning, 92.5% denied any urinary incontinence, and less than 1% were catheterised.

Strokes. 6% had a history of stroke, and 3% of all patients had right-sided weakness, 2% left-sided weakness and less than 1% had only speech impairment.

Mobility. 89% walked independently, 10% were only mobile with a walking aid and 1% were only mobile in a wheelchair.

Medication. 77% of patients were taking regular medication, and of these 91 patients, as Table 2.3 shows, 25% were taking three or more preparations. Of the 10 patients taking four or more preparations, six were taking four preparations, three were taking five preparations and one was taking six preparations. Of the 89 different preparations being used by the 91 patients taking medication, 21 contained more than one active constituent. Not all of the medication was prescribed by their doctor, and there was a striking contrast between the remarkably healthy state of the majority of the patients and the degree to which they took regular medication. As Table 2.4 shows, the most commonly used drugs were analgesics and diuretics, then hypnotics, and then hypotensive agents; 10% were taking digoxin. One quarter of the 'analgesics' taken also had an anti-inflammatory action (non-steroidal anti-inflammatory drugs). On later analysis of results by the chi-square distribution, to look for any relationship between the age of the patient and their medication, I was surprised to find that age had no effect on the likelihood of the patient being on medication, even when the different categories of drugs were looked at individually. Encouragingly

Table 2.3 Patients taking regular medication (77% of the total sample)

No. of preparations taken	% of those on medication
1	48
2	27
3	16
4 or more	9

Table 2.4 Classification of medication

Type of medication	% of total sample of patients
Any medication	77.0
Hypnotics	13.8
Anti-depressants	6.8
Other sedatives	4.0
Diuretics	21.4
Hypotensives	14.4
Analgesics	21.9
Digoxin	10.0

(though anecdotally), I can report that the oldest patient, aged 95, was on no medication whatsoever.

Blood pressure. The details of the mean blood pressure readings obtained in each of the three age strata are given for men and women separately in Table 2.5. Analysis of variance revealed no significant age effects on systolic blood pressure, but men showed a significant fall in mean diastolic pressure over 75 compared with the lowest stratum. Women showed some decrease in mean diastolic pressure in the older strata, but this difference was not statistically significant, at the 5% level.

Mental status questionnaires. The results of the abbreviated mental test (Hodkinson 1972; Qureshi & Hodkinson 1974) are given in Table 2.6. A score of 7 out of 10 is said to be the borderline score for dementia. The

Table 2.5 Blood pressure (Mean values for each stratum)

Men			
Age	65–74	75–84	85 and over
Systolic pressure	143	145	139
Diastolic pressure	82	71	71
Women			
Age	65–74	75–84	85 and over
Systolic pressure	152	159	145
Diastolic pressure	80	79	74

Table 2.6 Abbreviated mental test (Hodkinson 1972; Qureshi & Hodkinson 1974): percentage of patients scoring above, on and below the dementia borderline

Age	Scores (out of 10)		
	Over 7	7	Under 7
65 and over	91%	5%	4%
75 and over	85%	7%	8%

Table 2.7 The set test (Isaacs & Akhtar 1972). Percentage of patients scoring above, on and below the borderline (see text)

Age	Scores (out of 40)		
	Over 20	20	Under 20
65 and over	96%	0	4%
75 and over	90%	0	10%

results of the set test (Isaacs & Akhtar 1972) are given in Table 2.7. A score of 20 out of 40 is said to be the borderline score for dementia, and is said to represent the score below which the results of subsequent perceptual tests may be unreliable (Siev & Freishtat 1976).

Perceptual test results

Right/left orientation score (out of 3): 80% achieved a full score.

Stereognosis score (out of 4): 87% achieved a full score, with no difference between right and left.

Weight perception: 92% achieved a full score of 3 (no difference between right and left tested individually). 97% achieved a full score of 3 for weight comparison between hands.

Texture perception: 59% achieved a full score of 4 with the right hand: 57% with the left hand.

Size perception: 97% completed the test successfully.

Colour perception: 96% completed the test successfully.

Formboard: 77% succeeded with no re-positioning, and 18% succeeded after re-positioning some shapes (e.g. turning through at least a right angle after placing on the pegs).

Felt body: only 56% succeeded in correctly positioning the head, trunk and limbs. To be significant the errors had to be severe, e.g. limb attached half way down trunk, or separated from trunk by over 2 cm.

Shape posting box: 41% succeeded with no re-positioning, and 49% succeeded after re-positioning some shapes (e.g. turning through at least a right angle after placing on the slots).

Drawing tests

The analysis of success or failure depended on the following criteria: for the house, copying all the lines and connecting them, or not separating them by over 1 cm; for the clock, by drawing a clock with a face, two hands and the numbers 1 to 12; for the man: by drawing a human figure with head, trunk and four limbs in appropriate positions (as for felt body). The subjects were just told to 'copy the house', 'draw a clock' and 'draw a man' and further instructions were given on request only.

Table 2.8   Drawing test results (percentage of all patients)

	Failure	Success	No attempt
Copy a house	22%	76%	2%
Draw a man	18%	79%	3%
Draw a clock	47%	51%	2%

The results of this analysis are given in Table 2.8. Overall the results show that far more difficulty was experienced in drawing a clock than in copying a house or drawing a man. Certain variations on the drawing themes, such as a clock with a mirror image of the numerals, were only seen in association with either low mental test scores or previous hemiparesis; this association has been noted before (Gooddy & Reinhold 1952). Other variations, such as roman numerals on the clock, were often, but not always, asociated with other abnormalities of drawing such an absence of hands on the clock. One very important example of drawing test abnormality was that of the numbers which wander dramatically out of one side of the clock face. This has been suggested as being due to unilateral neglect due to stroke (Chalmers 1980, Johnston 1978), and may well have been so in previously quoted examples. In my study, however the three clear examples of this (e.g. Fig. 2.13) were clearly associated with neither stroke nor

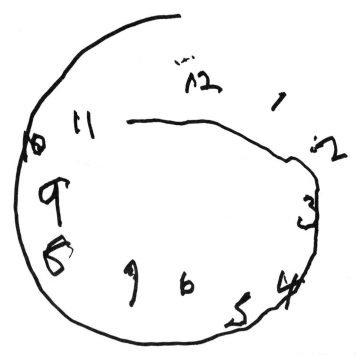

Fig. 2.13 Drawing test abnormality associated with impaired visual acuity. The patient was asked to draw a clock.

dementia, but with seriously impaired visual acuity (but without hemi-anopia or unilateral neglect). Observations of the patient performing the drawing confirmed this relationship, and once pen was taken off paper the subjects were uncertain of where to replace pen to continue the circle of numbers. The same mechanism of drawing failure, and relationship with *only* poor visual acuity only, was seen to produce a fragmented, jumbled drawing of a man, previously reported in association with stroke (Adams & Hurwitz 1963), but not found to be so in this case.

Constructional tests

Matchstick designs: 95.7% correctly constructed the triangle and 93.1% the zig-zag design but only 73.6% were able to construct the four-pointed star. All the designs were copied.

Cube designs: 96% correctly copied the three-cube steps, 94.3% the six-cube steps and 91.9% the 10-cube steps. Only 76.2% were able to copy the complex bridge design.

Hidden picture tests

Mixed pictures: 91.7% correctly identified the two mixed pictures, 90.2% the three mixed pictures, but only 72.8% the four mixed pictures.

Incomplete pictures: 87.2% correctly identified the vacuum cleaner, 61.3% the wheelbarrow, but only 25.3% the telephone (old-fashioned design) and only a mere 4.4% correctly identified the camera.

Analysis of the effect of age or sex or predictor variables

This was done by the chi-square distribution for most of the predicted variables. The following variables were analysed by the analysis of variance: blood pressure, power in the arms, mental test questionnaires, language and apraxia tests. The details of the levels of significance achieved for the results are summarised in Tables 2.9–2.12. The levels of significance are derived from the p value in the case of chi-square, and the F probability value in the case of analysis of variance. Only age and sex effects with p or F prob-

Table 2.9 Age differences (men and women)

Factor in decline with increasing age	Level of significance %
Physical stability (more falls)	5
Mobility out of home (more housebound)	1
Visual acuity	1
Proprioception	5
Shape box score	1
Ability to copy a house	5

Table 2.10   Age differences (men only)

Factor in decline with increasing age	Level of significance %
Diastolic blood pressure	5
Language test score	0.1
Colour test score	5
Ability to assemble felt body	5
Ability to draw a man	1
Ability to draw a clock	1
Ability to identify incomplete pictures	0.1

Table 2.11   Age differences (women only)

Factor in decline with increasing age	Level of significance %
Abbreviated Mental test ('Hodkinson') score	5
Set test score	1
Formboard score	5

Table 2.12   Sex differences

Female patients showed more impairment of:	Level of significance %
Stereognosis	1
Apraxia score	5

ability values of less than 0.05 (a 5% significance level) are given, higher values being regarded as indicating a lack of statistical significance.

Predictive power of the chosen predictor variables over the results of the perceptual tests

These effects were measured by a computer-assisted statistical technique known as logistic discrimination. Logistic discrimination is a stepwise multiple regression technique based on an equation for estimating the logistic form for posterior probabilities (Day & Kerridge 1967). In the first step all the predictor variables are fitted into the equation in turn, on their own. This provides a regression coefficient for each variable. In subsequent steps the best predictor variable from the first step is fixed in the equation with its regression coefficient, and the other variables are fitted in turn with the fixed one already in this equation. The usefulness of the variables as predictors is measured by a statistic called the scaled deviance which expresses the goodness of fit of the data to the model. If the scaled deviance is less than the number of degrees of freedom, then the results of that analysis are not to be relied upon (usually because of a skewed distribution of results).

The scaled deviance was less than half the value of the degrees of freedom for the following tests: weight, size and colour perception, the match triangle, the three-cube and six-cube steps and the incomplete camera picture. The results of logistic discrimination for these tests are not included here, because they are extremely unreliable, and they are not included in the summary of reliable predictors (given in Table 2.13). The cause of this was probably a skewed distribution of results in those tests, since they were all very easy tests, (except the camera picture, which was very difficult). Other tests were associated with a lower scaled deviance than there were degrees of freedom, though not less than half. These included stereognosis, and right/left discrimination (predicted by the ability to dress on ADL (activities of daily living) assessment), texture perception (predicted by the set test and language test scores) and the ability to construct the cube designs (predicted by the abbreviated mental test score (Hodkinson 1972; Qureshi & Hodkinson 1974)). These particular predictive relationships have to be regarded as possible but not wholly reliable.

The final results of this analysis were expressed as probabilities. These are the probabilities of the variables being significant predictors. In Table 2.13 I have shown the most significant predictor variables revealed for each perceptual test. The perceptual tests included in the table are only those

Table 2.13 Perceptual tests (reliable predictor variables)

More difficulty with (perceptual test)	If (predictor)	Level of significance %
Formboard	Increasing age	0.1
	Lower abbreviated mental test ('Hodkinson') score	0.1
Shape box	Increasing age	0.1
	Lower abbreviated mental test ('Hodkinson') score	5
	Lower set test score	5
Felt body	Lower apraxia score	0.1
Matchstick star	Increasing age	0.1
Mixed pictures	Poorer visual acuity	0.1
	Increasing age	0.1
Incomplete pictures	Lower abbreviated mental test ('Hodkinson') score	0.1
	Lower set test score	0.1
	Increasing age	0.1
Copying a house	Weaker arms	0.1
	Increasing age	0.1
Drawing a man	Increasing age	0.1
Drawing a clock	Increasing age	0.1

with a scaled deviance that is greater than the number of degrees of freedom, and are therefore thought to demonstrate statistically reliable predictive capability. Judgement on the effects of the predictor variables on several tests has to be reserved because of their skewed distribution, as described above.

The perceptual tests with reliable predictors are: felt body, formboard, matchstick designs, shape posting box, drawing tests (copying a house, drawing a clock and a man), mixed pictures and incomplete pictures (except camera). Several of these have been shown to be potentially unreliable when used with confused patients, since (as shown in Table 2.13) they may be affected by general mental impairment as shown by mental test scores. This will affect their selectivity when used to diagnose the effects of stroke. The following tests are affected by general mental impairment as described: formboard, shape posting box, matchstick tests, drawing a clock and incomplete pictures. Other effects on the tests include that of age itself, and imply increasingly impaired selectivity as age advances beyond 65. Tests affected in this way by age included formboard, shape posting box, matchstick tests, copying a house, drawing a clock, drawing a man, mixed pictures and incomplete pictures. The exclusion of individual perceptual tests from use with the confused or very elderly subject, based on the above findings, leaves only a few tests that appear unaffected by general mental impairment or age.

Only three reliably predicted perceptual tests were not affected by low mental test scores (with a few exceptions) and can therefore be recommended for use even with confused patients. They are: 1) The felt body test; 2) copying a house; and 3) drawing a man. Only one reliably predicted perceptual test was unaffected by ageing and can therefore be recommended for use with very elderly subjects. It is the felt body construction test, a test found to be significantly associated with apraxia (low scores on the apraxia test being associated with poor assembly of the felt body at a highly significant level).

Many of the perceptual tests which I examined may still show very distinctive individual results after stroke, e.g. when unilateral visual or tactile neglect is present, but the above findings and reservations about the tests should be considered in their interpretation. This is essential if such perceptual tests are still to be used to guide physicians and therapists in their assessment of the prognosis for successful rehabilitation after a stroke. The tests may help us to come to a greater understanding of the patient's sensory disability after stroke, but they become even more important when they are used to assess prognosis. We must critically examine any test which has such important implications for the management of our patients with stroke.

Acknowledgements

I wish to thank the following people who assisted me with my research: Professor J. C. Brocklehurst and Dr. K. Andrews for their advice and guidance, Brian Faragher for his expert help with the statistical analysis, Dr. Bodey and partners for permission to interview their patients, and Heather Hall for preparation of the manuscript. The line drawings were prepared by Keith Harrison, Department of Medical Illustration, University Hospital of South Manchester.

REFERENCES

Adams G F 1974 Cerebrovascular disability and the ageing brain. Churchill Livingstone, Edinburgh

Adams G F, Hurwitz L J 1963 Mental barriers to recovery from strokes. Lancet 2: 533–537

Adams G F, Merrett J D 1961 Prognosis and survival in the aftermath of hemiplegia. British Medical Journal 1: 309–314

Anastasi A 1968 Psychological testing, 4th edn. Collier MacMillan, London

Andersen A L 1951 The effect of laterality localization of focal brain lesions on the Wechsler-Bellevue sub-tests. Journal of Clinical Psychology 7: 149–153

Andrews K 1978 Understanding understanding. Physiotherapy 64: 132–134

Andrews K 1979 Perceptual disorders in stroke. Occupational Therapy (March): 62

Andrews K 1982 Clinical features of stroke. In: Caird F I (ed) Neurological disorders in the elderly. John Wright, Bristol, p 85–98

Andrews K, Brocklehurst J C, Richards B, Laycock P J 1980 The prognostic value of picture drawings by stroke patients. Rheumatology and Rehabilitation 19: 180–188

Arenberg D, Robertson-Tchabo E A 1977 Learning and aging. In: Birren J E, Schaie K W (eds) Handbook of the psychology of aging. Van Nostrand Reinhold, New York, p 421–449

Benton A L, Van Allen M W 1972 Aspects of neuropsychological assessment in patients with cerebral disease. In: Gaitz C M (ed) Advances in behavioural biology, vol. 3. Aging and the brain. Plenum Press, New York, p 29–39

Bergman M 1980 Aging and the perception of speech. University Park Press, Baltimore

Botwinick J 1977 Intellectual abilities. In: Birren J E, Schaie K W (eds) Handbook of the psychology of aging. Van Nostrand Reinhold, New York, p 580–605

Bromley D B 1966 The psychology of human ageing. Penguin Books, Harmondsworth

Chalmers G L 1980 Caring for the elderly sick. Pitman Medical, Tunbridge Wells

Chamberlain J O P 1973 Screening elderly people. Proceedings of the Royal Society of Medicine 66: 888–889

Cohen D, Schaie K W, Gribbin K 1977 The organization of spatial abilities in older men and women. Journal of Gerontology 32: 578–585

Corso J F 1971 Sensory processes and age effects in normal adults. Journal of Gerontology 26: 90–105

Corso J F 1977 Auditory perception and communication. In: Birren J E, Schaie K W (eds) Handbook of the psychology of aging. Van Nostrand Reinhold, New York, p 535–553

Cowdry E V (ed) 1939 Problems of ageing. Biological and medical aspects. Baillière, Tindall and Cox, London

Craik F I M 1977 Age differences in human memory. In: Birren J E, Schaie K W (eds) Handbook of the psychology of aging. Van Nostrand Reinhold, New York, p 384–420

Crandall R C 1980 Gerontology, a behavioural science approach. Addison-Wesley, London

Critchley M 1962 Clinical investigation of disease of the parietal lobes of the brain. Medical Clinics of North America 46: 837–857

Davies A D M 1967 Age and the memory-for-designs test. British Journal of Social and Clinical Psychology 6: 228–233

Davies A D M 1968 The influence of age on trail making test performance. Journal of Clinical Psychology 24: 96–98

Davison L A 1974a Current status of clinical neuropsychology. In: Reitan R M, Davison L A (eds) Clinical neuropsychology: current status and applications. Winston, Washington DC

Davison L A 1974b Introduction, In: Reitan R M, Davison L A (eds) Clinical neuropsychology: current status and applications. Winston, Washington DC

Day N E, Kerridge D F 1967 A general maximum likelihood discriminant. Biometrics 23: 313–323

Denham M J, Jeffreys P M 1972 Routine mental testing in the elderly. Modern Geriatrics (July): 275–279

Denny-Brown D, Meyer J S, Horenstein S 1952 The significance of perceptual rivalry resulting from parietal lesion. Brain 75 433–471

Eisdorfer C 1963 The WAIS performance of the aged: a retest evaluation. Journal of Gerontology 18: 169–172

Elias M F, Kinsbourne M 1974 Age and sex differences in the processing of verbal and non verbal stimuli. Journal of Gerontology 29: 162–171

Ettlinger G, Warrington E, Zangwill O L 1957 A further study of visuo-spatial agnosia. Brain 80: 335–361

Fox R L 1969 Some problems of ADL with parietal lobe syndrome. Occupational Therapy (October): 17–19

Fozzard J L, Wolf E, Bell B, McFarland R A, Podolsky S 1977 Visual perception and communication. In: Birren J E, Schaie K W (eds) Handbook of the psychology of aging. Van Nostrand Reinhold, New York, p 497–534

Fried I, Mateer C, Ojemann G, Wohns R, Fedio P 1982 Organization of visuospatial functions in human cortex: evidence from electrical stimulation. Brain 105: 349–371

Ghent L 1956 Perception of overlapping and embedded figures by children of different ages. American Journal of Psychology 69: 575–587

Gilleard C J, Pattie A H 1977 The Stockton Geriatric Rating Scale: a shortened version with British normative data. British Journal of Psychiatry 131: 90–94

Gooddy W, Reinhold M 1952 Some aspects of human orientation in space: (i) sensation and movement. Brain 75: 472–509

Gregory M E, Aitken J A 1971 Assessment of parietal lobe function in hemiplegia. Occupational Therapy 34 (7): 9–17

Herbst K G, Humphrey C 1980 Hearing impairment and mental state in the elderly living at home. British Medical Journal 281: 903–905

Heron A, Chown S 1967 Age and function. Churchill, London

Hertzog C K, Williams M V, Walsh D A 1976 The effect of practice on age differences in central perceptual processing. Journal of Gerontology 31: 428–433

Hobson W, Pemberton J 1955 The health of the elderly at home. Butterworth, London

Hodkinson H M 1972 Evaluation of a mental test score for assessment of mental impairment in the elderly. Age and Ageing 1: 233–238

Hodkinson H M 1973 Mental impairment in the elderly. Journal of the Royal College of Physicians of London 7: 305–317

Huppert F A 1982 Does mental function decline with age? Geriatric Medicine (January): 32–37

Isaacs B 1963 The diagnostic value of tests with toys in old people. Gerontologia Clinica 5: 8–22

Isaacs B, Akhtar A J 1972 The set test: a rapid test of mental function in old people. Age and Ageing 1: 222–226

Isaacs B, Marks R 1973 Determinants of outcome of stroke rehabilitation. Age and Ageing 2: 139–149

Isaacs B, Walkey F A 1964 Measurement of mental impairment in geriatric practice. Gerontologia Clinica 6: 114–123

Johnston M 1978 Restoration of motor function in the stroke patient. Churchill Livingstone, Edinburgh

Klisz D 1978 Neuropsychological evaluation in older persons. In: Storandt M, Siegler I C, Elias M F (eds) The clinical psychology of aging. Plenum Press, New York, p 71–95

Klove H 1974 Validation studies in adult clinical neuropsychology. In: Reitan R M, Davison L A (eds) Clinical neuropsychology: current status and applications. Winston, Washington DC

Knapp M E 1959 Problems in rehabilitation of the hemiplegic patient. Journal of the American Medical Association 162: 224–229

Levin H S, Benton A L 1973 Age effects in proprioceptive feedback performance. Gerontologia Clinica 15: 161–169

Lezak M D 1976 Neuropsychological assessment. Oxford University Press, New York

Lloyd Evans S 1976 A clinical trial of Piracetam in elderly patients. MSc Thesis, Manchester University

Lorge I 1957 Methodology of the study of intelligence and emotion in ageing. In: Wolstenholme G E W (ed) Colloquia on ageing, vol. 3. Methodology of the study of ageing. Churchill, London, p 170–187

Luria A R 1970 The functional organisation of the brain. Scientific American 222 (3): 66–78

Luria A R 1973 The working brain. Penguin Press, London

McFie J, Piercy M F, Zangwill O L 1950 Visual-spatial agnosia associated with lesions of the right cerebral hemisphere. Brain 73: 167–190

McMenamin P 1976 Assessment of visual-perceptual problems in relation to self-care activities. Occupational Therapy (January): 6–8

McMenamin P 1977 Tests of visual perception. Unpublished manual, Occupational Therapy Department, The London Hospital

Mashiah T 1978 The effect of ageing on colour vision in females. Age and Ageing 7: 114–115

Mayer-Gross W 1935 Some observations on apraxia. Proceedings of the Royal Society of Medicine 28: 1203–1212

Meier M J, Resch J A 1967 Behavioural prediction of short-term neurologic change following acute onset of cerebrovascular symptoms. Mayo Clinic Proceedings 42: 641–647

Meyrick R L, Cox A 1969 A geriatric survey repeated. Lancet 1: 1146–1149

Milner B, Teuber H-L 1968 Alteration of perception and memory in man: reflections on methods. In: Weiskrantz L (ed) Analysis of behavioural change. Harper and Row, New York, p 268–375

Moore V 1981 Analysis of drawing disability in senile dementia. British Society of Gerontology Annual Conference, University of Hull

Morgan E M 1972 Simple mental tests used with geriatric patients. Occupational Therapy (May): 319–324

Pfeffer R I, Kurosaki T T, Harrah C H et al 1981 A survey diagnostic tool for senile dementia. American Journal of Epidemiology 114: 515–527

Pfeffer R I, Kurosaki T T, Harrah C H, Chance J M, Filos S 1982 Measurment of functional activities in older adults in the community. Jounal of Gerontology 37: 323–329

Pfeffer R I, Kurosaki T T, Chance J M, Files S, Bates D 1984 Use of the mental function index in older adults. Reliability, validity and measurement of change over time. American Journal of Epidemiology 120: 922–935

Piercy M, Hecaen H, De Ajuriaguerra J 1960 Constructional apraxia associated with unilateral cerebral lesions — left and right sided cases compared. Brain 83: 225–242

Plutchik R, Conte H R, Weiner M B, Teresi J 1978 Studies of body image. IV. Figure drawings in normal and abnormal geriatric and non geriatric groups. Journal of Gerontology 33: 68–75

Qureshi K N, Hodkinson H M 1974 Evaluation of a ten-question mental test in the institutionalized elderly. Age and Ageing 3: 152–157

Rabbitt P 1977 Changes in problem solving ability in old age. In: Birren J E, Schaie K W (eds) Handbook of the psychology of aging. Van Nostrand Reinhold, New York, p 606–625

Reed H B C, Reitan R M 1963 Changes in psychological test performance associated with the normal aging process. Journal of Gerontology 18: 271–274

Reynell J K 1970 Children with physical handicaps. In: Mittler P (ed) The psychological assessment of mental and physical handicaps. Methuen, London, p 459

Royal College of Physicians, College Committee on Geriatrics 1981 Organic mental impairment in the elderly. Journal of the Royal College of Physicians of London 15 (3): 3–29

Schaie J P, Schaie K W 1977 Psychological evaluation of the cognitively impaired elderly. In: Eisdorfer C, Friedel R O (eds) Cognitive and emotional disturbance in the elderly. Clinical Issues. Year Book Medical Publishers, Chicago, p 55–73

Sheldon J H 1948 The social medicine of old age. Oxford University Press, London

Siev E, Freishtat B 1976 Perceptual dysfunction in the adult stroke patient. Charles Slack Inc, New Jersey USA

Silver C P 1978 Tests for assessment of mental function. Age and Ageing 7 (suppl): p 12–21

Steuer J, La Rue A, Blum J E, Jarvik L F 1981 Critical loss in the eighth and ninth decades. Journal of Gerontology 36: 211–213

Stonier P D 1974 Score changes following repeated administration of mental status questionnaires. Age and Ageing 3: 91–96

Strub R L, Black F W 1977 The mental status examination in neurology. Davis, Philadelphia

Walsh D A 1976 Age differences in central perceptual processing: a dichoptic backward masking investigation. Journal of Gerontology 31: 178–185

Walsh K W 1978 Neuropsychology. Churhill Livingstone, Edinburgh

Warrington E K 1970 Neurological deficits. In: Mittler P (ed) The psychological assessment of mental and physical handicaps. Methuen, London, p 279

Welford A T 1957 Methodological problems in the study of changes in human performance with age. In: Wolstenholme G E W (ed) Colloquia on ageing, vol. 3. Methodology of the study of ageing. Churchill, London, p 149–169

Welford A T 1958 Ageing and human skill. Oxford University Press, London

Welford A T 1977 Motor performance. In: Birren J E, Schaie K W (eds) Handbook of the psychology of aging. Van Nostrand Reinhold, New York, p 450–496

Whiteley A M: Warrington E K 1977 Prosopagnosia: a clinical, psychological, and anatomical study of three patients. Journal of Neurology, Neurosurgery and Psychiatry 40: 395–403

Wilkin D, Evans G, Hughes B, Jolley D 1982 The implications of managing confused and disabled people in non-specialist residential homes for the elderly. Health Trends 14: 98–100

Williamson J, Milne J S 1978 Research methods in aging. In: Brocklehurst J C (ed) Textbook of geriatric medicine and gerontology, 2nd edn. Churchill Livingstone, Edinburgh

Williamson J, Stokoe I H, Gray S et al 1964 Old people at home: their unreported needs. Lancet 1: 1117–1120

Wilson L A, Brass W 1973 Brief assessment of the mental state in geriatric domiciliary practice. The usefulness of the mental status questionnaire. Age and Ageing 2: 92–101

Wilson L A, Grant K, Witney P M, Kerridge D F 1973 Mental status of elderly patients related to occupational therapist's assessments of activities of daily living. Gerontologia Clinica 15: 197–202

Clinico-pathological correlations

There have been relatively few studies which have related clinical findings to pathological and biochemical changes in the post-mortem brain. The reasons for this are simple. In many countries it is difficult to muster the resources necessary for such studies and it is also difficult to obtain permission for post-mortem examination. In England and Wales post-mortem examination can only be performed with the consent of the relatives or by order of the coroner. Naturally, relatives are upset at the time of death and often are unwilling to give their permission for post-mortem. If permission is withheld the brain of a person who has been studied in life is lost for research purposes. If the aim of the research is to study as representative a sample of subjects as possible it is necessary to screen a large number of patients to obtain a modest collection of brains within the period of the usual research grant. The consequence of this is that it is only feasible to administer short tests that are simple to administer to large groups of subjects and inevitably these tests are measures of general intellectual deterioration rather than of specific psychological functions.

If more detailed psychological tests are employed it is sensible to choose subjects whose relatives have agreed in advance to post-mortem examination for the purposes of research. Patients selected in this way must be relatively fit to undertake the more sophisticated and lengthy testing and their expectation of life is likely to be longer than the duration of the average research grant.

A way of overcoming these difficulties is to test patients with early dementia who are willing to undergo brain biopsy to establish a diagnosis. However this procedure raises the important ethical question as to whether it is right to remove tissue from a failing brain when the diagnosis is immaterial because there is no known treatment for any of the main causes of dementia.

The majority of studies have had to rely on post-mortem examination and on relatively simple measures of dementia such as those described by the group working in Newcastle (Blessed et al 1968). They used two separate types of rating scales. One depended on nurses' and relatives' observations of the patient's behaviour and ability to cope with items of everyday living

(Dementia Scale) (DS) and the other on the patient's ability to recall information and to remember new material (Information–Memory–Concentration Test) (IMCT). These scales are simple and are easy to administer and have a high face validity, although there is some redundancy in the items as shown by Hodkinson (1972) in the case of the IMCT. In the Newcastle studies the scales provided a clear cut-off point between functional and organic illness: a score of 6 on the dementia scale and of 18 on the Information, Concentration and Memory Test. Further evidence of the validity of the dementia score is that Alzheimer's disease, which is progressive, provides a score that increases with the duration of the dementia (Mountjoy et al 1986).

The ease of administration and the utility of these scales in measuring overall disability justifies their use, but it is impossible to obtain from them specific sub-sets which can be directly related to particular behaviour so that the scores can be correlated with specific or localized biochemical or pathological changes.

NEUROPATHOLOGICAL CHANGES ASSOCIATED WITH ALZHEIMER'S DISEASE

The classical neuropathological changes associated with a diagnosis of Alzheimer's disease are the senile plaque (Blocq & Marinesco 1892) and the neurofibrillary tangle (Alzheimer 1907a,b). The senile plaque is spherical in shape and its diameter ranges from 5 to 200 μm across. A typical senile plaque consists of large numbers of altered neuronal processes or neurites which are intermingled with glial processes, an occasional microglial cell and a central core of amyloid fibrils (Tomlinson & Corsellis 1984). The neurofibrillary tangle is a change found within a neuron which appears to be the product of paired neurofilaments wound in a double helix within the neuron (Kidd 1964). More recently it has been claimed that the tangle is made up of a protein not normally found in the healthy neuron (Wischik et al 1985).

Both the tangle and the plaque are found in the hippocampus of normal elderly people. It is the greater number and wider distribution of the lesions, particularly in the neocortex, which distinguish a patient suffering from Alzheimer's disease or senile dementia of the Alzheimer type from the normal elderly person.

Although cortical neuronal loss associated with normal ageing is well established, there has been difficulty in demonstrating significant differences between demented patients and intellectually well-preserved individuals of comparable age. Thus Tomlinson and Henderson (1976) and Terry et al (1977) found no difference whereas Terry et al (1981) and Mountjoy et al (1983) did show significant differences in respect of the larger neurons in the frontal and temporal lobes. Mann et al (1985) found pyramidal neurons and the volume of their nucleolus to be reduced in the middle temporal gyrus and H1 sector of the hippocampus in 32 patients with Alzheimer's disease.

It is assumed, that the cortical atrophy seen macroscopically is due to loss of neurons. The atrophy is usually general though there is some suggestion that the pattern may be related to the age of the patient. Hubbard and Anderson (1981) showed that generalised cortical atrophy occurred in patients up to the age of 80 years but over that age the atrophy was often similar to that found in normal controls. Such atrophy as was present was usually confined to the temporal lobe. The greater atrophy found in the younger patients is also associated with greater numbers of plaques and tangles (Rothschild & Kasanin 1936, Corsellis 1962) and with significant neuronal cortical loss (Mountjoy et al 1983). Loss of neurons has also been shown to be greater in younger patients in the basal nucleus of Meynert (Tagliavini & Pilleri 1983), the cells of origin of the cholinergic innervation of the cortex, and in the locus ceruleus, the cells of origin of the noradrenergic innervation of the cortex (Bondareff et al 1982). These pathological differences between younger and older patients together with more severe biochemical lesions found in younger patients (Rossor et al 1984) have caused Bondareff (1983) to postulate that Alzheimer's disease may be two relatively distinct syndromes, the late variety, Type 1, and the younger, Type 2.

Correlations with plaque counts

Traditionally the plaques and tangles have been demonstrated by silver stains or by stains for amyloid such as thioflavine-S. Although different stains produce different absolute numbers of plaques in adjacent sections, there is high correlation between counts. The Newcastle group, who were pioneers in the quantitative investigation of plaques, favour the use of a modification of the von Braunmuhl method. With this method the plaque appears as a discrete area of dark silver impregnation. Tomlinson and his colleagues developed a method of counting which had a high inter-rater reliability ($r = +0.99$) between a trained neuropathologist on the one hand and two psychiatrists without previous experience of neuropathological techniques on the other hand (Blessed et al 1968). Slides taken from 12 samples of cortex were examined to find an area in each slide which was representative of the general density of plaques. Counts were then made by the use of a graticule in five fields in each of the sections and an average count for each person was derived by adding the total number of plaques and dividing by the number of fields.

Using this method Blessed et al (1968) showed an orderly relationship between plaque counts in the cortex and the severity of the dementia as measured by the Dementia Score and the IMCT. The correlations between the plaque counts and the two measures of dementia were high (DS: $r = +0.77$; IMCT: $r = -0.59$). However there was considerable scatter in the number of plaques, so that some patients showed a marked impairment on the dementia scales yet had a low plaque count, while others scored well within the range for normals but had high plaque counts. Nonetheless the correlation coefficients obtained were high and this suggested that plaque formation was directly related to the dementing process and could no longer be regarded as a mere epiphenomenon.

Wilcock and his colleagues (1982) counted plaques in the frontal, temporal, parietal and occipital lobes. They also studied several areas of the hippocampus, the H1, H2 and H3 areas, the subiculum and the parahippocampus. They correlated the plaque counts in each of these areas with a four-point dementia scale based on information obtained from relatives and the patients' performance on a mental test score (Hodkinson 1972) and/or the modified Kew test described by Hare (1978). The correlations obtained by these authors were lower than those obtained by Blessed et al (1968) and they were not statistically significant in the frontal or temporal lobes, or in the subiculum or the H2 sector of the hippocampus. In the other areas they were statistically significant, though the extent of the correlation was relatively small, and the highest correlation was found in the occipital lobe ($r = 0.43$), an area not well known to be related with intellectual function.

The studies of Wilcock et al and those of Blessed et al are not directly comparable because the rating instruments used to assess the degree of dementia were different and the method of relating these scores to pathological measures was different. The Newcastle study averaged counts for the whole brain whereas Wilcock and his colleagues correlated pathological changes in each lobe separately with the dementia score.

A later study (Mountjoy et al 1986) correlated the Dementia Score of Blessed et al with plaque counts and estimates of tangle formation in nine cortical areas. Plaque counts correlated highly and significantly in all areas with the Dementia Score.

Neary et al (1986) correlated plaque counts in biopsy material from the right middle temporal gyrus with a clinical rating scale, the Wechsler Adult Intelligence Scale (WAIS) (Wechsler 1944), a modified version of the Token Test (De Renzi & Vignolo 1962) and Visual Reaction Time task. The only significant correlation was between plaque count and the verbal subscales of the WAIS ($r = -0.45$). This finding cannot be explained by low plaque counts in early cases in whom the diagnosis is in doubt because the values for the individual cases show the plaques to be present in moderate numbers.

Correlations with tangles

Because the tangles are smaller than plaques and are less evenly distributed than the plaques it is hard to obtain a reliable figure for tangle counts unless the normal neurons are also counted. Such work is extremely tedious and few have attempted it. Some authors have found it satisfactory to estimate the density of tangles on a four-point scale (Corsellis 1962, Dayan 1970, Mountjoy et al 1983). Among the few who have counted the number of tangles are Wilcock et al (1982).

These authors were able to make tangle counts in the same areas of cortex as the plaque counts. The tangles were significantly correlated with the dementia score in all areas examined except the subiculum and H2 sector of the hippocampus. The highest correlation coefficient was $r = 0.59$ in the temporal lobe. Because the correlation coefficients between the dementia score and number of tangles were higher than for dementia score and number of plaques, the authors concluded that the tangle was of more importance in the dementing process than the plaque. Mountjoy et al (1986) correlated the Dementia Score of Blessed et al (1968) with estimates of neurofibrillary tangles rated on a four-point scale of none, mild, moderate and severe. This method lacks the rigour of that employed by Wilcock et al though it does overcome the difficulty of choosing a representative sample of cortex for the count of tangles. Like Wilcock et al, they found that the level of the correlation coefficient for the tangles was higher than that for the plaques.

Neary et al (1986) found that tangles correlated significantly with the verbal subscale of the WAIS ($r = -0.47$, $p < 0.05$) and the Token Test ($r = -0.65$).

It should be realised that there is a problem in making any correlation of tangles with anything else if the population studied includes both controls and dements. The reason for this is that although there is a steady scatter of scores between controls and dements in respect of psychological measures such as the dementia score there is a dichotomy in the distribution of the tangles. To a large extent the pathological diagnosis of Senile Dementia, Alzheimer's Type (SDAT) is made on the basis of neocortical tangles, and many pathologists feel that the presence of tangles is a necessary condition for making the diagnosis. Therefore the controls will have very few or no neocortical tangles and dements will have many. The result is that any correlation coefficient will be high because of a statistical 'dumb-bell' effect.

Test results for demented patients alone continue to show a statistically significant correlation between tangle formation and severity of dementia but the coefficient is lower than if dements and controls are combined.

Correlations with neuronal counts

Mountjoy et al (1986) sought correlations between the Dementia Score and neuronal counts made with the aid of an image-analysing computer. Neuronal counts made in this way correlated weakly and poorly with the Dementia Score and the only statistically significant correlation found in the nine cortical areas examined was in the anterior cingulate gyrus ($r = -0.5$,

$p <0.005$). The poor correlation between neuronal counts and Dementia Score may reflect problems associated with the method of making the neuronal counts or be the consequence of biochemical lesions preceding neuronal death, and being of greater importance in the aetiology of dementia than neuronal death.

By contrast Neary et al (1986), who studied biopsy material from the right middle temporal gyrus in 17 cases of Alzheimer's disease, found that a statistically significant correlation existed between cell loss in layers III and V, reductions in nuclear and nucleolar volume and cytoplasmic RNA content, and a number of psychological tests. The significant correlations with these various neuronal measurements do not necessarily reflect the predominance of the neuronal lesion but could be explained by the high intercorrelations of the neuronal measures. This study has the advantage of using biopsy rather than post-mortem tissue and this, together with the high intercorrelations and the decision to use one-tail tests of significance rather than the more stringent two-tailed tests, may explain the differences between this study and that of Mountjoy et al (1986).

BIOCHEMICAL DISORDERS ASSOCIATED WITH ALZHEIMER'S DISEASE

The cholinergic deficit in Alzheimer's disease has been well documented since 1976 (Bowen et al 1976, Davies & Maloney 1976, Perry et al 1977) and has been a consistent finding in all subsequent studies (Rossor et al 1982). Deficits in other neurotransmitters have been demonstrated. Concentrations of noradrenaline and its metabolite 3-methoxy-4-hydroxyphenyl glycol (MHPG) have been found to be reduced in the cerebral cortex at post-mortem examination. Similarly the activity of dopamine beta-hydroxylase (DBH), the specific biosynthetic marker of noradrenergic neurons (Rossor & Iversen 1986), at 5-HT binding sites is also reduced (Bowen et al 1983, Reynolds et al 1984). Gamma aminobutyric acid (GABA) is not generally reduced but there is some evidence that the level of the GABA is reduced in the temporal lobes of patients dying before the age of 79 (Rossor et al 1982). There appears to be no alteration in the levels of dopamine in the cortex. The only neuropeptide found to be significantly reduced in dementia is somatostatin (Rossor et al 1980, Davies et al 1980).

Correlations with biochemical lesions

The first effort to relate biochemical activity post-mortem with the severity of dementia registered in life was by Perry et al (1978). They showed that the IMCT (Blessed et al 1968) correlated highly and significantly with the measurement of choline acetyl transferase (ChAT), the biosynthetic enzyme for the cholinergic system ($r = 0.81$). By contrast the activity of glutamic acid decarboxylase (GAD) was not significantly correlated with the IMCT ($r = 0.16$).

In a later paper Perry et al (1981a) replicated their findings concerning the activity of both ChAT and GAD. It also showed low and statistically non-significant correlation coefficients between IMCT and DBH cholecystokinin, vasoactive intestinal peptide, Substance P and somatostatin. The finding regarding DBH was confirmed in a later publication (Perry et al 1981b).

Wilcock et al (1982) found a significant correlation between their four-point dementia score and ChAT activity. The ChAT activity was most reduced in the temporal lobe and the correlation of the dementia score here was better ($r = -0.67$) than in the frontal lobe ($r = -0.38$).

Gottfries et al (1983) measured 5-HT, 5-HIAA, NA, MHPG, DA, HVA, ChAT, MAO-A, MAO-B* in the hypothalamus, caudate nucleus, hippocampus and cingulate gyrus and correlated each of these measurements with a dementia scale completed by the head nurse the day after the death of the patient. These authors found that the most severely demented patients had positive correlations with NA and MHPG, in other words the most demented had the highest levels of these substances. They found ChAT activity in the caudate to be negatively but not quite significantly correlated with mental impairment ($r = 0.55$). There were no significant correlations in respect of the other measurements.

In a later study Mountjoy et al (1986) studied a group of 30 patients in whom ChAT and GABA activity had been measured in 16 areas of the cortex. ChAT activity correlated negatively and highly significantly with dementia score in all 16 areas of cortex, whereas GABA had a single significant correlation in Brodmann Area 9, which was just significant at the 5% level of probability. Although the dementia score correlated significantly with ChAT activity in all areas of the cerebral cortex it did not correlate significantly with the changes in ChAT activity in the cerebellar cortex. This is especially interesting because it demonstrates that it is changes in ChAT activity in the cerebral cortex alone which relate to the measure of intellectual decline.

In the same paper a more extensive series of patients and controls, varying in number between 60 and 74, was studied in Brodmann Areas 10, 21, and 24, in respect of ChAT and CABA activity, NA, DA, and somatostatin. Once again the ChAT activity correlated highly with the dementia score in each of these areas but GABA did not. Noradrenalin correlated significantly only in Brodmann Area 24, where the level of correlation was of the same order as that found for ChAT. In Brodmann Area 21 somatostatin and ChAT activity correlated equally well with the dementia score. A peculiar aspect of this study was a positive correlation between dopamine

---

* 5-HT, 5-hydroxytryptamine; 5-HIAA, 5-hydroxyindole acetic acid; NA, noradrenaline; DA, dopamine; HVA, homovanillic acid; MAO, monoamine oxidase.

activity and the dementia score — in other words, the higher the dopamine measurement in Brodmann Area 21, the more demented the subject.

The facts that the most consistent abnormality found in dementia is lowered ChAT activity and that this activity correlates most highly with measures of severity of dementia, suggest to some that an intervention in the cholinergic system should be the most promising therapeutic intervention. However clinical trials, carefully carried out, have failed to show any significant treatment effect (Hollander et al 1986). The rational treatment of dementia can only take into account the wide but selective deficits that have been described. A proper evaluation of the problems associated with dementia demands a prospective study of representative cohorts of elderly subjects.

SUMMARY

The papers reviewed here are almost impossible to compare because of differences in the rating scales used and in the methods employed to measure the pathological and biochemical variables. The post-mortem studies do have a number of features in common. There are usually high correlations between the measures of dementia and senile plaques and neurofibrillary tangles. This is reassuring in that it is these pathological changes which have been regarded as central to the pathological diagnosis of Alzheimer's disease. The high correlations between dementia measures and pathological changes indicate that these changes make a quantitative contribution to the dementing process and not just a qualitative one. It also suggests that the tangle is probably of greater importance than the plaque.

Similarly the constant and high correlations between ChAT activity and dementia measures show this biochemical marker not only to be the one which is reduced by the greatest amount in Alzheimer's disease but also the one that, in post-mortem studies, correlates most closely with the severity of dementia.

These clear findings have been called in question by the biopsy series of Neary et al, where more sophisticated psychological tests failed to show close correlation with plaque or tangle counts though they did with neuronal measures. These findings require replication and point to the need to elucidate the neuronal changes which may be the prelude to tangle formation in Alzheimer's disease.

REFERENCES

Alzheimer A 1907a Ueber eine eigenartige Erkrankung der Hirnrinde. Allgemeine Zeitschrift für Psychiatrie 64: 146–148
Alzheimer A 1907b Ueber eine eigenartige Erkrankung der Hirnrinde. Zentralblatt fur die gesamte Neurologie und Psychiatrie 18: 177–179
Blessed G, Tomlinson B E, Roth M 1968 The association between quantitative measures of

dementia and of senile change in the cerebral grey matter of elderly subjects. British Journal of Psychiatry 114: 797–811

Blocq P, Marinesco G 1892 Sur les lésions et al pathogénie de l'épilepsie dite essentielle. Semaine Medicale 12: 445–446

Bondareff W 1983 Age and Alzheimer's disease. Lancet 1: 1447

Bondareff W, Mountjoy C Q, Roth M 1982 Loss of neurons of origin of the adrenergic projection to the cerebral cortex (Nucleus locus coeruleus) in senile dementia. Neurology 32: 164–168

Bowen D M, Smith C B, White P, Davison A N 1976 Neurotransmitter-related enzymes and indices of hypoxia in senile dementia and other abiotrophies. Brain 99: 459–496

Bowen D M, Allen S J, Benton J S et al 1983 Biochemical assessment of serotonergic and cholinergic dysfunction and cerebral atrophy in Alzheimer's disease. Journal of Biochemistry 41: 266–272

Corsellis J A N 1962 Mental illness and the ageing brain. Oxford University Press, London

Davies P, Maloney A J F 1976 Selective loss of central cholinergic neurons in Alzheimer's disease. Lancet 2: 1403

Davies P, Katzman R, Terry R D 1980 Reduced somatostatin-like immunoreactivity in cerebral cortex from cases of Alzheimer disease and Alzheimer senile dementia. Nature 288: 279–280

Dayan A D 1970 Quantitative histological studies on the aged human brain. II. Senile plaques and neurofibrillary tangles in senile dementia (with an appendix on their occurrence in cases of carcinoma) Acta Neuropathologica (Berlin) 16: 95–102

De Renzi E, Vignolo L A 1962 The Token Test: a sensitive test to detect receptive disturbances in aphasics. Brain 85: 665–678

Gottfries C-G, Adolfsson R, Aquilonius S-M et al 1983 Biochemical changes in dementia disorders of Alzheimer type (AD/SDAT). Neurobiology of Ageing 4: 261–271

Hare M 1978 Clinical check-list for diagnosis of dementia. British Medical Journal 2: 266–267

Hodkinson H M 1972 Evaluation of a mental test score for assessment of mental impairment in the elderly. Age and Ageing 1: 233–238

Hollander E, Mohs R C, Davis K L 1986 Cholinergic approaches to the treatment of Alzheimer's disease. British Medical Bulletin 42: 97–100

Hubbard B M, Anderson J M 1981 Age, senile dementia and ventricular enlargement. Journal of Neurology, Neurosurgery and Psychiatry 44: 631–635

Kidd M 1964 Alzheimer's disease. An electron microscopical study. Brain 87: 307–320

Mann D M A, Yates P O, Marcyniuk B 1985 Some morphometric observations on the cerebral cortex and hippocampus in presenile Alzheimer's disease, senile dementia of the Alzheimer type and Down's syndrome in middle age. Journal of the Neurological Sciences 69: 139–159

Mountjoy C Q, Roth M, Evans N J R, Evans H 1983 Cortical neuronal counts in normal elderly controls and demented patients. Neurobiology of Ageing 4: 1–11

Mountjoy C Q, Rossor M N, Evans N J R, et al 1986 Biochemical and neuropathological changes in the brain and their correlation to the severity of dementia in Alzheimer's disease. In: Shagass C, Josiassen R C, Bridger W H, Weiss K J, Stoff D, Simpson G M (eds) Biological Psychiatry 1985. Proceedings of the Third Congress of Biological Pschiatry pp. 1415–1417. Elsevier, New York

Neary D, Snowden J S, Mann D M A et al 1986 Alzheimer's disease: a correlative study. Journal of Neurology, Neurosurgery and Psychiatry 49: 229–237

Perry E K, Perry R H, Blessed G, Tomlinson B E 1977 Neurotransmitter enzyme abnormalities in senile dementia — choline acetyltransferase and glutamic acid decarboxylase in necropsy brain tissue. Journal of the Neurological Sciences 34: 247–265

Perry E K, Tomlinson B E, Blessed G, Bergmann K, Gibson P H, Perry R H 1978 Correlation of cholinergic abnormalities with senile plaques and mental test scores in senile dementia. British Medical Journal 2: 1457–1459

Perry E K, Blessed G, Tomlinson B E et al 1981a Neurochemical activities in human temporal lobe related to ageing and Alzheimer-type changes. Neurobiology of Aging 2: 251–256

Perry E K, Tomlinson B E, Blessed G, Perry R H, Cross A J, Crow T J 1981b Neuropathological and biochemical observations on the noradrenergic system in Alzheimer's disease. Journal of the Neurological Sciences 51: 279–287

Reynolds G P, Arnold L, Rossor M N, Iversen L L, Mountjoy C Q, Roth M 1984 Reduced binding of (3H) ketanserin to cortical 5-HT2 receptors in senile dementia of the Alzheimer type. Neuroscience Letters 44: 47–51

Rossor M, Iversen L L 1986 Non-cholinergic neurotransmitter abnormalities in Alzheimer's disease. British Medical Bulletin 42: 70–74

Rossor M N, Emson P C, Mountjoy C Q, Roth M, Iversen L L 1980 Reduced amounts of immunoreactive somatostatin in the temporal cortex in senile dementia of Alzheimer type. Neuroscience Letters 20: 373–377

Rossor M N, Garret N J, Johnson A L, Mountjoy C Q, Roth M, Iversen L L, 1982 A post-mortem study of the cholinergic and GABA systems in senile dementia. Brain 105: 313–330

Rossor M N, Iversen L L, Reynolds G P, Mountjoy C Q, Roth M 1984 Neurochemical characteristics of early and late onset types of Alzheimer's disease. British Medical Journal 288: 361–364

Rothschild D, Kasanin J 1936 Clinicopathologic study of Alzheimer's disease: relationship to senile conditions. Archives of Neurology and Psychiatry 36: 293–321

Tagliavini F, Pilleri G 1983 Neuronal counts in the basal nucleus of Meynert in Alzheimer disease and in simple senile dementia. Lancet 2: 469–470

Terry R D, Fitzgerald C, Peck A, Millner J, Farmer P 1977 Cortical cell counts in senile dementia. Journal of Neuropathology and Experimental Neurology 36:633

Terry R D, Peck A, DeTeresa R, Schecter R 1981 Some morphometric aspects of the brain in senile dementia of the Alzheimer type. Annals of Neurology 10: 184–192

Tomlinson B E, Corsellis J A N 1984 Ageing and the dementias. In: Adams J H, Coresellis J A N, Duchen L W (eds) Greenfield's Neuropathology 4th edn. Arnold, London, p 951–1025

Tomlinson B E, Henderson G 1976 Some quantitative cerebral findings in normal and demented old people. In: Terry R D, Gershon S (eds) Neurobiology of aging vol. 3 Raven Press, New York p 183–204

Wechsler D 1944 The measurement of human intelligence. Williams and Wilkins, Baltimore

Wilcock G K, Esiri M M, Bowen D M, Smith C T 1982 Correlation of cortical choline acetyltransferase activity with the severity of dementia and histological abnormalities. Journal of the Neurological Sciences 57: 407–417

Wischik C M, Crowther R A, Stewart M, Roth M 1985 Subunit structure of paired helical filaments in Alzheimer's disease. Journal of Cell Biology 100: 1905–1912

Behavioural and clinical aspects — longitudinal studies

INTRODUCTION

The aim of this chapter is to illustrate age-related changes in intelligence, memory and personality, as well as the occurrence of definable mental disorders at age 70–80. In a wider perspective a psychological assessment of the elderly must take into account their state of health and also include an evaluation of the impact of the environment on psychological function and mental state.

Most of our observations are based on longitudinal studies of groups from the age of 70 onwards which have been performed in Göteborg, Sweden, since 1971. In these studies data are now available from three age-cohorts of 70-year-olds, namely those born in 1901/02, 1906/07 and in 1911/12 (Table 4.1). The first cohort has at the present time been followed up to age 83 and the second to age 75. An intervention programme has been added for the third age cohort. General descriptions of these studies are available in the literature (Rinder et al 1975, Svanborg 1977, Svanborg et al 1982, 1984).

The most impressive observations on psychological function and mental health are

— that previous ideas of cognitive ability successively declining with increasing adult age are not generally true;

Table 4.1 The present design of the gerontological and geriatric study of 70-year-olds in Göteborg, Sweden

Year of birth	Year of investigation									
	1971/ 72	1976/ 77	1980/ 81	1981/ 82	1982/ 83	1983/ 84	1984/ 85	1985/ 86	1986/ 87	1987/ 88
1901/02 (H 70)	70 yrs	75 yrs	79 yrs		81 yrs	82 yrs	83 yrs		85 yrs	86 yrs
1906/07 (H 70)		70 yrs		75 yrs				79 yrs		
1911/12 (IVEG)				70 yrs	intervention period	72 yrs	72 yrs		75 yrs	75 yrs

— that comparisons between age-cohorts (generations reaching the same age at different times) show marked differences in test results on cognitive functions. At the age of 70 and 75 these differences indicate an ongoing improvement.
— that affective and anxiety mental disorders are at least as common at age 70 as in middle age, and that dementia does not become the dominating mental syndrome until age 80.

METHODOLOGICAL CONSIDERATIONS

Methodological problems exist both when different groups reaching the same age at different times are compared, and when cross-sectional or longitudinal comparisons are made at different ages. Great efforts have been made to develop test methods that really assess basal functional abilities, as far as possible uncontaminated by environmental/cultural differences over time. Further methodological development is definitely needed in this respect.

Figure 4.1 illustrates positive age-cohort differences in verbal capacity at age 70 observed in Sweden over a period of 20 years. Such age-cohort differences stress the importance of good methodology. A prerequisite for an adequate comparison of different cohorts is the availability of samples representative of a whole population at a certain age, or at least a definable

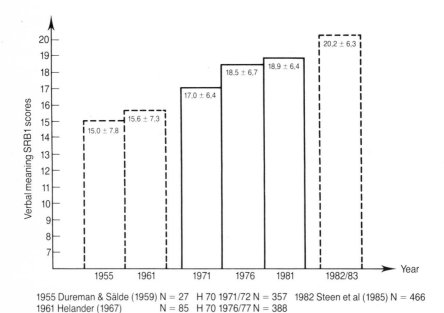

1955 Dureman & Sälde (1959) N = 27   H 70 1971/72 N = 357   1982 Steen et al (1985) N = 466
1961 Helander (1967)   N = 85   H 70 1976/77 N = 388
                                     H 70 1981/82 N = 501

Fig. 4.1 Cross-sectional (1955, 1961, 1982/83) and longitudinal (1971/72, 1976/77, 1981/82) comparison of verbal capacity in Swedish population samples.

part of such a population. The study of 70-year-olds in Göteborg, Sweden, has the advantage of proved representativity (Rinder et al 1975, Berg et al 1981, Persson 1980).

Further follow-ups of the three cohorts studied will show whether the observed positive age-cohort differences in intellectual functioning are also accompanied by cohort differences in the prevalence of definable mental disorders.

PSYCHOLOGICAL FUNCTIONING

The view that there is a general decrement in intelligence and memory in old age has been tenaciously held in the face of research evidence to the contrary. The predominant feature of functioning in the average or normal range of psychological abilities in old age is constancy or stability. Many people also believe that ageing is associated with personality changes such as increased introversion, increased rigidity and so forth.

There are many facets of psychological functioning. The following discussion will concentrate on intelligence, memory and personality in relation to the normal ageing process. In the Göteborg longitudinal study psychological and psychiatric examinations included intelligence and memory testing, personality questionnaires and an interview. In the following we will present examples of results to illustrate certain main conclusions.

Intelligence

The picture of declining intelligence with increasing age has not been corroborated in longitudinal and sequential investigations. In the Göteborg longitudinal study we have found no decline between the ages of 70 and 81 for an intelligence factor (SRB 7) called verbal meaning, and a small but significant change in a test measuring reasoning (Raven's Coloured Progressive Matrices) (Table 4.2). In general, tests show that the ability to store information is better maintained than perceptual integrative skills and the capacity to process new information. In addition, normal ageing generally means a slower speed of information processing, which may also

Table 4.2 Intelligence test results between the ages of 70 and 81

	70		81		
	$\bar{x}$	SD	$\bar{x}$	SD	N
Verbal meaning/SRB1[1]	19.3	5.7	18.5	7.3	67
Reasoning/Raven's Coloured Progressive Matrices[1]	23.4	4.9	20.5	6.8	71

[1] Significant difference $p<0.001$
SD = standard duration

affect certain aspects of intellectual functioning. These results are in line with previous studies on other groups of populations, for example by Schaie & Parham (1977). Thus intelligence tests show very little decline, and if there is one at all it seems to begin beyond the age of 75 for most intelligence factors.

Although ageing itself produces little change in intellectual functioning, there are factors which for some people may have a considerable influence on intellectual abilities. Health is one of them. Botwinick & Birren (1963) reported differences in intelligence test results between people with and without certain illnesses. In a 10-year follow-up of blood pressure, Wilkie & Eisdorfer (1971) found that people with high blood pressure showed a greater decline in intelligence test scores than those with normal blood pressure. They also noted a small improvement among persons with a mild elevation, and hypothesized that this elevation may be necessary to maintain adequate cerebral circulation. In the Göteborg longitudinal study, we found that subjects with cardiovascular disease had a greater decline in intelligence test scores between the age of 70 and 75 than subjects without such disease (Table 4.3) (Berg & Landahl 1979).

Table 4.3 Comparisons of change scores between the ages of 70 and 75 on intelligence and memory tests among subjects with and without cardiovascular disease including means and standard deviations for change scores (Berg & Landahl 1979)

	With cardiovascular disease			Without cardiovascular disease				
	$\bar{x}$	SD	N	$\bar{x}$	SD	N	t	$p(<)$
Verbal meaning/SRB 1	−1.84	6.51	38	−0.25	3.82	230	2.12	0.05
Reasoning/SRB 2	−2.58	6.02	38	−0.04	5.33	229	2.67	0.01
Spatial ability/SRB 3	−3.50	5.70	22	−0.44	4.23	118	2.94	0.01
Perceptual speed/Ps-if	−1.46	6.94	22	−0.38	6.54	117	0.70	NS

Organic brain disorders such as multi-infarct dementia and dementia of the Alzheimer type naturally produce a marked decline in cognitive test results. Such tests are usually sensitive to small changes in brain functioning, and through various tests of this kind it should be possible to detect onset of organic brain disorders early and certainly long before the illness affects behaviour in daily life. In the Göteborg study we have made a nine-year retrospective study of early cognitive signs of dementia (Berg et al 1985). The group used for the study consisted of those who at the age of 70 showed no evidence of dementia. This group was then divided into two: those who developed and those who did not develop dementia during the period up to 79. The results showed that those who developed dementia had significantly lower intelligence test results at the age of 70 than those who did not get dementia (Fig. 4.2). This retrospective analysis shows that signs of impending dementia might be found very early in intelligence test

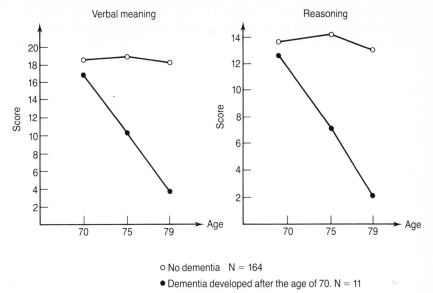

Fig. 4.2 A longitudinal analysis of results on two intelligence tests (Berg et al 1985).

results. Furthermore, this supports the view that cognitive decline in old age is due to specific illness rather than a more general ageing process.

Frequent observations in longitudinal studies have shown that those who died between two measurement points had lower test results in the measurement preceding their death, than the results from the same measurement for those who were still alive. This has been called 'terminal decline'. First reported by Kleemeier (1962), it has been confirmed in a number of studies, and seems to be related to bad health. Birren (1970) has written that 'change in intelligence in late life, as measured by conventional techniques, is not normally distributed. It may show little or no change in some healthy men in the seventh, eighth, and ninth decades of life, while, concurrently, individuals, possibly comprising a sub-population, suffering erosion of health, may show dramatic decline related to their likelihood of survival'.

In the Göteborg longitudinal study, intelligence test results have also been analysed in relation to death or survival (Berg 1985). The analysis showed that there is a relationship between proximity to death and the results of the intelligence tests. The distance from death can be regarded as an overall measure of health or biological age. It may, however, be hard to prove a specific disease-related cause for the decline, but one group of diseases that seems to be important is cardiovascular diseases. Thus, very much of what was believed to be normal deterioration of various intelligence factors during ageing is probably due to bad health and terminal decline (Fig. 4.3a, b).

A sociocultural factor that influences intellectual functioning is education. In analysis of intelligence test results from people between 25 and 64 years

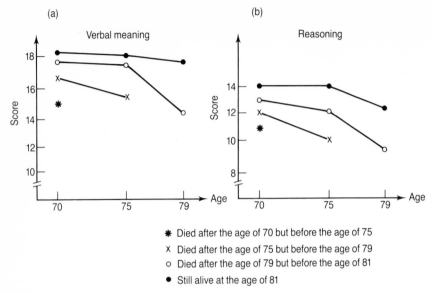

Fig. 4.3 a) The relation between survival and results of an intelligence test of verbal meaning. b) The relation between survival and results of an intelligence test of reasoning (Berg 1985).

of age, Birren & Morrison (1961) found that the number of years at school was a better predictor of intelligence test scores than age. A 20-year follow-up of people tested at a mean age of 64 (Jarvik & Blum 1974) showed that the better educated had less decline. In the Göteborg longitudinal study (Berg 1980) there was a marked difference in the test results between those with few and those with many years in school. In Sweden, there is a great difference between different generations in the average number of years at school. Those now in their eighties have had an average of little more than six years in school, while those in their twenties have had an average of 10 years in school. The fact that bad results in primary school usually also influence the length of further schooling will obviously limit the possibilities of drawing conclusions concerning direct causative relationships between length of education and cognitive ability in later life.

Memory

In studies of age and memory the three-stage information processing model is the most predominant. The three stages are: passage to sensory registers, primary or short-term storage, and secondary memory or long-term storage.

Information from the environment is processed through the sensory system and stored in sensory registers. A rapid forgetting rate is characteristic of these storages, but there seem to be only slight age differences in the functions of the sensory registers.

Because of the rapid forgetting rate in the sensory registers, only part of the information stored there will be selected and transferred to the primary memory. Operationally, the capacity of the primary memory is defined by the number of items that a person can remember without error (e.g. digit span). The items in the primary memory are in the conscious awareness and can be maintained by rehearsal. It can be regarded as a temporary holding and organization process rather than as a structured memory store. The primary memory also serves a control function for the secondary memory, during both the registration and the retrieval of information in that store. The age difference in the functioning of the primary memory seems to be small, at least up to the age of 70 and even later. In the results from the Göteborg longitudinal study the short-term storage seemed very stable.

Information that is rehearsed frequently or well organized is transferred to the secondary memory or long-term store. The capacity of this store is very large and the information must be organized in such a manner that it is possible to retrieve it on demand. The registration of information in the secondary memory involves not only the information itself, but also a retrieval plan. Most studies of the secondary memory report a slight decline in later life. Recent studies on a special form of learning, the so-called SPT or subject-performed tasks, also show very small differences between young and old people.

Thus, the research on memory and ageing has shown results similar to those of intelligence studies (i.e. that the age changes are small but that differences are sometimes found between generations). Health factors and terminal decline also have a great effect on memory functioning. There are, however, very few longitudinal studies on age and memory, but the results from the Göteborg study indicate small changes in memory with increasing age (Johansson 1985).

Psychomotor speed

The only psychological factor which more generally declines with increasing age is behavioural speed. It is usually measured by reaction time. Studies on reaction time and ageing usually show that the speed of response slows down with increasing age. The slowing often begins around the age of 20. Different cross-sectional studies suggest as much as 20–30% increase in simple reaction time between the ages of 20 and 70. In more complex reaction time situations the increase can be even greater.

The slowing of behavioural speed with increasing age seems to be due mainly to changes in the central nervous system. Illnesses like hypertension and cardiovascular diseases often negatively affect the reaction time.

The increased reaction time has an impact on certain cognitive functioning tests such as those measuring intelligence and memory. The time changes are often misinterpreted as qualitative changes in cognitive functioning.

Personality

In studying personality, however defined, structural concepts such as types and traits have been described and various tests have been constructed to quantify individual differences. In the last two decades personality assessments relying on traits and tests have been much criticized (Hogan et al 1977), and more process-oriented approaches have been advocated (Thomae 1980). Although many disappointed researchers in the psychological field have abandoned personality measurement, many clinicians still adhere to personality constructs and consider it meaningful to look for associations between personality and diseases such as mental disorders, myocardial infarctions, and cancer.

In theory, personality is fairly stable. This does not preclude developmental changes during the life-time. Most interest has been devoted to the study of changes in childhood, whereas changes in old age, although taken for granted, have rarely been explored. Most research aimed at elucidating age-related personality changes have compared findings from different age-strata, a cross-sectional approach. The results thus obtained have shown marked differences. It has been fairly well demonstrated that these age differences only reflect age changes to a limited degree (Schaie 1977). Longitudinal and sequential studies, on the other hand, have shown very small changes in personality over time. From a sequential study of people 21–34 years old, Schaie & Parham (1976) reported stability rather than change in most personality factors studied. In a follow-up study of college students 25 years after their first personality testing, Woodruff & Birren (1972) concluded that generational differences were larger than ageing differences. They also showed that consistency rather than change was typical of the follow-up group.

There are many methodological problems associated with longitudinal personality research (Moss & Susman 1980). In this context, it should be admitted that most instruments available for the study of personality are not designed to be used with elderly subjects. It should also be pointed out that some instruments are designed to measure preferably continuity, others preferably change. Many aspects of personality have been investigated but there are fairly few constant findings with regard to personality changes in old age (Neugarten, 1977).

In the Goteborg longitudinal study, results from the Eysenck Personality Inventory and the Cesarec-Marke Temperament Schedule are available (Persson 1980, Nilsson 1983a, Nilsson & Persson 1984a).

Eysenck Personality Inventory (EPI)

This measures extroversion/introversion and neuroticism and also has a lie-scale (Eysenck & Eysenck 1964). In other studies it has been found that, compared to younger subjects, old people score lower on extroversion and neuroticism and higher on the lie-scale (Nilsson 1983a). In our study EPI

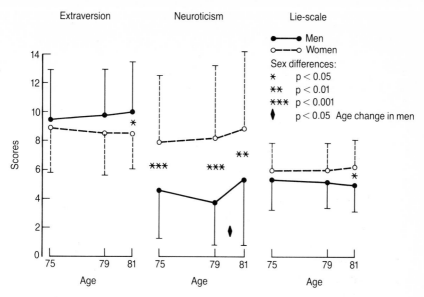

Fig. 4.4 EPI scores in an urban sample examined at the age of 75, 79 and 81.

was administered to the subjects when they were 75 and later at age 79 and 81. Results obtained from those subjects who completed the inventories on all occasions are given in Figure 4.4

With regard to age changes, a significant rise in neuroticism was found in men between 79 and 81; otherwise no significant changes were found. This rise may reflect personality changes associated with an increasing frequency of organic brain syndromes as subjects suffering from mild to moderate dementia were shown to score high on neuroticism (Nilsson 1983a). Towards the age of 81 there occurred a significant difference between the sexes in extroversion, (men being more extroverted) and in the lie-scale (men scoring lower). Contrary to other findings indicating decreasing sex differences in personality in old age (Gutmann 1977), our EPI-findings demonstrated increased sex differences in two scales.

Cesarec-Marke Temperament Schedule (CMPS)

This measures psychogenic needs (Murray, 1938) in 11 subscales, each consisting of 15 questions. The subscales have been arranged to five-factor indices (Cesarec & Marke 1968) and the results obtained from those subjects who completed the inventories when they were 70, 75, 79 and 81 years old have been depicted in Figure 4.5.

There was a fall in aggressive-nonconformance in men between 70 and 79, and a rise between 79 and 81 in both sexes. The fall is in accordance with other findings whereas the rise was unexpected. The rise might tentatively be explained by personality changes associated with increasing

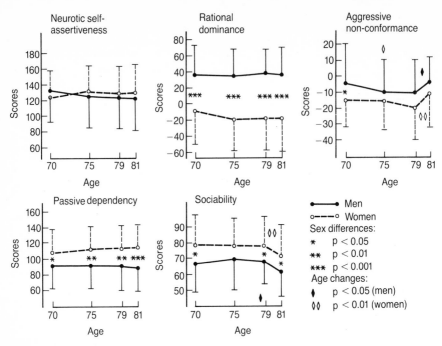

Fig. 4.5 CMPS scores in an urban sample examined at the age of 70, 75, 79 and 81.

frequency of organic brain syndromes. There was a fall in sociability in men between 75 and 81, and in women between 79 and 81, which seems to imply that there is a decrease in interpersonal involvement in old age, as previously stated by Cumming & Henry (1961), for example.

MENTAL DISORDERS

Earlier studies of the prevalence of mental disorders in adult populations have yielded widely differing figures. In recent studies the prevalence figures tend to be somewhat more alike. A constant finding has been a higher prevalence among women (Dohrenwend & Dohrenwend 1976). There still remain several methodological problems in estimating the prevalence of mental disorders (Williams et al 1980). One is the criteria for 'caseness'. Caseness might be defined on a qualitative level — which symptoms are required? — or on a quantitative level — a certain score or a certain degree of severity in symptoms are prescribed. Another problem is the choice of classification model.

In our study, operational criteria were used and diagnoses relied on relatively few symptoms and signs of a specified degree of severity (Persson 1980, Nilsson 1983b). Contrary to other investigations, cases were also defined if the subjects used psychotropic drugs in prescribed doses, even if the patient had no or few symptoms. Compared to other case definitions,

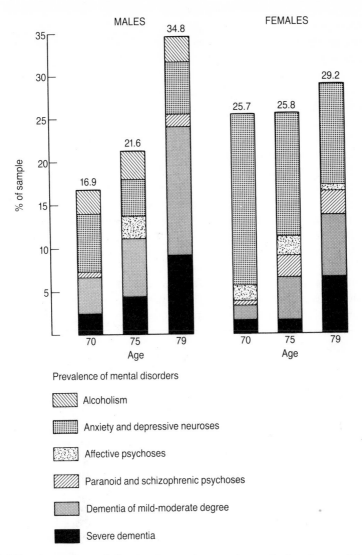

Fig. 4.6 Prevalence of mental disorders in an urban sample examined at the age of 70, 75 and 79.

ours should have a somewhat higher sensitivity. Results are given in Figure 4.6.

The main trends in prevalence figures at 70, 75 and 79 years of age (Nilsson & Persson 1984b) might be summarized as follows. Prevalence of mental disorders increased with increasing age, especially among men. This rise was due to a significant increase in dementia. In women there was a significant decrease in prevalence of neuroses between 70 and 79 years of age. In both sexes, there was a slight and non-significant increase in paranoid and schizophrenic syndromes. With regard to significant sex differences, the total prevalence was higher at 70 in women, the prevalence of neuroses was higher in women at age 70 and 75, and paranoid and schizophrenic psychoses were more common in women at age 75.

As far as concerns diagnostic instruments for mental disorders in the elderly, the fact that only limited changes in personality and cognitive function occur in the healthy elderly indicates that the customary diagnostic instruments can also be used for them. It should however be emphasized that the physiological lowering of psychomotor speed must be taken into consideration in order to avoid overdiagnosis of e.g. depression and dementia.

On the other hand, the exploration of causative factors, relevant for the understanding of the nature of the disorders and ways of treatment, is generally more complicated in the elderly. The impact of somatic impairment and disorders on psychological functioning mentioned above, as well as the impact of age-associated changes in living circumstances on mental functioning and health, are generally greater in older patients. Perceived loneliness was also related to a higher consumption of medical services and psychotropic drugs in the Göteborg studies (Berg et al 1981), and the loss of a spouse caused dramatic increases in morbidity and mortality (Mellström et al 1982).

CONCLUSION

Growing old will obviously change functional capacity sooner or later. Recent studies of samples proved to be representative for populations, and therefore allowing generalizations, have shown that age-related decline of many functions occurs later in life than was usually believed.

It has generally been considered that intellectual function, personality and mental health are markedly influenced by ageing processes. Although the collection of experiences during life must contribute positively to our cognitive ability and to our personalities, ageing processes have previously been considered to cause functional decline and weakened personality.

In healthy individuals decline in psychological functioning occurs rather late in life, if ever. Rapid changes are usually signs of physical or mental disease, and appear unrelated to age. Most people have good mental health up to very old age although the risk of organic brain disorders increases. Adjustment and life satisfaction are not related to age *per se* but to health and environmental factors.

Separating the normal from the abnormal and health from disease, is still a challenge in gerontological research. Adequate epidemiological methods, ideally using a cross-sequential approach, will help us to shed light upon the no-man's-land between health and disease. Results from the Göteborg study given in this chapter contradict the stereotype that ageing produces various decremental changes. Instead, two separate patterns emerge: in the eighth decade the majority of healthy individuals have well-preserved mental abilities but a growing minority of individuals suffer from somatic and/or mental diseases together with decremental changes in intellectual functioning and personality.

REFERENCES

Berg S 1980 Psychological functioning in 70- and 75-year-old people. Acta Psychiatrica Scandinavica 62: suppl 288
Berg S 1985 Intelligence and terminal decline. Paper presented at the XIIIth International Congress of Gerontology, New York, 1985
Berg S, Landahl S 1979 Psychological functioning in 70- and 75-year-old people. Intellectual functions and cardiovascular disease. Reports from the Department of Applied Psychology. University of Göteborg, 4 (2)
Berg S, Mellström D, Persson G, Svanborg A 1981 Loneliness in the Swedish aged. Journal of Gerontology 36: 342–349
Berg S, Nilsson L, Svanborg A 1985 Early cognitive signs of dementia: a nine year follow-up study. IInd International Congress of Psychogeriatric Medicine, Umeå, 1985
Birren J E 1970 Toward an experimental psychology of aging. American Psychologist 25: 124–135
Birren J E, Morrisson D F 1961 Analysis of the WAIS subtests in relation to age and education. Journal of Gerontology 6: 365–368
Botwinick J, Birren J E 1963 Cognitive processes: mental abilities and psychomotor responses in healthy aged men. In: Birren J E et al (eds) Human aging: a biological and behavioral study (USPHS publ. 986). Government Printing Office, Washington DC, p 97–108
Cesarec Z, Marke S 1968 Mätning av psykogena behov med frågeformulärsteknik. Skandinaviska testförlaget, Stockholm
Cumming E, Henry W E 1961 Growing old. Basic Books, New York
Dohrenwend B P, Dohrenwend B S 1976 Sex differences and psychiatric disorders. American Jounal of Sociology 81: 1447–1454
Eysenck H J, Eysenck S B G 1964 Manual of the Eysenck personality inventory. University of London Press, London
Gutmann D 1977 The cross-cultural perspective: notes toward a comparative psychology of aging. In: Birren J E, Schaie K W (eds) Handbook of the psychology of aging. Van Nostrand, New York, p 302–326
Hogan R, Desoto C B, Solano C 1977 Traits, tests, and personality research. American Psychologist 32: 255–264
Jarvik F, Blum J E 1974 Intellectual performance of octogenarians as a function of education and initial ability. Human Development p 364–375
Johansson B 1985 Memory and memory measurement in old age. Institute of Gerontology, Jönköping
Kleemeier R W 1962 Intellectual change in the senium. Proceedings of the Social Statistics Section of the American Statistical Association, p 290–295
Mellström D, Nilsson Å, Odén A, Rundgren Å, Svanborg A 1982 Mortality among the widowed in Sweden. Scandinavian Journal of Social Medicine 10: 33–41
Moss H A, Susman E J 1980 Longitudinal study of personality development. In: Brim O G, Kagan J (eds) Constancy and change in human development. Harvard University Press, Cambridge, Mass, p 530–595
Murray H A 1938 Explorations in personality. Oxford University Press, New York
Neugarten B L 1977 Personality and aging. In: Birren J E, Schaie K W (eds) Handbook of the psychology of aging. Van Nostrand, New York, p 626–649
Nilsson L V 1983a Personality changes in the aged. A transectional and longitudinal study with the Eysenck Personality Inventory. Acta Psychiatrica Scandinavica 68: 202–211
Nilsson L 1983b Prevalence of mental disorders in a 70-year-old urban sample. A cohort comparison. Journal of Clinical and Experimental Gerontology 5: 101–120

Nilsson L V, Persson G 1984a Personality changes in the aged. A longitudinal study of psychogenic needs with the CMPS. Acta Psychiatrica Scandinavica 69: 182–189

Nilsson L V, Persson G 1984b Prevalence of mental disorders in an urban sample examined at 70, 75 and 79 years of age. Acta Psychiatrica Scandinavica 69: 519–527

Persson G 1980 Prevalence of mental disorders in a 70-year-old population. Acta Psychiatrica Scandinavica 62: 119–139

Rinder L, Roupe S, Steen B, Svanborg A 1975 Seventy-year-old people in Gothenburg. A population study in an industrialized Swedish city. I. General presentation of the study. Acta Medica Scandinavica 198: 397–407

Schaie K W 1977 Quasi-experimental research designs in the psychology of aging. In: Birren J E, Schaie K W (eds) Handbook of the psychology of aging. Van Nostrand, New York, p 39–58

Schaie K W, Parham I A 1976 Stability of adult personality traits. Fact or fable? Journal of Personality and Social Psychology 34: 146–158

Schaie K W, Parham I A 1977 Cohort-sequential analyses of adult intellectual development. Developmental Psychology 13: 649–653

Svanborg A 1977 Seventy-year-old people in Gothenburg. A population study in an industrialized Swedish city. II. General presentation of social and medical conditions. Acta Medica Scandinavica suppl 611: 5–37

Svanborg A, Berg S, Nilsson L, Persson 1984 A cohort comparison of functional ability and mental disorders in two representative samples of 70-year-olds. In: Wertheimer J, Marois M (eds) Modern aging research vol. 5. Senile dementia: outlook for the future. Alan R Liss, New York, p 405–409

Svanborg A, Landahl S, Mellström D 1982 Basic issues of health care. In: Thomae H, Maddox G L (eds) New perspectives on old age. A message to decision makers. Springer, New York, p 31–52

Thomae H 1980 Personality and adjustment to aging. In: Birren J E, Sloane R B (eds) Handbook of mental health and aging. Prentice Hall, Englewood Cliffs, N J, p 285–309

Wilkie F, Eisdorfer C 1971 Intelligence and blood pressure in the aged. Science 172: 959–962

Williams P, Tarnopolsky A, Hand D 1980 Case definition and case identification in psychiatric epidemiology: review and assessment. Psychological Medicine 10: 101–114

Woodruff D S, Birren J E 1972 Age changes and cohort differences in personality. Developmental Psychology 6: 252–259

Measuring levels of disability — the Clifton Assessment Procedures for the Elderly

INTRODUCTION

The Clifton Assessment Procedures for the Elderly (CAPE) were first published under that name in 1979 by the author and colleague (Pattie & Gilleard 1979). They were the result of various smaller research projects, publications and papers which had attracted a great deal of attention nationally and internationally, illustrating the increasing awareness of the need for new and more appropriate measures of cognitive and behavioural functioning in the elderly. The CAPE, which has two parts, a Cognitive Assessment Scale (CAS) and a Behaviour Rating Scale (BRS), can measure cognitive and behavioural disabilities either separately or in a combined form as deemed appropriate to the situation and nature of the investigation. A shortened form, the CAPE Survey Version, was published at a later date (Pattie 1981). The scales are now widely used and despite some occasional criticism are generally seen as well standardised and relevant for use in studies of the elderly (Brewer 1984, Kellett 1982, Cooper & Bickel 1984, Gibson et al 1980, Wilkinson & Graham-White 1980, Woods & Britton 1985).

Background to the CAPE

The CAS (Cognitive Assessment Scale) is a short psychometric test, devised for use initially with a group of chronic patients (Pattie et al 1975); with only minor modifications it was found to be a valid and reliable measure of cognitive functioning in the elderly, and shown to have both diagnostic and prognostic value (Pattie & Gilleard 1975, 1976). It was renamed the Cognitive Assessment Scale when it became part of the CAPE. The BRS was derived from the Stockton Geriatric Rating Scale (Meer & Baker 1966), first published as the Shortened Stockton Rating Scale (SSRS) (Gilleard & Pattie 1977) and renamed the CAPE Behaviour Rating Scale when the two scales, the CAS and BRS, were published in 1979 as the Clifton Assessment Procedures for the Elderly, CAPE (Pattie & Gilleard 1979). Some later studies have referred to the scales by a variety of names and titles, but it should be recognised that the SSRS is in fact the same scale as the CAPE BRS and that the CAS and BRS together form the CAPE. In the present chapter the scales will be described by their correct titles, to avoid further confusion, even if they have been named differently in other studies.

Description of the scales (see Appendices, pp. 76–80)

The CAPE Cognitive Assessment Scale (Appendix 5.1). This has three subtests: Information/Orientation (I/O) with 12 items; Mental Ability (measuring counting, saying the alphabet, reading and writing); and the Psychomotor test, which is the Gibson Spiral Maze (Gibson 1977) with amended administration.

The CAPE Behaviour Rating Scale (Appendix 5.2) has 18 items measuring four main areas of behavioural disability, namely Physical Disability (Pd), Apathy (Ap), Communication Difficulties (Cd) and Social Disturbance (Sd). Four subscale scores can be obtained, and a total score measuring overall behavioural disability. The items are rated by a relative or carer, who knows the subject, on a three-point scale (0,1,2); the total scores therefore can range from 0–36. A grading system (Appendix 5.3) is offered with grades A–E (which can be further subdivided in the case of the BRS, for clearer classification, particularly of the frail elderly, into 11 grades), which may be seen as indicating levels of impairment in functioning. In describing the grades initially the authors suggested that certain grades were characterised by patients in particular locations needing particular types of care. While in practice this has been largely substantiated, the CAPE has been criticised for appearing to suggest that patients can actually be allocated on the basis of these scores and grades, a claim which was never made by the authors.

The Survey Version of the CAPE (Appendix 5.4) (Pattie 1981) resulted from a survey of 400 elderly people which demonstrated that a significant single factor of 'disability' accounted for 60% of the variance of the scores, and that the Information/Orientation score of the CAS and Physical Disability score of the BRS contributed most to the factor scores. A score based on I/O minus Pd correlated highly significantly ($r = 0.964$, $n = 400$, $p < 0.001$) with total scores on the CAPE and was recommended for use in large-scale surveys or projects: hence the Survey score; it is particularly useful where other tests and questionnaires are being used. This is an extremely brief test and easy to administer, though it should be recognised that even the full version of the CAPE is not time-consuming or too tiring, making it very acceptable to both the user and the subject. A grading system for the CAPE Survey score is also offered, though it has recently (McPherson & Tregaskis 1985) been criticised as having too narrow a range of scores within each grade.

STUDIES USING THE CAPE

One of the largest projects using the full CAPE is the study carried out by the author and colleagues (Pattie et al 1979, Pattie 1980). Four hundred subjects were tested three times over a two-year period, and have been followed up again more recently. Some of the data for these subjects (100 each in the community, under the social services, in geriatric and psychiatric hospitals) were used both for standardisation data and in investigating various theoretical topics to be discussed below.

Parts of the CAPE have been used extensively by some authors, notably Clarke et al (1981, 1984'), who have investigated the incidence of dementia both in homes for the elderly and in the community.

Several projects have used CAPE scores as corroborative measures of diagnoses or level of functioning (Gilleard et al 1984, Simpson 1981), while others have looked at efficacy of treatment in relation to CAPE scores and grades (Baines et al 1987, Holden & Sinebruchow 1978, Power et al 1987, Miller 1985).

Other important uses of CAPE are surveys of the elderly for the purposes of management and planning (Pattie et al 1983) and use of resources (MacDonald et al 1982; Warne et al 1984; McPherson et al 1985). The tests have also proved useful with other populations, eg. non-elderly chronic psychiatric patients (Pattie et al 1983, Flett 1981) and the mentally handicapped. (Smith et al 1981).

A few studies (Twining & Allen 1981, McPherson et al 1985, McPherson & Tregaskis 1985) have looked at further validation of the CAPE, but remarkably few have compared the CAPE results with those of other tests (Kendrick 1985, Moore & Wyke 1984).

One of the least documented, but perhaps most significant, achievements of the CAPE was to have its evidence of disability levels in homes for the elderly accepted by the Department of the Environment, resulting in rate relief of £10 000 per annum for one local authority! (Lord, 1983).

Several of the 'Rising Tide' projects funded by the Department of Health & Social Services for studying services for the elderly and some of the 'Care in the Community' studies are currently using the CAPE; the results of this work and comparison of the CAPE with other data should be interesting.

The CAPE and senile dementia

One of the earliest findings established was the diagnostic value of the CAPE I/O score. A cut-off point on this scale was shown to correctly classify over 90% of cases diagnosed as functional or organic, and a later study showed an accuracy of over 80% over a two-year period (Pattie & Gilleard 1975, 1977, 1978a). A follow-up of psychiatric patients over a six-year period showed a very high relationship between scores and diagnosis, possibly as high as 92%. The death rate was high, but 'borderline' cases and patients classified incorrectly when followed up were found to support the psychometric diagnosis (Pattie 1984a). McPherson et al (1985), using a different style of investigation, supported the CAPE's ability to distinguish between levels of impairment specifically associated with dementia.

The CAPE has been widely used as a measure of the prevalence of dementia in community and hospital settings. In 1979 Pattie and her colleagues reported a 4% incidence of dementia in their community study of 100 subjects. This was somewhat lower than would have been expected from earlier reports of incidence (Kay et al 1964, and various other studies reviewed by Cooper & Bickel 1984), particularly as the sample was not random, but included a substantial proportion of more elderly and more disabled community residents. This group was followed up over a two-year period, and again 5–6 years later; the original findings were largely supported.

Clarke et al (1984) included the CAPE I/O measure in their study of the general health and dependency of 1073 elderly people living at home. The incidence of dementia according to the CAPE criteria was surprisingly low — 1.6% — but 40 subjects 'could not be classified'. Subsequent personal contact with those authors suggests that at least some of these subjects should have been classified as low scorers. Even if the prevalence of dementia were raised to 2%, it would still be well below expected rates. A possible explanation is that the investigation studied only those over the age of 75: many studies suggest that dementia frequently shows itself well before this age (e.g. the average age of patients in psychiatric beds is usually in the seventies), and those in the community at 75+ are often the 'fit survivors' (cf. Power et al 1984).

Briggs (1985) reports a prevalence of 3–4% based on I/O score on a population of nearly 2000 people over 65 in the community drawn from age-sex registers in general practice. Gibbons (1985), in the Northampton 'Rising Tide' project, found an incidence of 2% for a smaller sample of a similar population. Unfortunately few studies have had psychiatric diagnosis or other corroborative evidence to support the findings, but one very recent study (Johnston et al 1987) found an 82% agreement in a non-psychiatric sample (district hospital). The consistency of the lack of conflict in the evidence using this or other indicators suggests that earlier studies may have been unduly pessimistic; they had methodological problems and assumed that mild impairment would lead to dementia. Too little account may be taken, even now, in looking at the increasing proportion of the elderly, of the facts that the present 60- and 70-year-olds are often in better health, the 'fit elderly' also survive in increasing proportions, the risk of mortality is decreased, and the onset of dementing illness and changes due to normal ageing are delayed. More research is clearly needed in this area, and the CAPE may have a sound contribution to make.

Borderline dementia/mild impairment

The question and validity of detecting dementia in its early stages has been discussed by Bergmann (1979), who suggested that early cases were difficult to identify, and by others interested in screening procedures for the elderly (Cooper & Bickel 1984). The assumption that mild impairment leads to dementing illness clearly has major implications for planning.

The research sample of 400 subjects (Pattie et al 1979, Pattie 1980) provided an opportunity for a follow-up study of this topic. Those who scored 8 or 9 on the I/O score at any of the four surveys over a six-year period were investigated. The pattern of their scores over time was not similar to that of a dementing process as seen in the psychiatric population, or indeed in the four community cases identified at the first survey. At subsequent surveys one or two subjects went on to develop a series of lower scores, but the majority had died or improved. Among the community sample 15 subjects obtained borderline scores (8 or 9) at one time over the six-year period; all but one were over the age of 75, and all but one died within the period. Only one subject could be identified as having an apparent dementing illness, and she was the only subject who had been transferred to a psychiatric hospital. The picture was similar for the subjects in residential homes and for those initially in psychiatric care, where only two subjects with mild impairment went on to a pattern of increasingly lowered scores. Although tentative, these findings are considered to be important, and to indicate that mild impairment does not necessarily lead to a long dementing illness, that it may indicate normal or 'benign' ageing, or may be an indication of impending mortality (cf. terminal drop data, Kleemeier 1962, Pattie 1980).

Disability and level of care

The attraction of matching disability to level of care required is seen by the number of studies which have used the grading system of the CAPE for this purpose. The notion of 'continuum of care' and appropriate use of resources is even more important at times of increasing demand and financial constraint.

Early work on the CAPE (Pattie 1980) showed a clear relationship between disability and care offered, even within a community sample where only minor differences in disability were noted. Those receiving help from general practitioners, social services or other sources were significantly more disabled on CAPE scores (though still within grades A and B) than those who did not receive help, and there was some shift in allocation of resources over the two-year period which more accurately reflected apparent need. (This was not substantiated over the 6-year follow-up, but the numbers were low, and more work in this area is needed.)

The demonstrated relationship between disability and provision of care has been well supported, though McPherson et al (1985) suggested that the grades based on the shorter survey score may not be sufficiently accurate for identification of individual need.

A different approach has been used by Wilcock & Wiltshire (1982), who, while recognising that criteria for assessment of fitness would vary between homes for the elderly, attempted to define these through multi-disciplinary assessment and CAPE scores. Of the 260 residents assessed in homes for the elderly, 190 were considered fit, 45 borderline and 25 unfit. Several criteria on the BRS were identified as closely classifying the fit residents, but the Pd and total BRS scores were best, the former giving a 91% accurate classification, and a total score of 13 or over correctly classifying 88% of fit residents. They found a high correlation between Pd and total score on this and a subsequent sample (0.87, 0.92). They used the total cut-off of 13 for a group of potential admissions, finding again a high level of agreement, 33 out of 34 from a group of 47 being correctly classified as suitable. Wilcock and Wiltshire pointed out that the score for their project was considerably different from that found by Pattie & Gilleard (1978b) in identifying a group of 'high adjustment–minimal deterioration' residents on admission and follow-up. This earlier study was, however, an attempt to identify a group who might have been considered 'too fit' for such accommodation, since they showed no deterioration over an 18-month period. Further investigation of this showed that most of the low adjustment subjects in the Pattie & Gilleard group would have been correctly classified by Wilcock and Wiltshire's data and that the mean score of 13.9 for the vulnerable group who died or were hospitalised is not dissimilar to the latters' 'unfit' subjects.

Booth et al (1982), using other scales in a very large survey (6947 residents in local-authority homes), commented on the problems of comparison of studies, since so little collaborative work has occurred, and so many different methodologies have been used. They found that their scales did not correlate very highly with others, and gave lower levels of disability than did the CAPE and several others. Follow-up and further validation of any set of assessment procedures is vital, and further work on admission and adjustment criteria is clearly necessary.

Another study (Gilleard et al 1980) compared behavioural disability in psychogeriatric patients and inhabitants of residential homes. Using the CAPE Behaviour Rating Scale, they found a high degree of overlap, but evidence of significantly greater disability in the hospital population, particularly in ratings of incontinence, confusion, communication difficulties and need for supervision. Others have commented on the overlap between homes and hospital, and Kellett (1982), in stressing the need for matching resources to need, suggested that the CAPE, along with a centrally appointed assessor and committee, should be used to ensure a reasonably consistent application of criteria for dementia, and that allocation of benefits and care be made accordingly.

An interesting Australian study of a geriatric sample by Warne et al

(1984) found correlations of $r = 0.71$ and 0.70 for team rating of disability and the BRS and CAS/BRS combined scores respectively. They noted that teams paid less importance than they should to cognitive function, and, in a comparison of team and 'score' recommendations, found the CAPE scores could frequently have improved the allocation of resources. They felt higher scores on social disturbance items identified those who need psychiatric rather than geriatric care.

Clarke et al (1981) identified, from a sample of 247 residents in local-authority homes, a fairly large number (105) who had scores of ≤ 5 on the I/O score. The CAPE BRS scores on Pd, Ap and Sd were found to differ significantly between two groups ($n = 60$), classified by staff as 'problem' or 'non-problem' residents. The behavioural deficits which made residents difficult to manage were seen as not being confined to social disturbance but to relate to disability generally, and seemed to provide further support for the need for overlap between National Health Service (NHS) and Social Services staff.

The usefulness of CAPE for planning and management

There are few published studies on this topic, though much applied work is known to have been done. Several studies mentioned in the preceding section are relevant, as is a large-scale hospital survey by nursing and psychology staff (Pattie et al 1983) which used BRS scores to assist in the reorganisation of hospital wards. The nurses found that the BRS scores provided an excellent objective database which facilitated change in hospital policy.

The BRS grades were accepted by the ward nursing staff as a valid measure of their patients' functioning, with very few exceptions. Patients can be allocated according to nursing/hospital policies; in this case mixed disability wards were chosen for some groups of patients, notably the elderly or psychogeriatric wards, whereas grades determined the allocation of chronic psychiatric patients to different styles of wards according to disability levels. Earlier work by the CAPE authors has used the BRS extensively in similar surveys, and the scale has been found helpful in making across-ward and across-hospital comparisons. BRS results have been shown to be equally useful in identifying younger psychiatric patients whose levels of disability suggested they might be suitable for more active intervention, more intensive rehabilitation and/or discharge from hospital.

Smith et al (1981), in assessing the reliability and validity of the CAPE for the elderly mentally handicapped, also refer to the use of the scales in assessing need for care; they found significant correlations between the test results and estimated levels of independence. They also found a significant relationship between the CAPE and IQ measures and it seems, therefore, that the CAPE may also be valid and useful in screening the mentally handicapped.

Test results on large-scale surveys can also be used to monitor change in hospital patients. For example, the York survey (Pattie & Gilleard 1977) showed that moving wards had a deleterious effect on behavioural functioning in the elderly, but did not appear to adversely affect the risk of mortality. This study was carried out made over a one-year period with a large number of patients. An advantage of the brevity of the CAPE is that large populations can be assessed quickly, facilitating comparisons of populations rated close together in time.

It must be stressed that the CAPE provides a means of screening and identifying individuals and their possible needs — the match can never be perfect. To expect this from any test is unrealistic, and would deny the importance of clinical and social factors and be an injustice to staff and patients alike.

Evaluation of treatment

Several studies have used the CAPE as a pre- and post-'treatment' measure, thus allowing for the matching of control subjects and objective measurement of change.

Miller (1985) reported a study which used CAPE scores to match patients for disability before comparing changes related to two different nursing regimes, 'task allocation' and 'individualised nursing care' (the nursing process). For patients who had been in hospital for more than one month, there was apparently a significant increase in both cognitive and behavioural disability for those in the 'task allocation' wards as compared with those in wards using the nursing process. A longer term study in the same setting showed some improvement over a two-year period for the patients in the wards with the individualised approach. Some items of the BRS — e.g. being in bed, incontinence and some aspects of self care — were seen to be influenced by ward practice. This is an important study as it shows that some but not all aspects of disability are potentially reversible. The link between environmental factors and dependency has also been discussed by Booth et al (1982), for the case of residential homes.

Expectations of change in the more cognitive aspects of the functioning of the elderly due to psychological interventions have not generally been met. Greene et al (1983) reported some improvement in CAPE I/O scores following 'Reality Orientation' programmes, but this change was not lasting. Holden & Sinebruchow (1978) using the CAPE, and Hanley et al (1981) using different cognitive measures, also found no consistent evidence of change, particularly in behaviour.

Baines et al (1987) found different patterns of change in a study evaluating reality orientation (RO) and reminiscence therapy (REM), with only the group who received RO followed by REM showing improvement on CAPE cognitive and behavioural measures. They, like many others, comment on the other benefits of such programmes, e.g. improvements in staff morale and in the quality of life of the patients.

Chanfreau-Rona et al (1984) reported stability in CAPE cognitive scores for a group of patients on a continence programme, by comparison with matched groups who showed some deterioration over time. They stressed the need to start programmes before incontinence, cognitive impairment and morale became too low for benefits to occur.

Power et al (1984) also found (as have other unpublished studies on similar topics) that intervention (in his case volunteers visiting inmates of residential homes) has much less impact if offered to people showing evidence of fairly severe deterioration on CAPE scores.

MacDonald et al (1982), using a comparable style of investigation but different scales to investigate dementia, disability and outcome, concluded, as had Gilleard & Pattie (1980) using the CAPE, that type of care did not greatly affect mortality or deterioration, both of which are more determined by the initial levels of cognitive and behavioural competence.

Only one drug trial using the CAPE has been traced in published form (Martin et al 1983) — this showed no change in CAS scores as a result of administering a synthetic peptide to patients.

DISABILITY AND DEPENDENCY

Rating scales have been accused of confusing these two issues, and sometimes further problems are caused by trying to include measures of depression and psychiatric disturbance in an attempt to get an overall view of the elderly. Townsend (1979) offered five ways of looking at or defining disability, and the recent NHS Financial Information Project (1984) again stressed the need for definition and clarity of use in discussing disability in the elderly. The CAPE deals with cognitive impairment and behavioural disability — it does not attempt to measure depression, which can, of course, affect functioning. It does, however, take account of behavioural disturbance in its Sd scale, seeing it as relevant to overall disability, though it may offer a slightly different dimension from the other sub-scales (Gilleard & Pattie 1980). Dependency and need for care reflect disability, but the type of care needed by an individual is not necessarily directly indicated. It is therefore important to recognise which aspects of cognitive and behavioural disability are subject to change through environmental, medical and other factors (cf. Miller 1985). While disability in the elderly is not always permanent, the potential for change does seem to be limited, and current and future studies may look more at possibilities for slowing down deterioration and optimising potential.

Pattie (1980) found a close relationship between level of care and measured disability, and considered it meaningful to think in terms of a continuum of care and dependency. This study also showed the existence of a general factor of cognitive and behavioural disability, accounting for a large degree of variance in several groups of elderly people. This was less noticeable in the narrow range of less disabled community residents, and more so for the very disabled and those about to die, possibly confirming the increasing homogeneity or 'dedifferentiation' of abilities with increasing deterioration. The CAPE offers a fairly global measure of disability and has limitations for measurement of smaller or more specific changes. Here other scales may be more useful, though the CAPE's brevity, fairly wide coverage and extensive UK validation (Woods & Britton 1985) may justify its inclusion, even when other scales are used, to increase comparability of findings.

Factors other than methodological ones also make it difficult at times to investigate the relationship of disability to dependency, particularly in settings such as residential homes.

Local authority homes for the elderly

While several studies mentioned above have referred to work in residential homes, it is perhaps worth considering this topic again. The CAPE has been used, as have other tests, to measure the prevalence of senile dementia in such homes with even more varying results than community surveys!

In the original standardisation work on the CAPE, the residents in several homes were assessed, and the incidence of residents scoring I/O $\leq$ 7, i.e. showing evidence of cognitive impairment, was usually of the order of 33%. Power et al (1984) in Bristol obtained a very much lower figure, whereas the Leicester survey (Clarke et al 1981) found a much higher proportion (51%) of residents scoring within the dementia range. Both these studies used the CAPE I/O score, and the results may be a reflection of different local policies. Other studies using different techniques have also come up with widely varying figures: Mann et al (1984) supporting a prevalence rate of about 33%, Masterson et al (1979) finding 27%–66% and Booth (1985) reported a 48% prevalence of confusion ($n = 6891$). Some studies (e.g. Pattie et al 1979, Wilkin et al 1978) have found evidence of increasing disability among residents in residential homes, whereas others have not supported this (Masterton et al 1981). Booth (1985) found that only mental confusion showed increased prevalence; there was no apparent change in other aspects of disability. Since mortality risk is associated with increased cognitive impairment, the problem may not be one of great need for extra places, but one of appropriate staffing for such homes where the level of disability clearly merits different skills (e.g. community psychiatric nurses) than those usually available (cf. Masterton et al 1979, Mann et al 1984).

It was noted too (Pattie 1980) that change in disability was not necessarily associated with transfer of residents of such homes; staff seem willing to continue to care for quite deteriorated residents, so that the match of disability and appropriateness of care is further confused.

Clearly local policy (and more recently, the proliferation of private nursing homes) makes it difficult to utilise the data available, but nonetheless it is essential to continue to monitor cognitive and behavioural levels in different types of care provision for the elderly.

Changes in disability over time and with age

Early psychological studies concentrated on the apparent decline in intellectual functioning with age, and there is still great interest in the nature of dementing illness and 'normal ageing'. Pattie (1980) found significant but extremely small changes in cognitive and behavioural functioning as measured by the CAPE in her cross-sequential study of 400 elderly. This was true across all age-groups and almost all levels of disability, but it was noted that, particularly among those living in the community or comparatively unimpaired subjects, mean differences in scores were often due to a number of subjects deteriorating more markedly and some not at all. The recent follow-up study six years after the initial survey confirmed that many fit, even very elderly, subjects show little evidence of change in their scores over time. Even small differences in scores were seen to be reflected in change in care however; e.g. six out of seven subjects who had moved from their own homes to other care had 'deteriorated', i.e. their survey scores (I/O − Pd) had dropped by two points or more.

Although there is clearly an association between age and increasing disability, the correlation between age and scores is usually low: age and CAS total score, $r = -0.216$; age and BRS total score, $r = 0.258$ ($n = 400$, $p < 0.001$ in both cases) (Pattie 1980). While age was shown to have an effect on both cognitive and behavioural scores, the sex of the subject had an effect on cognitive scores only. Factor analysis of the results of the 400 subjects showed that age contributed more to behavioural than to cognitive decline. Interestingly, the factor structure in this survey was slightly different for men and women; men's scores yielding two factors, a strong cognitive first factor and a second factor loading more on physical disability and apathy, whereas women's scores produced only one overall disability factor. Although the scores of all subjects deteriorated over time, it seemed that men could rarely survive after a certain level of impairment had been reached. There was very tentative evidence that this related more to cognitive than behavioural deterioration. This sex difference may account in part for the much greater numbers of elderly women who suffer from long-term dementing illness than men. Sex differences in the nature of disability have also been noted in the elderly mentally handicapped by Smith et al (1981); again this is an area meriting further study.

COMPARISON WITH OTHER TESTS

As already stated, there is little systematic validation of the CAPE against other studies, particularly in terms of its diagnostic and prognostic value. Several fairly small studies have shown correlations between the CAPE and other tests, e.g. Kendrick (1985) reports correlations of $r = 0.66$, ($p < 0.001$) for the Kendrick object Learning Test and the CAS and $r = -0.63$ ($p < 0.01$) with the BRS; Moore & Wyke (1984) reported 'highly significant correlations' between drawing ability, CAS scores and three of four Wechsler Adult Intelligence Scale (WAIS) subtest scores: and Skelton-Robinson & Jones (1984) found a correlation of $r = 0.578$, $(p < 0.01)$ for the BRS and a test of nominal dysphasia. Pattie & Gilleard (1979) reported higher correlations between the CAS and the WAIS performance scale than between the CAS and the verbal scale; they also found a high correlation $(r = 0.90, p < 0.01)$ between the CAS I/O score and the Wechsler Memory Scale total score. Despite its wide use, the WAIS itself has not proved of great value in predictive diagnosis in the elderly (Bolton et al 1966) or in predicting outcome (Pattie & Gilleard 1979). More work is needed to justify the subjective comparisons often made between tests; the CAPE scales still seem to offer as reliable and valid a measure as any other, and are, of course, shorter than most. It is comparatively easy to get group differences on tests of cognitive and behavioural functioning for the impaired and non-impaired elderly; outcome and follow-up studies are essential in their further evaluation and are rarely carried out.

CRITICISM OF THE CAPE

As mentioned earlier in this chapter, the CAPE scales were derived from earlier work, proved to be reliable and valid, and have been extensively used clinically and in research projects. At a practical level some users have questioned the usefulness of the Gibson Spiral Maze (Hamilton 1982), whereas others have queried the grading system, particularly for the Survey Version (McPherson et al 1985); and the factor structure of the BRS has also been disputed (Twining & Allen 1981). It is, however, debatable whether such points should lead to any radical alterations in the scales, since revisions and and amendments to standardised scales often create as many problems as they solve.

THE FUTURE FOR THE CAPE

The CAPE is still seen as useful in screening procedures and surveys and for the individual patient. Unevenness in CAPE scores can lead to appropriate therapeutic interventions; for instance, to increasing activity and therapeutic intervention where Apathy scores are lower than the overall level of functioning would seem to indicate, whether for an individual or ward; alerting caring staff to the possibility of depression or understimulation and apathy where behavioural scores are worse than cognitive, etc., etc. The identification of behaviours which can be changed by manipulation of the environment and the relationship of stress on the part of carers to measured disability and other factors are promising areas of current and future research (Gilleard et al 1984).

The work of Ballinger et al (1982) on cluster analysis of symptoms in elderly demented patients, which involved some parts of the CAPE, is also a promising development.

The aim of this chapter has been to review the CAPE and some of its applications. It cannot be comprehensive, but one can hope it will act partly as a reference point for those interested in working with the elderly, in the CAPE and in the need for attempts to rationalise methodological issues, and in limitations in assessing the elderly. New psychological developments will continue to need objective measures and constant evaluation. Short scales such as the CAPE offer an opportunity for rapid and non-intrusive measurement, giving clinicians opportunity for applied research. Hopefully the CAPE can continue to make a contribution to the evaluation and maintaining of services, and to the care of the individual elderly person.

REFERENCES

Baines S, Saxby P, Ehlert K 1987 Reality orientation and reminiscence therapy: a controlled cross-over study of elderly confused people. British Journal of Psychiatry (in press)

Ballinger B R, Reid A H, Heather B B 1982 Cluster analysis of symptoms in elderly demented patients. British Journal of Psychiatry 140: 257–262

Bergmann K 1979 The problem of early diagnosis. In: Alzheimer's disease: Early Recognition of Potentially Reversible Deficits Eds. Glen A I M & Whalley, L J Ch. 16, pp 68–77, Churchill Livingstone, Edin.

Bolton N, Britton P G, Savage R D 1966 Some normative Data on the WAIS and its Indices in an Aged Population. Journal of Clinical Psychology 22: 183–188

Booth T 1985 Home truths; old people's homes and the outcome of care. Gower, Aldershot

Booth T, Barritt A, Berry S, Martin D N, Melotte C, Stone S 1982 Levels of dependency in local authority homes for the elderly. Journal of Epidemiology and Community Health 36: 53–57

Brewer P 1984 Brief assessments for the elderly mentally infirm. Occupational Therapy (June): p 168–171

Briggs R 1985 Personal communication

Chanfreau-Rona D, Bellwood S, Wylie B 1984 Assessment of a behavioural programme to treat incontinent patients in psychogeriatric wards. British Journal of Clinical Psychology 23: 273–279

Clarke M, Williams A J, Jones P A 1981 A psychogeriatric survey of old people's homes. British Medical Journal 283: 1307–1310

Clarke M, Clarke S, Odell A, Jagger C 1984 The elderly at home: health and social status. Health Trends 16: 3–7

Cooper P and Bickel H 1984 Population screening and the early detection of dementing disorders in old age: a review. Psychological Medicine 14: 81–95

Flett S 1981 Elderly dependency survey Report for Health Care Planning Team Unpublished report, South Lincolnshire Health Authority

Gibbons R 1985 Personal communication

Gibson A J, Moyes I C A and Kendrick D 1980 Cognitive assessment of the elderly long-stay patient. British Journal of Psychiatry 137: 551–557

Gibson H B 1977 Manual of the Gibson Spiral Maze (2nd edit). Hodder and Stoughton, Sevenoaks

Gilleard C J, Pattie A H 1977 The Stockton Geriatric Rating Scale: a shortened version with British normative data. British Journal of Psychiatry 131: 90–94

Gilleard C J and Pattie A H 1980 Dimensions of disability in the elderly: construct validity of rating scales for elderly populations. British Psychological Society Annual Conference, Aberdeen.

Gilleard C J, Pattie A H, Derman G 1980 Behavioural disabilities in psychogeriatric patients and residents of old people's homes. Journal of Epidemiology and Community Health 34: 106–110

Gilleard C J, Gilleard E, Whittick J E 1984 Impact of psychogeriatric day hospital care on the patient's family. British Journal of Psychiatry 145: 487–492

Greene J G, Timbury G C, Smith R, Gardiner M 1983 Reality orientation with elderly patients in the community: an empirical evaluation. Age and Ageing 12: 38–43

Hamilton M 1982 Use of rating scales in geriatric patients. Gerontology 28: 42–48

Hanley I G, McGuire R J, Boyd W D 1981 Reality orientation aɴd dementia: a controlled trial of two approaches British Journal of Psychiatry 138: 10–14

Holden U P, Sinebruchow A 1978 Reality orientation therapy: a study investigating the value of the therapy in the rehabilitation of elderly people. Age and Ageing 7: 83–90

Johnston M, Wakeling A, Graham N, Stokes F 1987 Cognitive impairment, emotional disorder and length of stay of elderly patients in a district general hospital (in press)

Kay D W K, Beamish P, Roth M 1964 Old age mental disorders in Newcastle Upon Tyne. British Journal of Psychiatry 110: 146–158, 668–682

Kellett J M 1982 A new approach to the elderly. British Medical Journal 285: 1588–1589

Kendrick 1985 The Kendrick Cognitive Test for the Elderly. NFER Nelson, Windsor

Kleemeier R W 1962 Intellectual changes in the senium. Proceedings of the Social Statistics Section of the American Statistical Association, p 290–295

Lord R 1983 Gaining some relief for old people's homes. Local Government Chronicle (April) p 416–417

MacDonald A J D, Mann A H, Jenkins R, Richard L, Godlove C, Rodwell G 1982 An attempt to determine the impact of four types of care upon the elderly in London by the study of matched groups. Psychological Medicine 12: 193–200

McPherson F M, Tregaskis D 1985 The short-term stability of the Survey Version of CAPE. British Journal of Clinical Psychology 24: 205–206

McPherson F M, Gamsu C V, Kiemle G, Ritchie S M, Stanley A M, Tregaskis D 1985 The concurrent validity of the Survey Version of the Clifton Assessment Procedures for the Elderly. British Journal of Clinical Psychology 24: 83–91

Mann A H, Graham N, Ashby D 1984 Psychiatric illness in residential homes for the elderly: a survey in one London borough. Age and Ageing 13: 257–265

Martin J C, Ballinger B R, Cockram L, McPherson F M, Pigache R M, Tregaskis D 1983 Effect of a synthetic peptide, ORG 2766, on in-patients with severe senile dementia. Acta Psychiatrica Scandinavica 67: 205–207

Masterton G, Holloway E M, Timbury G C 1979 The prevalence of organic cerebral impairment and behavioural problems within local authority homes for the elderly. Age and Ageing 8: 226–230

Masterton G, Holloway E M, Timbury G C 1981 Role of local authority homes in the care of the dependent elderly: a prospective study. British Medical Journal 283: 523–524

Meer B, Baker J A 1966 The Stockton Geriatric Rating Scale. Journal of Gerontology 21: 392–403

Miller A 1985 A study of the dependency of elderly patients in wards using different methods of nursing care. Age and Ageing 14: 132–138

Moore V, Wyke M A 1984 Drawing disability in patients with senile dementia. Psychological Medicine 14: 97–105

NHS Financial Information Project 1984 Support paper — Disability in the Elderly. West Midlands Regional Health Authority

Pattie A H 1980 Disability in the elderly and patterns of care: a psychological study. D.Phil Thesis, University of York

Pattie A H 1981 A Survey Version of the Clifton Assessment Procedures for the Elderly (CAPE). British Journal of Social and Clinical Psychology 20: 173–178

Pattie A H 1984a Evaluating the CAPE in the assessment of dementia. Paper presented at a conference on the Clinical Methodology of Psychiatric Treatment Trials, Department of Psychiatry, University of Birmingham, September 1984

Pattie A H 1984b Psychological instruments in the diagnosis of dementia and the management of change. Symposium on Dementia in Old Age, Department of Psychiatry, University of Leeds, October 1984

Pattie A H, Gilleard C J 1975 A brief psychogeriatric assessment schedule — validation against psychiatric diagnosis and discharge from hospital. British Journal of Psychiatry 127: 489–493

Pattie A H, Gilleard C J 1976 The Clifton Assessment Schedule — further validation of a psychogeriatric assessment schedule. British Journal of Psychiatry 129: 68–72

Pattie A H, Gilleard C J 1977 Ward survey, Clifton Hospital. Psychology Department, York Health Authority, York

Pattie A H, Gilleard C J 1978a The two year predictive validity of the Clifton Assessment Schedule and the Shortened Stockton Geriatric Rating Scale. British Journal of Psychiatry 133: 457–460

Pattie A H, Gilleard C J 1978b Admission and adjustment of residents in homes for the elderly. Journal of Epidemiology and Community Health 32: 212–214

Pattie A H, Gilleard C J 1979 Manual of the Clifton Assessment Procedures for the Elderly (CAPE). Hodder and Stoughton, Sevenoaks

Pattie A H, Williams A, Emery D 1975 Helping the chronic patient in an industrial therapy setting: an experiment in inter-disciplinary co-operation. British Journal of Psyciatry 126: 30–33

Patie A H, Gilleard C J, Bell J H 1979 The relationship of the intellectual and behavioural competence of the elderly to their present and future needs from community, residential and hospital services. Report for Yorkshire Regional Health Authority, York

Pattie A H, Irvine E, Wilk R, McAndrew P 1983 Three articles, Hospital Surveys 1, 2, 3, in Nursing Times 79 (46,47,48)

Power M J, Clough R, Gibson P, Kelly S 1984 Helping lively minds — a volunteer experiment in residential care of the elderly. Report to DHSS, available from University of Bristol Social Care Research

Simpson S, Woods R, Britton P 1981 Depression and engagement in a residential home for the elderly. Behaviour Research and Therapies 19: 435–438

Skelton-Robinson M, Jones S 1984 Nominal dysphasia and the severity of senile dementia. British Journal of Psychiatry 145: 168–171

Smith A H W, Ballinger B R, Presly A S 1981 The reliability and validity of two assessment scales in the elderly mentally handicapped. British Journal of Psychiatry 138: 15–16

Townsend P 1979 Poverty in the United Kingdom: A Survey of Household Resources and Standards of Living. Peregrine.

Twining T C, Allen D G 1981 Disability factors among residents of old people's homes. Journal of Epidemiology and Community Health 35: 305–307

Warne R W, Thomas T, Shepherd S J 1984 The Clifton Assessment Procedures for the Elderly 19th Annual Conference of the Australian Association of Gerontology, University of Sydney August 1984

Wilcock G K, Wiltshire M 1982 Criteria for assessing a client's fitness for admission to a welfare home: a practical proposition. Journal of Epidemiology and Community Health 36: 303–305

Wilkin D, Mashiah T, Jolley D J 1978 Changes in the behavioural characteristics of elderly populations of local authority homes and long-stay hospital wards 1976–1977. British Medical Journal 2: 1274–6

Wilkinson I M, Graham-White J 1980 Psychogeriatric Dependency Rating Scales (PGDRS), a method of assessment for use by nurses. British Journal of Psychiatry 137: 558–565

Williamson J, Stokoe I H, Gray S, Fisher M, Smith A 1964 Old people at home: their unreported needs. Lancet I: 1117–1120

Woods R T, Britton P G 1985 Clinical psychology with the elderly. Croom Helm, London

APPENDIX 5.1

CLIFTON ASSESSMENT PROCEDURES FOR THE ELDERLY (CAPE)

Cognitive Assessment Scale

Name: ....

Current address/placement: ....

....

Date of birth: .... **Occupation:** ....

Information/Orientation

Name:	Hospital/Address:	Colour of British Flag:
Age:	City:	Day:
D.o.B.	P.M.:	Month:
Ward/Place:	U.S. President:	Year:

I/O Score . . . .

Mental Ability

Count 1-20	*Time:*........*Errors:*........		Alphabet	*Time:*........*Errors:*........	
	≤10 secs - no errors	3		≤10 secs - no errors	3
	≤30 secs - no errors	2		≤30 secs - no errors	2
	≤30 secs - 1 error	1		≤30 secs - 1 error	1
		0			0
Write name:			Reading:	(See overleaf)	
	Correct and legible	2		10 words or more	3
	Can write but not correctly	1		6-9 words	2
	Not able to	0		1-5 words	1
				0 words	0

MAb Score . . . .

Psychomotor   *Time:* .... *Errors:* ....   Pm Score . . . .

Scoring

Errors:	0-12	13-24	25-36	37-48	49-60	61-72	73-84	85-96	96 +	N/C	N/A
Score:	10	9	8	7	6	5	4	3	2	1	0

Add Bonus 2 if 60 secs or under;
          1 if 120 secs or under

Assessed by: ....   **Date:** ....

APPENDIX 5.2

CLIFTON ASSESSMENT PROCEDURES FOR THE ELDERLY (CAPE)

Behaviour Rating Scale

Name: .... **Date of birth:** ....

Current address/placement: ....

....

Please ring the appropriate **number** for each item

1. When bathing or dressing, he/she requires:
   - no assistance   0
   - some assistance   1
   - maximum assistance   2

2. With regard to walking, he/she:
   - shows no signs of weakness   0
   - walks slowly without aid, or uses a stick   1
   - is unable to walk, or if able to walk, needs
     frame, crutches or someone by his/her side   2

3. He/she is incontinent of urine and/or faeces (day or night):
   - never   0
   - sometimes (once or twice per week)   1
   - frequently (3 times per week or more)   2

4. He/she is in bed during the day (bed does **not** include couch, settee, etc):
   - never   0
   - sometimes   1
   - almost always   2

5. He/she is confused (unable to find way around, loses possessions, etc):
   - almost never confused   0
   - sometimes confused   1
   - almost always confused   2

6. When left to his/her own devices, his/her appearance (clothes and/or hair) is:
   - almost never disorderly   0
   - sometimes disorderly   1
   - almost always disorderly   2

7. If allowed outside, he/she would:
   - never need supervision   0
   - sometimes need supervision   1
   - always need supervision   2

8. He/she helps out in the home/ward:
   - often helps out   0
   - sometimes helps out   1
   - never helps out   2

9. He/she keeps him/herself occupied in a constructive or useful activity (works, reads, plays games, has hobbies, etc):
   - almost always occupied   0
   - sometimes occupied   1
   - almost never occupied   2

10. He/she socialises with others:
    - does establish a good relationship with others   0
    - has some difficulty establishing good relationships   1
    - has a great deal of difficulty establishing good
      relationships   2

11. He/she is willing to do things suggested or asked of him/her:
    - often goes along   0
    - sometimes goes along   1
    - almost never goes along   2

12. He/she understands what you communicate to him/her (you may use speaking, writing, or gesturing):

— understands almost everything you communicate 0
— understands some of what you communicate 1
— understands almost nothing of what you communicate 2

13. He/she communicates in any manner (by speaking, writing or gesturing):

— well enough to make him/herself easily understood at all times 0
— can be understood sometimes or with some difficulty 1
— can rarely or never be understood for whatever reason 2

14. He/she is objectionable to others **during the day** (loud or constant talking, pilfering, soiling furniture, interfering with affairs of others):

— rarely or never 0
— sometimes 1
— frequently 2

15. He/she is objectionable to others **during the night** (loud or constant talking, pilfering, soiling furniture, interfering in affairs of others, wandering about, etc.):

— rarely or never 0
— sometimes 1
— frequently 2

16. He/she accuses others of doing him/her bodily harm or stealing his/her personal possessions — if you are **sure** the accusations are true, rate zero, otherwise rate one or two:

— never 0
— sometimes 1
— frequently 2

17. He/she hoards apparently meaningless items (wads of paper, string, scraps of food, etc.):

— never 0
— sometimes 1
— frequently 2

18. His/her sleep pattern at night is:

— almost never awake 0
— sometimes awake 1
— often awake 2

Eyesight:
(tick which applies)

— can see (or can see with glasses)
— partially blind
— totally blind

Hearing:
(tick which applies)

— no hearing difficulties, without hearing aid
— no hearing difficulties, though requires hearing aid
— has hearing difficulties which interfere with communication
— is very deaf

Rated by: . . . . Date: . . . .
Staff/Relative

APPENDIX 5.3

CAPE DEPENDENCY GRADES

A — no impairment: independent elderly — comparable to those living without support in the community

B — mild impairment: low dependency — likely to include those needing some support in the community, warden-supervised accommodation and the better residents in residential accommodation

C — moderate impairment: medium dependency — people functioning at this level are likely to need residential care or considerable support and help if at home

D — marked impairment: high dependency — it is within this category that there is the greatest overlap between those in social services accommodation and those in hospital care

E — severe impairment: maximum dependency — this level is seen most often in psychogeriatric wards and the ones who remain in community homes/E.M.I. hostels often present considerable problems to staff in terms of their demands on staff time

Grades	A	B	C	D	E
I/O	12,11	10,9	8,7,6	5,4,3	2,1,0
MAb	11	10,9,8	7,6	5,4	3,2,1,0
Pm	12,11,10	9,8,7	6,5,4	3,2	1,0
CAS total	35-30	29-24	23-16	15-9	8-0
BRS total	0-3	4-7	8-12	13-17	18+
Pd	0,1	2,3	4,5	6,7	8-12
Ap	0,1	2,3	4,5	6,7	8-10
Cd	0	0	0	1	2-4
Sd	0	1	2	3,4	5-10

APPENDIX 5.4

CLIFTON ASSESSMENT PROCEDURES FOR THE ELDERLY (CAPE)
Survey Version

Name: ....

Current address/placement ....

Date of birth:... **Age:**..

Information/Orientation

Name:	Hospital/Address	Colour of Flag:
Age:	City:	Day:
D.o.B.	P.M.:	Month:
Ward/Place:	U.S. President:	Year:

I/O Score . . .

Physical disability

1. When bathing or dressing, he/she requires:
   - —no assistance — 0
   - —some assistance — 1
   - —maximum assistance — 2

2. With regard to walking, he/she:
   - —shows no signs of weakness — 0
   - —walks slowly without aid, or uses a stick — 1
   - —is unable to walk, or if able to walk, needs frame, crutches or someone by his/her side — 2

3. He/she is incontinent of urine and/or faeces (day or night):
   - —never — 0
   - —sometimes (once or twice per week) — 1
   - —frequently (3 times per week or more) — 2

4. He/she is in bed during the day (bed does **not** include couch, settee, etc):
   - —never — 0
   - —sometimes — 1
   - —almost always — 2

5. He/she is confused (unable to find way around, loses possessions, etc):
   - —almost never confused — 0
   - —sometimes confused — 1
   - —almost always confused — 2

6. When left to his/her own devices, his/her appearance (clothes and/or hair) is:
   - —almost never disorderly — 0
   - —sometimes disorderly — 1
   - —almost always disorderly — 2

Pd Score . . .

CAPE Survey Score: (I/O — Pd):................................... **Grade**....................................

Assessed by:... **Date:**...

Measuring levels of disability — an hierarchical approach

INTRODUCTION

Diseases are specific morbid processes. Disabilities on the other hand, refer to inabilities to perform essential tasks. In the aged, diseases are important, but it is often disabilities which are of utmost concern to patients and carers. Thus, examination of the elderly should emphasize functional assessment as well as diagnosis of disease states.

Old age is a time of decline for many mental and physical abilities. In a recent Health Interview Survey (NCHS 1975), 5% of the aged were so disabled they had to live in institutions and another 17% who lived in the community were unable to carry on essential activities. Similarly, Gurland et al (1983) reported that 30% of the elderly in New York and 31% in London were 'Personal Time Dependent (PTD)': they had mental or physical disabilities requiring someone to provide services essential to the dependent's existence in the given setting. Furthermore, the frequency of PTD increased with age: 17 and 18% of the elderly aged 65 to 69 in New York and London respectively were Personal Time Dependent, compared to 53% and 34% respectively of those aged 80+. Inevitably, provision of services to this large group of disabled elderly will become a major pre-occupation of health care planners and health care providers. Such service delivery will require accurate assessment of disability. Brief, reliable and valid measures of disability will have to be developed.

In attempting to measure this inability to perform certain tasks (disability), it is useful to consider how task performance is organized. At one level, the performance of a task involves the integrated participation of a number of tissues and organs in a functional process resulting in the performance of the task (Luria 1966). At another level, task performance depends on the mastery and integration of a number of simpler performances. Thus, task performances are at the top of functional hierarchies of progressively less complex performances. For example, if walking is an essential task one might construct a simple 'Walking hierarchy':

Walk	Sit
Stand	Head control

In this functional hierarchy, the ability to walk follows, and is dependent at least in part on, mastery of the ability to stand, which in turn follows, and is dependent on, mastery of the ability to sit, then mastery of head control.

Interestingly, these functional hierarchies often reflect human developmental sequences. In the infant, head control precedes and is prerequisite to the ability to sit, which in turn precedes and is prerequisite to the ability to stand, then walk. Similarly, the eventual performance of complex hand and finger gestures depends first on central, then more peripheral neurological-neuropsychological development: i.e. first the development of co-ordinated body movements, then independent arm, hand and finger movements, then visual-motor coordination, then simultaneous coordinated movements of hands, then fingers.

Increasing disability often involves reverse progression through these functional hierarchies — when complex physical and mental tasks are no longer able to be performed, more simple tasks in the hierarchy may be conserved depending on the level of disability: i.e. the subject who can no longer walk may be able to stand or sit. If functional hierarchies could be described for a number of task performances, then the functional level in the hierarchy or the level of disability could be determined. Moreover, the hierarchical nature of such functional levels would mean that successful performance at a given level would automatically result in successful performance at levels lower in the hierarchy.

During the past century, a number of authors have referred to the apparent hierarchical organization of the mental functions. At the turn of the century Hughlings Jackson (1958) described the hierarchical organization of motor function; Luria (1966) described the hierarchical organization of higher mental functions; Hubel (1963) described the apparent hierarchical organization of the visual cortex of the cat. Similarly, Piaget (Flavel, 1963) described an hierarchy of human cognitive development: the sensory-motor stage (the most primitive stage of development) was followed by a preoperative stage, by a stage of concrete operations and then by a stage of formal operations. A child who successfully passed tests at the concrete operative level could pass tests at lower levels in this cognitive hierarchy but could not necessarily pass tests at the higher formal operative level.

As dementia progresses, there seems to be a fairly consistent hierarchical decline in mental function. Ajuriaguerra et al (1964) have demonstrated that functional decline in demented subjects approximates to Piaget's developmental stages in reverse: there is a reverse progression of test performance characteristic of each developmental stage. Impairment of dissociation of weight and volume precedes impairment of conservation of weight which precedes impairment of conservation of the horizontal, which in turn precedes impairment of conservation of the vertical. Furthermore, there is some evidence that decline in neuropsychological and neurological functions follows a similar hierarchical pattern (Constantinidis & Richard, 1978): for example, in the decline of language functions nominal aphasia usually precedes the appearance of paraphasias: which usually precede the appearance of deformed words. This apparent hierarchical organization and decline of mental functions was extended to the measurement of cognitive impairment in dementia, resulting in the development of an Hierarchic Dementia Scale (Cole et al 1983)

THE HIERARCHIC DEMENTIA SCALE

The first step in the development of the Hierarchic Dementia Scale (HDS) (see Appendix 6.1, pp. 90–91) was the compilation of a list of mental functions in which hierarchies might be constructed. Clinical experience was used to delineate 45 mental functions covering amnesic, cognitive and psychomotor spheres, and these were initially investigated. With further experience in testing, 25 of these functions were excluded because they were found to contribute little information or were functions for which it seemed impossible to construct hierarchies (i.e. estimation, auditory gnosis, social behaviour and continence, etc.). The final list comprises 20 functions which include orienting reflexes, looking behaviour, orientation, personal remote memory, registration, recent memory, ideomotor praxis, ideational praxis, graphic praxis, constructional praxis, concentration, denomination, comprehension (written and verbal), reading, writing, gnosis, calculation, similarities, pre-frontal signs and motor system.

The next step was to construct tentative hierarchics for each of the above functions. Based on the work of Piaget and the Geneva school and on clinical experience, a list of 10–15 items ranking in order of increasing difficulty in each hierarchy was prepared. Items at the bottom of these hierarchies were those on which even the most demented patient could score (score 1) and items at the top were those on which only the least demented patient could score (score 10).

These tentative hierarchical subscales were then administered to 30 patients with differing levels of cognitive decline ranging from the minimally demented to those with severe dementia. Correct responses to each item in each hierarchy (subscale) were recorded and a frequency distribution of correct responses to the items within each hierarchy was determined. An item analysis for each subscale was performed to determine the rank order of item difficulty. Whenever there were discrepancies the hierarchy was rearranged by deletion of some items or insertion of others, always with the same principle in mind: that the number of correct responses to each item was progressively graded. This procedure was repeated several times. In this way, functional hierarchies were constructed each with 5 or 10 items which gave the best and most useful distribution of correct response frequencies. Each item carries a score of 2 or 1, depending on the number of items in the hierarchy. The maximum score for each hierarchy is 10 and the maximum for the whole scale is 200.

In using the hierarchical subscales (Appendix 6.1), the idea is rapidly to determine or pinpoint the highest level of performance for each mental function. Being able to start at an item appropriate to the functioning level of the patient economizes on testing time. For a mildly demented patient, the examiner might start at the top of the subscale and if the response is correct, the patient would score 10 for that subscale. If, on the other hand, the patient was unable to respond correctly, the examiner would proceed to test him on subsequent items lower in the subscale until the patient could respond to two consecutive items correctly. For a more demented patient, the examiner might start at the lower end of the subscale and proceed upwards until the patient was unable to respond correctly to two consecutive items. For example, in the Ideomotor subscale, the examiner could start at 'Double Rings' or 'Reversed Hands' for a mildly demented patient, but start at 'Clap Hands' for a more demented patient.

Whatever the level of functioning of the patient, the examiner always tries to maximize patient performance by repeating instructions, rewording instructions, demonstrating what should be done, imitating the patient's response, etc. Depending on the condition of the patient and the skill of the examiner, the highest level of performance in any hierarchy can be determined in from 10s to 3 min.

The use of such hierarchies in the rating scale allows at least a partial solution to many of the difficulties involved in assessing the demented patient. By being able to start at an appropriate level and by maximizing patient performance (which does not seem to prejudice test results), problems arising from the presence of numerous physical, sensory and emotional handicaps and problems of cooperation and fatigue can be overcome. The hierarchies allow optimum patient functioning to be determined rapidly and in a broad range of areas.

To determine the reliability and concurrent validity of the HDS, 50 consecutively admitted patients with senile dementia of the Alzheimer type or multi-infarct dementia (Roth 1978) were examined. Each patient was assessed independently by two trained examiners using the Hierarchic Dementia Scale and two other established dementia scales: the Blessed Dementia Scale (Blessed et al 1968) and the Crichton Geriatric Rating Scale (Robinson 1961). Fifteen days following the initial assessment, each patient was reassessed on the Hierarchic Dementia Scale. In addition, because electro-encephalographic changes have been related to degree of mental impairment (Obrist & Busse 1965), the dominant occipital alpha frequency of patients was recorded when possible.

Scores on the HDS ranged from 11 to 191, with mean of 113 and a standard deviation of 50. Inter-rater reliability was 0.89. Test/re-test reliability was 0.84. Coefficient alpha, a measure of the internal consistency of the scale, was 0.97.

With respect to concurrent validity, the correlation coefficient of scores of the HDS and the Blessed Scale was 0.72 and of the HDS and the Crichton Scale 0.74. Thirty-four patients had EEGs at the time of the dementia ratings and the correlation coefficient of total HDS scores with alpha frequency was 0.57.

APPLICATION OF THE HIERARCHIC DEMENTIA SCALE

The scale has already been used to study the 4-year course of Alzheimer's disease (AD) (Dastoor & Cole, 1986). Thirteen subjects (6 men and 7 women aged 47 to 88) with AD (American Psychiatric Association 1980) were referred by physicians in the community for a research project on 'lecithin treatment in early memory deficits' (Etienne et al 1979) and were investigated at the Montreal Neurological Institute. The intellectual deterioration had been obvious to their families for less than three years. Except for the dementia, their medical history was unremarkable. All treatable causes of dementia were ruled out and there was no evidence of vascular dementia. The computed tomography scans were consistent with Alzheimer's disease. At the time of initial contact, all the subjects were autonomous, living in the community with their family, but would have been able to live on their own. Prior to their entry in the study they had no language or praxic impairments, but had mild deficits of recent memory (i.e. able to recall two or three out of five objects after a five-minute delay) and mild disorientation to time (i.e. disoriented to current date and month).

Cognitive disabilities were assessed initially on the Hierarchic Dementia Scale and every 12 months thereafter for a period of 48 months.

Each HDS assessment was completed without knowledge of the previous HDS score. The 12-month scores of each subject were examined and for the purpose of comparing individual courses, total scores for each subject (A-M) were plotted (Fig. 6.1) as percentages of the initial (100%) score.

With one exception (case A), the total scale scores and the subscale scores declined consistently and progressively over time, but, as indicated in Figure 6.1, there was considerable variation between individuals in patterns of decline. Three subjects (cases K-M) had demonstrated severe decline after 24 months while at least four other subjects (cases B-E) had demonstrated only mild decline after 48 months. The remainder had demonstrated an intermediate pattern of decline. Moreover, while the rate of decline seemed to remain relatively constant over time in eight subjects (cases B-E, G, H, I, M), it increased in four subjects (caaea F, J, K, L).

Similarly, the decline of individual mental functions was far from uniform. Writing, ideational praxis, graphic praxis, constructional praxis, concentration, calculation, motor and pre-frontal functions declined linearly but reading and gnosis declined rapidly initially and seemed to level off after 36 months. In contrast, denomination, ideomotor praxis, registration, similarities and orienting reflexes were conserved initially but declined

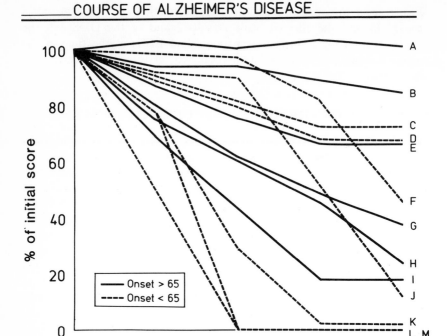

Fig. 6.1 Progression of Alzheimer's disease in 13 subjects as measured by the Hierarchic Dementia Scale (percentage of initial score)

rapidly after 24 months. The lower initial scores for recent memory substantiated the clinical impression that this function is impaired first and most severely in AD patients.

When the 13 subjects were divided into two groups — an early onset group (cases C, D, F, J, K-M) whose mean age at initial contact was 56.1 years, range 47–64 years, and a late onset group (cases B, E, G, H, I) whose mean age was 78.0 years, range 69–88 years — the pattern of decline for these two groups was dissimilar: over time, the rate of decline for both young and old subjects was variable but often more rapid in younger subjects.

POSTSCRIPT

In addition to such descriptive longitudinal studies, the scale may be applied to clinical and epidemiological studies of prognostic factors, treatment strategies, treatment efficacies, or to studies of need and service requirements in relation to levels of disability.

As well, using the same empirical methodology as in the development of the 'Hierarchic Dementia Scale', similar functional hierarchies and measurement scales might be developed for any number of tasks such as walking, dressing, eating, grooming, continence, or other aspects of cognitive function. The result would be a series of scales for the rapid and accurate assessment of disability.

This principle of hierarchical organization of functions is potentially useful not only in the measurement of disability but in the management of disability. For example, if the ability to walk is seen as a function at the top of a 'Walking hierarchy' composed of Standing, Sitting and Head Control, the examiner could not only measure or rate the inability to walk at one of the lower levels in the hierarchy but identify the prerequisites or 'interventions' necessary for moving up the hierarchy — thus, moving from a level of 'Standing' to the level of 'Walking' might require improved joint mobility, improved coordination or improved balance.

A table of a functional hierarchy and 'interventions' might be constructed (Table 6.1).

Table 6.1

Walking hierarchy	Interventions
Walking	
	← Joint mobility and coordination
Standing	
	← Leg strength
Sitting	
	← Neck and trunk strength
Head control	

Similar tables might be constructed for drawing (Table 6.2) or ideomotor functions (Table 6.3)

Table 6.2

Drawing hierarchy	Interventions
Cube	
Cube (difficulty with perspective)	
	← Relation of consistent angles
2 rectangles	
	← Relation of angles
Square and circle	
	← Relation of figures
Rectangle	
	← Relation of line length
Square	
	← Relation of lines to form angles
Circle in circle	
	← Relation of inside-outside
Circle	
	← Relation of lines
Line	
	← Motor control
Scribble	

Table 6.3

Ideomotor hierarchy	Interventions
Reversed hands	
	← Synchronous hand-finger orientation
Double rings	
	← Synchronous finger control
Double fingers	
	← Two finger control
Opposed hands	
	← Synchronous arm and hand control
Single ring	
	← Finger and thumb control
Single finger	
	← Single finger control
Clap hands	
	← Synchronous arm control
Wave	
	← Hand control
Raised hands	
	← Arm control
Open mouth	

The more precise are the functional hierarchies, the more precise are the interventions.

Thus, an hierarchical approach to organization of functions and disabilities may provide simple and useful tools not only for measuring disability but for organizing and focusing re-educational or rehabilitative efforts.

REFERENCES

Ajuriaguerra J de, Rey M, Bellet-Muller, Tissot R 1964 A propos de quelques problèmes posées par le déficit opératoire des vieillards atteints de démence dégénérative en début d'évolution. Cortex 1: 232–256

American Psychiatric Association 1980 Diagnostic and Statistical Manual of Mental Disorders, 3rd edn. (DSMIII) American Psychiatric Association, Washington DC

Blessed G, Tomlinson B E, Roth M 1968 The association between quantitative measures of dementia and of degenerative changes in the cerebral grey matter of elderly subjects. British Journal of Psychiatry 114: 797–811

Cole M G, Dastoor D P, Koszyoki D 1983 The Hierarchic Dementia Scale. Journal of Clinical Experimental Gerontology 5: 219–234

Constantinidis J, Richard J 1978 Dementia with senile plaques and neurofibrillary changes. In: Isaacs A D, Post F (eds) Studies in geriatric psychiatry. Wiley, New York

Dastoor D P, Cole M G 1986 The course of Alzheimer's disease: an uncontrolled longitudinal study. Unpublished

Etienne P, Gauthier E P, Dastoor D P et al 1979 Alzheimer's disease: clinical effects of lecithin treatment. In: Barbeau A, Growdon J, Wurtman R (eds) Nutrition and the brain 5. Raven Press, New York

Flavel J 1963 The developmental psychology of Jean Piaget. Van Nostrand, New York

Gurland B, Copeland J, Kelleher M, Kuriansky J, Sharpe L, Dean L 1983 The mind and mood of aging. Haworth Press, New York

Hubel D 1963 The visual cortex of the brain. Scientific American 209: 54–58

Jackson J H 1958 Selected writings of John Hughlings Jackson. Taylor J (ed) Basic Books, New York

Luria A 1966 Higher cortical functions in man, 2nd edn. Basic Books, New York
NCHS (National Center for Health Statistics) Health interview survey. 1975 U.S. Department of Health Education and Welfare Health Resources Administration, Washington D.C.
Obrist W, Busse E 1965 The electroencephalogram in old age. In: Wilson W (ed) Applications of electroencephalography in psychiatry: a symposium. Duke University Press, Durham, North Carolina
Robinson R 1961 Some problems of clinical trials in elderly people. Gerontology Clinic 3: 247–257
Roth M 1978 Diagnosis of senile and related forms of dementia. In: Kayzman R, Terry R, Bick K (eds) Alzheimer's disease: senile dementia and related disorder. Raven Press, New York

APPENDIX 6.1

THE HIERARCHIC DEMENTIA SCALE

1. Orienting
- 10. No impairment
- 8. Shakes Examiner's Hand
- 6. Reacts to Auditory Threat
- 4. Reacts to Visual Threat
- 2. Reacts to Tactile Threat

2. Prefrontal
- 10. None
- 8. Tactile Prehension
- 6. Cephalobuccal Reflex
- 4. Orovisual Reflex
- 2. Oral Tactile Reflex

3. Ideomotor
- 10. Reversed Hands
- 9. Double Rings
- 8. Double Fingers
- 7. Opposed Hands
- 6. Single Ring
- 5. Single Finger
- 4. Clap Hands
- 3. Wave
- 2. Raise Hands
- 1. Open Mouth

4. Looking
- 10. Finds Images
- 8. Searches for Images
- 6. Grasps content of Picture
- 4. Scans Picture
- 2. Looks at Picture

5. Ideational
- 10. Imaginary Match and Candle
- 9. Imaginary Nail and Hammer
- 8. Imaginary Scissors
- 7. Imaginary Comb
- 6. Match and Candle .
- 5. Nail and Hammer
- 4. Scissors
- 3. Comb
- 2. Put on Shoes
- 1. Open Door

6. Denomination
- 10. No Errors
- 9. Nominal Aphasia — Parts
- 8. Nominal Aphasia — Objects
- 7. Use of Parts
- 6. Use of Objects
- 5. Conceptual Field — Parts
- 4. Conceptual Field — Objects
- 3. Sound Alike — Parts
- 2. Sound Alike — Objects
- 1. Deformed Words

7. Comprehension
Verbal:
- 5. Close eyes and touch left ear
- 4. Clap hands three times
- 3. Touch your right eye
- 2. Touch your nose
- 1. Open mouth

Written:
- 5. Close eyes and touch left ear
- 4. Clap hands three times
- 3. Touch your right eye
- 2. Touch your nose
- 1. Open mouth

8. Registration
- 10. Spoon, candle, scissors, button, whistle
- 8. Spoon, candle, scissors, button
- 6. Spoon, candle, scissors
- 4. Spoon, candle
- 2. Spoon

9. Gnosis
- 10. Superimposed Words
- 9. Superimposed Images
- 8. Digital Gnosis
- 7. Right-Left — Examiner
- 6. Right-Left — Self
- 5. Body Parts — Examiner
- 4. Body Parts — Self
- 3. Touch (pinch)   5 cm
- 2. Touch (pinch)   5 — 15 cm
- 1. Response to Touch (pinch)

10. Reading
- 10. Paragraph
- 8. Paragraph with error (s)
- 6. The cat drinks milk.
- 4. Receive
- 2. M

11. Orientation

10. Date
8. Month
6. Year of Birth
4. Morning or Afternoon
2. First Name

12. Construction

10. Four Blocks Diagonal
8. Four Blocks Square
6. Two Blocks Diagonal
4. Two Blocks Square
2. Form Board Circle

13. Concentration

10. Serial 7's (100, 93, ...)
9. Serial 3's (30, 27, ...)
8. Months of Year Backwards
7. Days of Week Backwards
6. 93 — 85
5. 10 — 1
4. Months of Year Forwards
3. Days of Week Forwards
2. 1 — 10
1. Actual Counting

14. Calculation

10. 43 — 17
9. 56 + 19
8. 39 — 14
7. 21 + 11
6. 15 — 6
5. 18 + 9
4. 9 — 4
3. 8 + 7
2. 2 — 1
1. 3 + 1

15. Drawing

10. Cube
9. Cube (difficulty with perspective)
8. Two Rectangles
7. Circle and Square
6. Rectangle
5. Square
4. Circle Inside Circle
3. Circle
2. Line
1. Scribble

16. Motor

10. No Impairment
9. Increased Muscle Tone — Repeated
8. Increased Muscle Tone — Initial
7. Loss of Rhythm
6. Loss of Associated Movements
5. Contractures of Legs
4. Kyphosis
3. Vertical Restriction of Eye Movement
2. Non-ambulatory
1. Lateral Restriction of Eye Movement

17. Remote Memory

10. Amount of pension
8. Number of grandchildren
6. Year of marriage or of first job
4. Father's Occupation
2. Place of Birth

18. Writing

Form:
5. Flowing Style
4. Loss of Flow
3. Letters Misshappen
2. Repetition or Substitution of Letters
1. Scribble

Content:
5. No Error
4. Word Substitution
3. Missing Preposition
2. Missing Verb or Noun
1. Missing 3 or 4 Words

19. Similarities

10. Airplane — Bicycle
8. Gun — Knife
6. Cat — Pig
4. Pants — Dress
2. Orange — Banana

20. Recent Memory

10. All Five
8. Any Four
6. Any Three
4. Any Two
2. Any One

Quantifying clinical observation. Geriatric Mental State — AGECAT package

INTRODUCTION

The development of semi-structured and reliable methods for assessing and recording mental state has represented a significant advance in psychiatric research. Such techniques were pioneered by Spitzer et al (1970), and Wing et al (1974). The criticisms that standardized methods interfere with the free-flow of the interview and impair communication by imposing a rigid format on the questioning have proved groundless. For studies which require accurate recording of the types of behaviour and effect necessary for diagnosis, measuring response to physical treatments, and to some extent predicting outcome, they have proved invaluable.

Since it was first described (Copeland et al 1976, Gurland et al 1976) the Geriatric Mental State, a standardized method of diagnosis and assessment for the elderly, has been in continual demand. The interview has been gradually refined in the light of data derived from the examination of several hundred hospital in-patients and several thousand community subjects, and a second edition is now available. The spur to provide a second edition has come from the increasing request for training in its application, from studies in the United Kingdom, Australia, the continent of Europe and elsewhere, which have required not only the hospital edition but also a shorter version for community use and case finding. An increasing number of translations into languages other than English have been made, and complementary interviews have been developed and piloted, such as the History and Aetiology, the Social Status and the Physical Examination Schedules. A Psychological Assessment Schedule is being developed. Finally, a computerised diagnostic system, AGECAT (Copeland et al 1986), can now be applied to the GMS and its associated interviews in order to achieve a standardised diagnosis which can be used for epidemiological comparisons, longitudinal studies, the recognition of early cases and as a diagnostic guide for use by non-psychiatrists.

THE DEVELOPMENT OF THE GERIATRIC MENTAL STATE — AGECAT PACKAGE

The Geriatric Mental State (GMS)

Development

When the US–UK Cross-National (Diagnostic) Study turned its attention to the elderly in hospital, the research workers found that existing interviews for eliciting and recording mental state were not suitable for older aged subjects. For example, organic areas of pathology were not adequately covered, questions tended to be long and complicated with no provision made for the termination of an unsatisfactory interview if the subject was too ill or too old to continue. Consequently a method for covering major symptom areas briefly at the start was required, so that all subjects received a basic interview before the more detailed examination. Some provision was also required for the examination of drowsy or unconscious patients.

The project members were already experienced in the use of two mental state interviews developed for younger subjects, the Present State Examination (PSE) (Wing et al 1974) and the Psychiatric Status Schedule (PSS) (Spitzer et al 1970), in the hospital studies of those aged under 60 (Cooper et al 1972). These two interviews, to some extent, complemented one another. It was decided to form the 'Geriatric Mental State' (GMS) using some items from both schedules with a range of new items covering important areas of organic pathology. The overall structure of the PSE was retained and much of the method of its administration. The final interview contained in all 541 items: 268 PSE, 64 PSS and 209 new items. The form of many of the PSE and PSS items was simplified, and detailed rating instructions added, because elderly subjects tended to make vague responses which were difficult to rate reliably.

In order to overcome the problem of the premature termination of the interviews due to frailty, inattention or cognitive failure, the more important symptoms were selected to be given to the subject first. These 'boxed items' cover the major symptom areas briefly and allow for an overall view of the subject's mental state. The interview is terminated at the end of this section if the patient gives unintelligible replies or there are other reasons for doubting the validity of the responses. Other interview problems concerned the recognition of normal ageing, the influence exerted by physical symptoms, and the concept that depression accompanied by severe physical illness may not justify a psychiatric diagnosis. Because the influence of normal ageing is largely unknown and many studies will be undertaken without physical examination, it was decided not to try to build-in judgements of aetiology. A more detailed description of the Geriatric Mental State can be obtained from earlier publications (Copeland et al 1976, Gurland et al 1976, Copeland & Gurland 1978, Copeland et al 1985).

The GMS was used by the project in several hundred interviews in hospitals in New York and London, including both psychiatric and geriatric facilities.

Validation

Reliability studies for the GMS have been reported (Copeland et al 1976, Copeland & Gurland 1978). In the two original studies undertaken, using six principal categories (affective disorder, schizophrenia and paranoid states, organic psychoses, alcoholism, neuroses and personality disorders, and 'other diagnoses'), diagnostic agreement on Study 1 occurred in 17 out of 20 patients, and in 69% of rater pairs in Study 2. By general consent, the patients in Study 2 presented more serious diagnostic problems. Because historical data were not used in the reliability studies the distinction between main and alternative diagnoses was difficult. Taking 'partial' agreement, where one rater's main diagnosis was another's alternative diagnosis, in Study 1 agreement was reached on 19 out of 20 cases, and in Study 2 on 85% of the New York pairs and 80% of the London pairs. In these studies the psychiatric raters used their own intuitive diagnoses based on the findings of the standardised interviews.

The agreement on individual items or symptoms was examined using the total number of questions rated positively by each psychiatrist for each patient. The role of interviewer/observer or follow-up interviewer was not shown to have any effect on the number of ratings made. The product–moment correlation co-efficients between interviewer and observer for all the positive ratings was 0.87 and for the re-interview comparison 0.78. In order to examine for a systematic lack of agreement between the raters due to patient variables, agreement indices kappa were calculated for each patient. The mean kappa value for all items was 0.73 for interviewer/observer comparisons and 0.48 for interviewer versus re-interviewer, with ranges of 0.50–0.89 and 0.11–0.66 respectively. It was not surprising, in view of the tendency for the mental state of elderly subjects to fluctuate, that differences should be found between the initial and the re-interview values. As shown in previous studies, behavioural and speech items produced less agreement than direct questions; the mean kappas for the former were 0.56 and for the latter 0.80.

Weighted kappa (Cohen 1968) was used in order to examine which items in the schedule produced consistently less agreement than others. The mean values of weighted kappa for the commonly used items with sufficient positive ratings were better for items in the main part of the schedule than those for the seventh edition of the PSE (Kendell et al 1968). Re-interview kappas were lower than those for the observer comparison, and behavioural items lower than those in the rest of the schedule where only two questions had weighted kappas of less than 0.50 (Copeland & Gurland 1978).

Assessing the validity of psychiatric diagnosis is a more difficult problem than assessing reliability. It is usually measured against psychiatric judgement, but unfortunately psychiatrists tend to disagree amongst themselves. Alternative methods, if biological or pathological confirmation was not possible, usually involved studies of outcome. Such studies may examine the outcome for a single episode of illness or record the progress of a disease over a number of years. They require sensitive instruments which can record change over time. Below, changes in GMS symptom profiles with time are shown to provide some validation of intuitive psychiatric diagnosis.

Some further validation of diagnosis can be obtained from statistical methods such as cluster analysis. Seventy-five patients forming a consecutive series admitted to a psychiatric hospital in London and interviewed using the GMS were subjected to the Wolfe formal mixture analysis procedure (NORMIX). Nine patients had to be omitted because they had outlying scores, i.e. scores high on all forms of belligerence, alcohol abuse and visual hallucinations. Four clusters emerged from this analysis. When discriminant function analyses were calculated between the groups they revealed a remarkably high degree of separation. Group 1 had 22 members, of whom 18 had a psychiatric diagnosis of dementia and two of confusional states. Group 2 consisted mainly of mild depressive cases, but with some early dementia and some cases of schizophrenia. Group 3 contained only five cases, of which four had a psychiatric diagnosis of manic depressive depressed. Group 4 was a 'ragbag' of diagnoses with the members scoring highly on retarded speech or hypomania. It was clear, however, that, by applying such a procedure to GMS items, cases of dementia and severe depression could be distinguished one from another.

One way of describing the clinical picture of an illness is to divide the symptoms — here the items of the GMS — into groups which tend to associate together, and to plot the profile of the resulting group scores. Not only is such a procedure useful for comparing one type of illness with another or different sub-types of illness within the same diagnostic category, but the change in the profile over time provides a record of the course of the illness and the response to therapeutic intervention. Gurland et al (1976) describe the derivation of 21 symptom groups or factors from data gathered from 100 recently hospitalised psychiatric patients examined using the GMS. Using partly the results of a factor analysis and partly a correlation procedure, 21 'factors' were identified which were judged as having clinical relevance.

Figure 7.1 shows a simplified symptom profile of GMS items for three diagnostic groups: depression, dementia and other organic states. The unbroken line represents the symptom profile at the initial mental state examination on admission and the broken line that undertaken three months later. It will be seen that the symptom profiles for each of the diagnostic groups differ from one another and that most show substantial changes towards normality after three months. The exception is dementia, where there is evidence of deterioration, the peak on the aphasia factor having been replaced by one on disorientation.

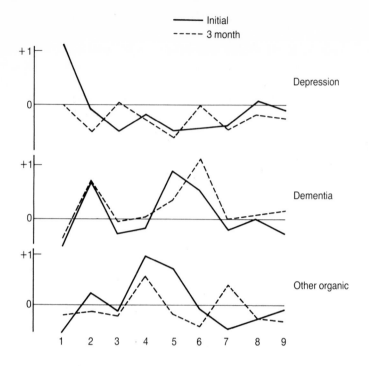

Fig. 7.1 GMS. Simplified symptom profiles at initial interview and after three months. Reproduced and adapted with permission, from Copeland et al (1976).

These symptom or factor profiles were found particularly helpful in a study comparing admissions to London mental hospitals with those to state mental hospitals in New York. In New York the project psychiatrists disagreed with the New York psychiatrists' diagnoses of organic disorder on a number of subjects. The project members diagnosed these subjects as having affective disorder. Figure 7.2 shows the profiles of patients agreed by both project members and New York psychiatrists to be organic, those agreed to be functional and those where the psychiatrists disagreed. It will be seen that the profiles of this last group follow closely those of the agreed functional cases for six of the eight factors, while for the remaining two, 'observed belligerence' and 'paranoid delusions', there is wide divergence. The outcome of these patients at three months was similar to that of the functional group. It was concluded that angry patients with paranoid affective disorders had been misdiagnosed as organic cases by the New York hospital psychiatrists.

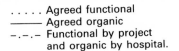

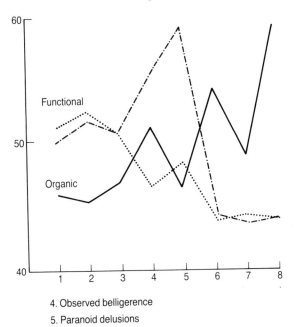

4. Observed belligerence

5. Paranoid delusions

Fig. 7.2 GMS. A comparison of patients agreed and diagnosed to be either functional or organic by project and hospital psychiatrists in two New York hospitals. Reproduced and adapted, with permission, from Gurland et al (1976).

How the Geriatric Mental State was used and developed in the studies of the US–UK Cross-National (diagnostic) Project

The GMS was used, with the addition of a history and informant interview, for the studies comparing consecutive series of admissions to London area mental hospitals and New York state hospitals, in order to investigate the apparent excess of organic cases admitted to the latter. Patients were interviewed within 72 hours of admission and again three months later, in hospital or at home. The project demonstrated that the proportions of patients with organic and affective disorders admitted to hospitals in both cities were remarkably similar. When the known higher prevalence of alcoholism in New York was taken into account the proportions were found to be almost identical (Copeland et al 1975). It was possible to say with some confidence that differences in the hospital diagnoses were not due to differences in the patients, but to different diagnostic criteria applied by the hospital psychiatrists. As we have seen above, the comparison of symptom profiles between initial interview and three month follow-up lent some validation to the project diagnoses.

For the next stage of its work the project was to examine random samples of elderly subjects living at home in the communities of the two cities. An interview which dealt at length with functional psychotic symptoms was clearly inappropriate for community residents. The study also wished to relate psychiatric diagnosis to expressed physical symptoms, degrees of immobility, social isolation and service requirement. A community version was therefore prepared, omitting those items judged to be of less importance for community subjects, but including minor symptoms. To make the interview more acceptable, the GMS items were dispersed among the non-mental state items. The resulting schedule was named the Comprehensive Assessment and Referral Evaluation schedule (CARE).

Because it was no longer possible to depend upon the intuitive diagnosis of psychiatrists, as half the subjects in New York were interviewed by social scientists (trained in the method and found to be reliable with the interviewing psychiatrists), two algorithms were devised, one for dementia and one for depression. The method of their derivation has been described by Gurland et al (1983). The subjects were classified on five levels of severity of illness categorised as 'limited' and 'pervasive'. Copeland and Gurland (1985) have shown that for the London sample the proportions of subjects with pervasive depression and dementia are similar to the proportion nominated when the criteria of the Diagnostic and Statistical Manual III (DSMIII) of the American Psychiatric Association (1980) are used: pervasive depression in London, 12.4%, DSMIII depression (major affective disorder, dysthymic mood and bereavement) reached 12.7%; pervasive dementia in London, 2.3%, DSMIII dementia 2.8%.

Against expectation, as the life suffered by the elderly in New York was thought to be more stressful than that suffered by the elderly in London, the levels of pervasive depression in the two cities were found to be similar, 13.0% in New York and 12.4% in London. However, the figures for pervasive dementia, 4.9% in New York and 2.3% in London, showed this disease to be twice as frequent in New York as in London. This highly significant difference was also confirmed when 'limited' forms of depression and dementia were examined. A number of possible causes for the increased prevalence of dementia in New York were sought. Differences in age, sex, race, country of origin, being non-white or foreign-born, were not found to account for the discrepancy. Levels of education and occupational attainment were both found to have an inverse relationship to dementia. If the known higher prevalence of arterio-sclerotic disease in New York had resulted in a higher proportion of multi-infarct dementia, then the prevalence of stroke ought to have been higher in New York, but was found to be the same in both cities. The unlikely possibility that the hospitals or nursing homes in London were admitting a larger proportion of dementing patients than in New York was examined further. A substantially reduced version of the CARE schedule, 'Institute CARE', was used to examine random samples of subjects in the hospitals and nursing homes of both cities (Gurland et al 1979). The prevalence of dementia was found to be higher in the New York than in the London nursing homes.

The large number of items describing physical illness and grades of immobility in the CARE schedule have allowed scales for assessing these to be derived. A modified form of the CARE schedule has been used to examine random samples of the elderly in rural Cheshire. Tentative results suggest that the prevalence of mental disorders is lower in this rural community. A shortened version, 'CORE-CARE' (see chapter six), has been prepared, from which the 'pervasive/limited' diagnoses can be extracted. Unfortunately it is not possible to derive the computer diagnosis AGECAT (described below), from this interview. AGECAT can however be applied to the original and modified forms of CARE.

The Geriatric Mental State modified for community interviewing

For larger-scale studies, it became clear that a shorter interview than the CARE interview was required. The comparatively low prevalence of dementia in the community, and the increasing cost of community surveys (including that of employing psychiatrists to interview whole samples) meant the introduction of a case-finding instrument was desirable. Such an instrument could be used as the first stage of a two-stage procedure in which a psychiatrist would follow-up nominated cases. Under ideal conditions one instrument should be developed to fulfil one function. However, conditions are rarely ideal, and in these days of shortage of funds such purity is impracticable. We therefore decided to develop, for community surveys, an instrument which would have three basic purposes in one, to identify and categorise case and sub-case levels of illness, that is to say, have a case-finding purpose, record levels of symptoms and provide symptom profiles, and lastly produce a tentative diagnosis allowing comparison to be made between different studies.

At the same time Henderson and his co-workers in Canberra, Australia, had a similar idea. They extracted the GMS questions from the CARE schedule, formed them into a separate interview by incorporating some of the CARE social items, and used it to interview 274 community residents (Henderson et al 1983).

A longitudinal study of depression and dementia was due to start in Liverpool in which a random sample of over 1000 elderly subjects living at home would be identified, examined and followed up at intervals over succeeding years. This provided an opportunity to try out the new instrument.

Having the London data available for analysis, we performed a series of linear discriminant function analyses, distinguishing between dementia and depression; dementia and depression together against other diagnoses; and dementia, depression and other diagnoses together against non-cases. On the basis of these analyses, items were selected for the community version.

Further items were then added for the recognition of obsessional, hypo-chondriacal, phobic and anxiety neuroses and for the crude identification of psychotic states other than organic. Cutting scores were developed for organic states and depression which identified the cases in the London community study. This community version (GMSA) was then applied to a random sample of 1070 subjects as part of the longitudinal study of dementia and depression in Liverpool. When used as a case-finding device by trained non-psychiatrists, it provided organic and depressive scores and a 'Dementia Depression Index' which allowed the immediate identification of subjects for further study as part of a two-stage interview procedure. As this instrument also provided symptom profiles, it could be used to assess change over time. The AGECAT diagnostic system (see below) could be applied to it in order to provide a tentative computer diagnosis, identify levels of 'caseness' and levels of confidence in diagnosis. By a simple restriction of the case categories it could be adapted to provide a close approximation to a DSMIII diagnosis.

Early reliability studies of the community version of the GMS

In Canberra, Henderson and his colleagues (1983) reported an extensive reliability study of their community version of the GMS. Fifty-two attenders at a geriatric day hospital were examined by two psychiatrists separately, and their interviews were audiotaped. For cases where items were recorded with sufficient frequency mean phi coefficients were calculated. For within-interview assessments these mean coefficients reached 0.84 and for between-interview assessments, 0.56. Henderson et al report that the items recording cognitive impairment and depression were generally satisfactory.

A reliability study is now being analysed in Liverpool, comparing the ratings of non-psychiatrists and psychiatrists using videotapes of community subjects.

History and Aetiology Schedule (HAS)

Mental state alone cannot provide a satisfactory method for making a diagnosis. Some diagnoses demand historical data. In the early studies of the US/UK Project, a history schedule was used alongside the mental state interviews, but none proved sufficiently satisfactory to recommend to other users. With the development of the AGECAT diagnostic system, a schedule for historical data became essential for refining the diagnoses beyond the simplest categories. It is possible however that the contribution of historical items to diagnosis can be overemphasised. Simon and his colleagues (1971) found that when a history schedule was given subsequent to the Present State Examination it only rarely resulted in a change of diagnosis.

Nevertheless, it was decided to develop a History and Aetiology Schedule (HAS) for the elderly. Such an interview would be best given to an informant, but it should be possible to give some items directly to the subject if an informant were not available.

The HAS was developed with the following aims; 1. to provide information from an informant as an alternative view of the patient's illness; 2. to gain a clearer insight into 'caseness' by describing the length and form of the illness from the onset; 3. to clarify the diagnosis, e.g. distinguish acute from chronic organic states, where the onset and previous history are crucial factors; 4. to allow questioning on previous alcohol intake, trauma, physical illness and endocrine abnormality; 5. to attempt to distinguish between progressive dementia and other causes of the dementia syndrome, and between Alzheimer type and multi-infarct dementia, using a modification of the Hachinski score based partly on suggestions by Roth (1981); 6. to distinguish between cases of depression, bereavement and fluctuating states of sadness; 7. to provide a family history of mental illness and suicide etc.; and 8. to provide some assessment of concomitant physical illness. The interview made no attempt to assess life events as aetiological factors, as there seemed to be no satisfactory method of doing this in abbreviated form.

A pilot survey was carried out on a small community sample, and the HAS was then modified and applied to a consecutive series of hospital admissions and used in the 3-year follow-up of 1070 Liverpool community subjects. It was programmed for the AGECAT diagnostic system. Data are at present being analysed and results will become available during the coming year. (Copeland et al, in preparation)

Physical Examination Schedule

The relationship between physical and psychiatric illness is well established although ill understood. A physical assessment of the individual is desirable in any investigation although not always possible in community studies. Where a physical examination has been performed in our studies, it has not seemed to play an important part in clarifying the psychiatric state. The Physical Examination Schedule, however, consists of a check list of important items of physical state relevant to diagnosis. Additional schedules are being developed to assess disability and physical illness scales, using the data from the London community sample.

Social Status Schedule

A Social Status Schedule has been developed by extracting items from the CARE schedule based on the results of the London sample. It aims to gather the usual demographic data and gives an assessment of self-care, ability to shop, dress, cook and perform other social functions. It also records help required to assist in these functions, frequency of contact with relatives and friends, household problems and financial difficulties.

Other interviews under development

During the Liverpool community study, a range of simple psychological tests was undertaken with each of the 1070 subjects. Subsamples were more extensively investigated with a battery of such tests in order to attempt to assess their success: 1. in recognising early cases of dementia, and 2. in delineating change over time. (Binks and Davies, 1984). On the whole, the psychological tests available at present do not appear to contribute much to the recognition of early cases or to diagnosis. Suitable tests which will acccurately measure differential changes in psychological functions over follow-up periods are only now being developed. Such tests are urgently awaited. A schedule of Early Behavioural Change is being prepared on the assumption that changes in social behaviour may precede psychological changes. In any event, most subjects developing dementia will be recognised initially by changes in social performance.

The need for standardised diagnosis — the computerised diagnostic system AGECAT

In order to standardise the diagnostic process fully, the step between the collection of standardised data, and the choice of a diagnostic category must also be standardised. Methods for doing this have already been introduced. The 'pervasive dementia' and 'pervasive depression' algorithms developed by the US-UK Cross-National Project and reported by Gurland et al (1983) represent one such attempt. Using research diagnostic criteria is another, but unfortunately these have not been developed for dementia. The criteria for DSMIII allow wide interpretation of individual criteria so that estimations from comparative studies using these criteria cannot be relied upon.

Computerised diagnostic systems for psychiatric diagnosis are not new. Spitzer & Endicott (1968) developed the Diagno system, and Wing et al (1974) the Catego system and later the ID case identification. It was necessary to develop such a system for the GMS and its companion schedules.

The first aim of the AGECAT system was to replicate a psychiatric intuitive diagnosis sufficiently closely to retain clinical validity whilst at the same time providing a completely reliable and repeatable diagnostic method. The second aim was to identify syndrome cases of psychiatric illness and to allot them to levels of certainty for each diagnostic group. This would allow comparison between different studies performed in like manner using the GMS-AGECAT package. It is also important to be able to show change in diagnosis and level of certainty over time. At present the AGECAT system can be applied to the full GMS, the community version (GMSA), the full CARE schedule and the modified CARE schedule. The History and Aetiology Schedule has been programmed and incorporated in the AGECAT system, although its success in breaking down the main diagnostic groups into subgroups is still being tested. Ultimately, the Social States Schedule, the Physical Examination Schedule and psychological tests will be incorporated.

The construction of AGECAT

It was decided to construct AGECAT according to a theoretical model and then test its success at replicating psychiatric diagnoses on samples diagnosed by psychiatrists. In the preliminary stage, GMS symptom scores are condensed to form 157 symptom components. Usually the symptom scores on a comparatively small number of symptoms are added together to form the symptom component score. In some cases only one symptom is involved but rarely a much larger number of symptoms are aggregated into one symptom component by adopting the score on the most severe symptom. The allocation of symptoms to symptom components was done on a theoretical basis, not using any statistical procedure.

In stage 1 the symptom components are arranged to form eight diagnostic 'clusters'. In the first of the two substages the symptom components are brought together into groups. For example, in the organic cluster one group consists of 'mild memory disturbance', containing such items as memory for interviewer's name on the first occasion, rater's opinion of memory, knowledge of the length of time living at the current address, being evasive etc. Another group is 'moderate memory disturbance and time disorientation', consisting of the following: complaining of muddled thinking, memory for interviewer's name on the second occasion, knowledge of current month, current year and Prime Minister's name, identification of objects, discrepancy between stated birthdate and age, being bland and indifferent to errors, and perseveration. The third group, 'place and person disorientation and organic thought disorder', consists of disorientation for persons, confabulation, disorientation for place (although this is only included if severe or if the items on Prime Minister's name or 'indifference to errors' have already been scored), rambling (only included if the 'moderate memory' group scores more than four and the 'mild memory group' more than one).

The second substage uses a logical decision tree operating on the group scores, in order to arrive at a level of confidence (from 0 to 5) for each of the syndrome 'clusters'. The eight syndrome clusters are: organic, schizophrenia, mania, depression (psychosis and neurosis), obsessional, hypochondriacal, phobic, and anxiety neurosis.

In stage 3, the levels of confidence are compared one with another in the hierarchical sequence listed above. 'Organic' is compared first with 'schizophrenic' levels and this result stored by the computer, and then compared with the levels of confidence on 'mania' and so on across all eight clusters. If, when depressive psychosis has been reached a firm psychotic diagnosis has already been made, comparison is not made with the neurotic clusters.

At this point also, a number of symptom components are examined to determine whether to nominate the case 'other psychosis'. Such a category is used if isolated psychotic symptoms appear to be present but no firm diagnosis is possible. In a very few cases, symptom components are used in stage 2 for making decisions between diagnoses. For example, where levels of organic disorder are equal to levels of depressive disorder, the dominant diagnosis may be determined by the presence or absence of the symptom component of retardation.

When compared with psychiatric diagnosis, confidence level 3 and above seems to indicate a syndrome case (Copeland et al 1986).

At present the computer prints out a primary diagnosis, secondary and alternative diagnoses if appropriate, and the confidence levels on all eight syndrome clusters. In addition, it is possible to compute symptom profile scores, the organic and depression scores, and the Dementia Depression Index (see below). Whether the individual represents a syndrome case of illness depends on whether level 3 or above has been attained on any of the syndrome clusters or whether a diagnosis 'other psychosis' has been made.

It has been stressed elsewhere that the definition of a case must depend upon the requirements of the study for which that case is sought (Copeland 1981). However, psychiatrists seem to agree that, at a certain level of intensity, symptoms tend to group to form a recognisable psychiatric syndrome. We have termed these 'syndrome cases' (Copeland et al 1986). Two or more of such syndromes may be present in the same subject at any one time. Of course, a syndrome case does not necessarily indicate the need for therapeutic intervention. Bereavement may be recorded as a syndrome case of depression, but a decision may be made not to treat with antidepressant medication. The recognition of a syndrome case of depression as a case of bereavement does not occur until the stage where AGECAT is applied to the data from the History and Aetiology Schedule.

AGECAT's levels of confidence are not strictly speaking levels of severity, although they do have some relationship to the latter as might be expected. Severe cases tend to have a range of symptoms and are therefore likely to be more confidently diagnosed. However, the criterion for attaining the highest level of confidence in schizophrenia is the presence of 'first-rank symptoms'. It is conceivable that a top level of '5' might be attained by a patient with a 'mild' illness who happens to exhibit two first-rank symptoms. In the organic states it would seem likely that levels of confidence do approximate closely to stages of severity. The concept of severity, however, is complex and would need careful validation by outcome studies. As it stands, AGECAT provides two levels of confidence below syndrome case level. These may be useful for identifying early cases of illness.

We believe that the design of the AGECAT system is innovative in computing terms (Dewey & Copeland 1986). The descripton of the system which those unsophisticated in computer language can read is always in step with the actual computer program which the machine is obeying, and has the precision of an algorithm language. Because it is possible to derive several texts from the same original it is also possible to derive different computer versions for different languages and machines.

Two systems have been developed for presenting the GMS itself on the computer and feeding the results into the AGECAT system. One which runs under RTll is a flexible program, but unfortunately the computer is not portable. For community studies a program has been developed (Jones 1984) to present the schedule to the interviewer on a portable microcomputer. At present, the results must be transferred to one of the larger machines for the AGECAT analysis, but when AGECAT is transferred to run under MSDOS this step should be eliminated. A reliability study comparing this method of data collection with orthodox pencil and paper methods is being analysed.

THE VALIDITY OF AGECAT DIAGNOSIS

The AGECAT diagnostic system, having been developed on a theoretical model, was applied to two samples of 75 recent admissions to a London psychiatric hospital and a geriatric hospital, interviewed with the GMS and 396 random community subjects living at home in London, interviewed using the CARE schedule. Using the major categories of affective, schizophrenic, organic and 'other diagnoses' and non-cases, agreements reached over 60%. Simple adjustments only were necessary in order to correct omissions in the theoretical model. It was found, for example, that a proportion of subjects had been diagnosed by AGECAT as non-cases even though they had expressed substantial depressive symptoms because they had denied depressive mood. It was also found that where depressive neurosis had reached confidence level 3, it had tended to prevail in the psychiatrist's diagnosis against the highest levels of the other neurotic conditions. AGECAT was adjusted accordingly.

Concordance on subjects with pure anxiety was not good. On further examination it was found that the psychiatrists disagreed widely on what level of anxiety should be recognised as a 'case'. When those designated 'mild' or 'uncertain' were removed, concordance rates were improved.

When these minor modifications had been made, AGECAT was compared again with the psychiatrists' diagnoses for the psychiatric hospital patients. AGECAT's concordance with the psychiatrists' diagnoses on depression and dementia reached 91%; AGECAT identified 97% of the the patients as 'cases'. The overall agreement reached a kappa value of 0.84 (Copeland et al 1986). Kappas for depression were 0.80, organic 0.86, schizophrenia and paranoid 0.88. In a number of other instances the diagnostic cluster was agreed but differences arose on level of caseness between confidence levels 2 and 3. If these latter are accepted as agreements, and the two cases where data were inadequate for AGECAT to perform properly are excluded, the best partial concordance on the diagnostic 'clusters' overall reaches 94%.

Overall agreement on the random community sample of 396 subjects living at home reached 89%. AGECAT agreed on 77% of the psychiatric cases. Agreement on depression and dementia specifically reached 88% and the overall concordance on psychiatrists' cases regardless of diagnosis was 80%. Cohen's kappa for overall agreement reached 0.74 and for specific syndromes, depression 0.80, organic 0.88 and non-cases 0.74. The problems of case versus non-case discrimination also applied to this sample. The main disagreements are in the case levels of neurotic disorders other than depression. This time AGECAT tends to overdiagnose depression by not discriminating between depression and bereavement at this stage, rather than by identifying depression in response to physical illness. There were also 13 subjects whose depression was longstanding and fluctuating, where the symptoms were nevertheless substantial but appeared to clear rapidly during the interview. The psychiatrists had not made a diagnosis of depression in these cases. Whatever condition these subjects had, the History and Aetiology Schedule now attempts to recognise it.

Taking into consideration those cases which were followed up one year later, AGECAT was probably correct in six of the disagreed cases, so that AGECAT could be said either to have agreed with the psychiatrists or to have made the correct diagnosis in 91% of subjects, and specifically on 91% of cases of depression and dementia.

Tables 7.1 to 7.4 group the same data in alternative form: by diagnosis. Table 7.1 shows the concordance between AGECAT and the psychiatrists' diagnoses of depression. Five cases from the geriatric hospital sample have been removed because they were too physically ill to be interviewed. AGECAT agrees on 90% of the psychiatrists' diagnoses of depression across all three studies. Table 7.2 shows the agreement with psychiatrists on the AGECAT cases of depression. Here agreement is less satisfactory, reaching only 73%. This is because 19 AGECAT cases of depression are rated as non-cases by the psychiatrists. The reasons for this discrepancy have already been explained. AGECAT tends to overdiagnose depression at this stage. However, it should be said that in any study of depression, investigators

Table 7.1 Syndrome: depression. Concordance on psychiatrists' cases

Psychiatrists' diagnosis	No. of cases	AGECAT diagnosis			
		Depression	Organic	Non-case	Total
Psychiatric hospital	75	25		1	26
Geriatric hospital	70	9	1	1	11
Community	396	60		8	68
Total	541	94	1	10	105

Concordance 90%

Table 7.2 Syndrome: depression. Concordance on AGECAT cases

AGECAT diagnosis	No. of cases	Psychiatrists' diagnosis						
		Dep	Org	Schiz/Par	Man	Neur	Non-case	Total
Psychiatric hospital	75	25	4	1	1	1		32
Geriatric hospital	70	9		3		1	6	19
Community	396	60	1	1		2	13	77
Total	541	94	5	5	1	4	19	128

Concordance 73%

would probably wish to identify those subjects having substantial depressive symptoms and to make their own judgements on whether they fit their particular case criteria.

Table 7.3 shows AGECAT's agreement on the psychiatrists's diagnoses of organic disorders. Five psychiatrists' cases are designated non-cases by AGECAT but at level of confidence 2, the borderline syndrome case level. Overall concordance reaches 82%. Table 7.4 shows the agreement between the psychiatrists and the AGECAT organic diagnoses. Overall agreement is 91%.

Table 7.3 Syndrome: organic. Concordance on psychiatrists' cases

Psychiatrists' diagnosis	No. of cases	AGECAT diagnosis			
		Organic	Depression	Non-case	Total
Psychiatric hospital	75	27	4		31
Geriatric hospital	70	22	3	5	30
Community	396	15	1	1	17
Total	541	64	8	6	78

Concordance 82%

Table 7.4 Syndrome: organic. Concordance on AGECAT cases

AGECAT diagnosis	No. of cases	Psychiatrists' diagnosis				
		Organic	Depression	Schiz/Par	Non-case	Total
Psychiatric hospital	75	27		1		28
Geriatric hospital	70	22	1		2	25
Community	396	15			2	17
Total	541	64	1	1	4	70

Concordance 91%

Both the psychiatrists and AGECAT reach full agreement on the four cases of schizophrenia in the samples, and AGECAT agrees on five cases out of eight of paranoid disorders, while the psychiatrists agree on all nine cases falling into AGECAT's combined schizophrenia/paranoid category. Two out of the three manic cases are concordant.

The concordance on the neuroses is not good. Only six of the psychiatrists' cases of neurosis are agreed by AGECAT out of 20, and only six out of 10 of the AGECAT cases are agreed by the psychiatrists. The distinction between syndrome cases and non-cases of neurotic illness is likely to be a matter of where the psychiatrist chooses to define his cut-off point. The research psychiatrists in these studies had little opportunity for training in this distinction due to the comparative rarity of such cases, even in the community. Two of the three cases of neurosis admitted to the mental hospital, presumably with more severe illness, were both recognised by AGECAT and agreed as cases of hypochondriasis and anxiety respectively. Overall concordance on non-cases reached 91%.

Some validation of the AGECAT diagnoses is possible from the follow-up studies. Each subject in the hospital studies was followed up three months later and 60% of the community sample were followed up one year later.

In the psychiatric hospital, the psychiatric follow-up diagnoses are not available, and therefore AGECAT initial diagnoses are used. Of the depressive cases at the three-month follow-up, almost two-thirds moved to a lower depressive level of confidence or were no longer classed as cases. Four depressive cases emerged with other diagnoses (schizophrenia, dementia) inconsistent with the original diagnosis. Four patients developed conditions (mania or neurosis) which were crudely consistent with the original diagnosis of depression. For the organic cases it was necessary to divide the illnesses into acute and chronic conditions. This was done using the psychiatrists' initial diagnoses. Sixty-eight percent of the cases concordant for dementia had shown no improvement three months later and four cases only slight improvement on hospital treatment. Of the seven cases specified as 'other organic' (mainly confusional states), five had shown improvement.

In the community sample, psychiatrists' follow-up diagnoses were not available, but of the 36 cases of AGECAT depression followed up, one-fifth were found to be worse or to show no improvement, the rest were better, two had changed to a diagnosis considered inconsistent with the previous diagnosis of depression. None of the nine organic cases followed up showed any improvement.

It may be said therefore, that the follow-up studies provide some validation for AGECAT diagnoses insofar as the patients tended to progress according to expectation.

Replication samples

Because some simple adjustments were required to the AGECAT system after it had been applied to the above samples, and because the results quoted reflect these changes, it was necessary to apply AGECAT to a number of replication samples. One of these is reported here. It consisted of an interim follow-up of 122 subjects from the random sample of 1070 subjects interviewed in their own homes in Liverpool (Copeland et al 1987). The subjects in this subsample were taken from the portion of those nominated by AGECAT as syndrome cases of organic and depressive disorder at confidence level 3 and above, and approximately twice as many non-cases, selected randomly. These were interviewed 'blind' by a group of psychiatrists in training. The interviews were conducted in the subjects' own homes and each of the psychiatrists made a diagnosis according to their own intuitive judgement.

Using six diagnostic categories, overall agreement reached 87%. The agreement for cases of organic states, schizophrenia, depression, neuroses and 'other psychotic' conditions as a whole reached 78%. The overall agreement on non-cases was 85%. AGECAT agreed with the psychiatrists on 84% of the cases of depression and dementia. Four of the psychiatrists' cases of dementia and one of depression were recognised by AGECAT on the correct diagnostic cluster but at confidence level 2. If the 'cutting point' deciding cases were lowered to level 2, as might be sensible for a community sample identifying subjects for further examination, AGECAT identified 97% of the psychiatrists' cases of depression and dementia with the addition of only five false positives. The psychiatrists agreed on 82% of the AGECAT cases of depression and dementia. In order to look at the discrepant cases more closely, Table 7.5 shows the distribution of non-concordant cases of depression on AGECAT's levels of confidence. All the disagreed cases were of depressive neurosis except one, which achieved a rating of level 0. No symptoms are recorded for this case and it must be assumed that the illness was so severe that the interview had to be abandoned. The interviewer had probably forgotten to make the appropriate explanatory rating. The remaining subjects are nearly all those who denied depressive mood and also had few other symptoms. The three remaining cases which scored level 0 had summaries which clearly indicated that they suffered from mood changes but were otherwise active people. One was thought to underplay her symptoms and the others were described as 'mild'. It seems likely that all three cases were incorrectly assessed by the psychiatrists as achieving the criteria of syndrome case level.

Table 7.5 Psychiatrists' cases of depression and organic disorder with which AGECAT disagreed, distributed on AGECAT levels of confidence (n = 541)

Disagreed psychiatrists' cases	AGECAT confidence levels						Total disagreed	Total in sample
	0	1	2	3	4	5		
Depression	4	3	3	1			11	105
Organic disorder	2		6	6			14	76

Table 7.5 also shows the distribution for psychiatrists' cases of organic disorder not agreed by AGECAT, in the original three studies. They will be seen to cluster around the borderline at levels 2 and 3. Six of the subjects achieved caseness on the organic syndrome cluster although they were finally allotted to other diagnoses. Both of the cases which initially achieved AGECAT Organic Level 0 had a follow-up assessment: one, three months later, and the other, one year later. Both were then agreed to be cases of depression.

THE DETECTION OF EARLY CASES OF DEMENTIA

Dementia must be detected in the population early in its course if treatment is to have the maximum therapeutic effect, and decisions on management taken at a time which will avoid social crises during the later stages. Early detection is also necessary in order to describe the natural history of these conditions, which is still imperfectly known, and to allow the circumstances surrounding the onset of dementia to be studied. As it is unlikely that biochemical markers suitable for mass screening will be discovered, early detection will generally be by relatives and friends, based on social behaviour. How far it is possible to detect early cases of dementia by minor variations in mental state and behaviour is now being investigated in a longitudinal study. Preliminary results on the follow-up of a small interim sample of 126 subjects selected as possible early cases of dementia and pseudo-dementia are hopeful. Although this small sample contains only 16 cases, whom the psychiatrists diagnosed as dementing between 9 and 12 months after the initial interview, 10 had been recognised as cases of dementia by AGECAT in the original interviews, four others had scored on the Organic cluster but had not at that time reached case level, and only two were unrecognised at initial interview. Most of the subjects scoring confidence level 3 on the Organic cluster on the initial interview were diagnosed by the psychiatrists at the follow-up as dementing. Others had recovered, indicating that they had had acute confusional states which the AGECAT system, based purely on mental state at that time, did not discriminate from the dementias. Most of the subjects scoring at Organic level 2 (below case level) were seen to develop depressive illness, especially if the Organic levels had been associated with even minimum levels of depression at the original interview. Two non-cases initially scoring Organic level 2 had progressed to cases of dementia at level 3 at follow-up.

It would appear therefore, that although the AGECAT system recognises a number of subjects at Organic confidence levels of 1 or 2 (approximately 10% of the sample), at follow-up the majority of these have either reverted to level 0 or progressed to depression. Nevertheless, some have developed dementia. The biggest challenge for any case-finding instrument in this field is to detect early, mild or prodromal stages of dementia and distinguish them from normal ageing. AGECAT appears to have some success in this, although two subjects, who were missed at initial interview, later became cases. These could have suffered acute strokes between interviews but this remains to be investigated (Copeland et al 1986).

An aid in detecting cases of pseudo-dementia would be helpful. Some preliminary data are becoming available, suggesting that a simple calculation based on the depression and organic scores, the 'Dementia Depression' Index, may not only aid in this distinction but may also have some predictive power for selecting those subjects who may later develop dementia. We shall know more about the success of the GMS-AGECAT package as a whole in detecting dementia when the results of the three-year follow-up of the Liverpool sample become available during 1987.

THE PRESENT STAGES OF DEVELOPMENT OF THE GMS-AGECAT PACKAGE AND FUTURE PLANS

The Geriatic Mental State is at present available in its original form, in its community form and as part of the modified CARE schedule. The second edition of the History and Aetiology Schedule is available, and the Physical Examination and Social Status Schedules are also available. The Geriatic Mental State has been translated into German, Danish, Icelandic, Dutch, French and Spanish, and the shortened version into Italian and Norwegian. Versions are also being prepared in Portuguese, Spanish and Mandarin. The need for these translations reflects the use of the instrument in different parts of the world. Detailed manuals (Copeland et al 1985) are available for the full and community schedules and a computer programme for the AGECAT diagnostic system will soon be available for distribution. Training sessions for potential users are held in Liverpool, lasting four to five days, as required, but at least every six months. The second revised edition of the full GMS has been completed. The extensive data now accumulated have been used to eliminate unsatisfactory and redundant items, and some new items have been added. Analyses are proceeding in order to discover if the extensive battery of psychological tests undertaken in some of these studies contributes to the detection of early cases, to the diagnostic distinction or to the ability to map out the deficits and patterns of the illness over time. Other studies are in progress, examining the stages of dementia.

The GMS-AGECAT package has developed gradually in response to our own needs and those of others, so the author and his colleagues are always pleased to receive comments and suggestions for improvements.

Acknowledgements

The author would like to acknowledge the contribution of the members of the US-UK teams on both sides of the Atlantic: in New York: B. J. Gurland, L. Sharpe, R. Simon, J. Kuriansky, L. Dean, P. Stiller, R. Bennett, D. Wilder, J. Teresi, R. Golden and D. Cook; in London: M. J.

Kelleher, M. L. Robinson, R. Parker, A. Smith, A. Mann, Y. Tsegos and B. Robinson. Throughout the studies reported here B. J. Gurland directed the US team. J. R. M. Copeland directed the UK team from 1970–77, including the community study and the subsequent AGECAT studies in Liverpool.

The AGECAT studies were developed in association with M. E. Dewey, H. M. Griffiths-Jones, I. A. Davidson, C. McWilliam, D. Forshaw and other colleagues in the University of Liverpool Department of Psychiatry.

The studies were conducted in the US at the Center for Geriatrics and Gerontology of the Faculty of Medicine of Columbia University and the New York State Office of Mental Health, and at the Department of Geriatric Research, New York State Psychiatric Institute; and in the UK at the Department of Psychiatry, Institute of Psychiatry, University of London, and the Department of Psychiatry and the Institute of Human Ageing, University of Liverpool.

The studies were funded mainly by grants from the National Institute of Mental Health (Grant No. 5R1MH09191), and Administration on Aging (Grant No. 93-P-57467) Washington DC, by the New York State Office of Mental Health, the Department of Health and Social Security, London, the Wellcome Trust, the World Health Organization and the Mersey Regional Research Committee.

REFERENCES

American Psychiatric Association 1980 Diagnostic and Statistical Manual of Mental Disorders (DSMIII), 3rd edn. American Psychiatric Association, Washington DC

Binks M G, Davies A D M 1984 The contribution of the National Adult Reading Test to the detection of dementia amongst community dwelling old people. Paper delivered at the British Society of Gerontology, Leeds

Cohen J 1968 Weighted Kappa: nominal scale agreement with provision for scaled disagreement or partial credit. Psychological Bulletin 70: 213–220

Cooper J E, Kendell R E, Gurland B J, Sharpe L, Copeland J R M, Simon R 1972 Psychiatric Diagnosis in New York and London: A Comparative Study of Mental Hospital Admissions. Maudsley Monograph Series, No 20, Oxford University Press, London

Copeland J R M 1981 What is a case, a case for what? In: Wing J K, Bebbington P, Robbins L N (eds) What is a Case, the problems of definition in psychiatric community surveys. Grant McIntyre, London, pp 7–11

Copeland J R M, Gurland B J 1978 Evaluation of diagnostic methods: an international comparison. In: Isaacs A D, Post F (eds) Studies in Geriatric Psychiatry. Wiley, Chichester, pp 189–209

Copeland J R M, Gurland B J 1985 International comparative studies. In: Arie T (ed) Recent Advances in Psychogeriatrics. Churchill Livingstone, Edinburgh, pp 175–195

Copeland J R M, Dewey M E, Griffiths-Jones H M 1986 Computerised psychiatric diagnostic system and case nomenclature for elderly subjects: GMS and AGECAT. Psychological Medicine 16: 89–99

Copeland J R M, Kelleher M J, Kellett J M, Gourlay A J, Barron G, Cowan D W, De Gruchy J, Gurland B J, Sharpe L, Simon R, Kuriansky J, Stiller P 1975 Cross-national study of comparison of the diagnosis of elderly psychiatric patients admitted to mental hospitals serving Queens County in New York and the old Borough of Camberwell, London. British Journal of Psychiatry 126: 11–20

Copeland J R M, Kelleher M J, Kellett J M, Gourlay A J, Gurland B J, Fleiss J L, Sharpe L 1976 A semi-structured clinical interview for the assessment of diagnosis and mental state in the elderly. The Geriatric Mental State Schedule. 1. Development and reliability. Psychological Medicine 6: 439–449

Copeland J R M, Dewey M E, Henderson A S, Kay D W K, Neal C D, Harrison M A M, McWilliam C, Forshaw D, Shiwach R 1987 The Geriatric Mental State used in the community: Replication studies of the computerised diagnosis AGECAT. Psychological Medicine (in press)

Copeland J R M, McWilliam C, Dewey M E, Wood N, Forshaw D M, Sharma V K, Abed R, Shiwack R 1986 The early recognition of dementia and depression in the elderly: a preliminary communication of a longitudinal study using the GMS AGECAT Package (Community version). International Journal of Geriatric Psychiatry 1: 63–70

Dewey M E, Copeland J R M 1986 Computerised psychiatric diagnosis in the elderly: AGECAT. Journal of Microcomputer Applications 9: 135–140

Gurland B J, Copeland J R M, Kelleher M J, Kuriansky J, Sharpe L, Dean L 1983 The Mind and Mood of Ageing: The Mental Health Problems of the Community Elderly in New York and London. Haworth Press, New York; Croom Helm, London

Gurland B J, Cross P, Defiguerido J, Shannon M, Mann A M, Jenkin R, Bennett R, Wilder D, Wright H, Killeffer E, Godlove C, 1979 A cross-national comparison of the institutionalized elderly in the cities of New York and London. Psychological Medicine 9: 781–788

Gurland B J, Fleiss J L, Goldberg K, Sharpe L, Copeland J R M, Kelleher M J, Kellett J M 1976 A semi-structured clinical interview for the assessment of diagnosis and mental state in the elderly. The Geriatric Mental State Schedule 2. A factor analysis. Psychological Medicine 6: 451–459

Henderson A S, Duncan-Jones P, Finlay-Jones R A 1983 The reliability of the Geriatric Mental State examination. Acta Psychiatria Scandanavica 87: 1–9

Jones J R 1984 A microcomputer version of the Geriatric Mental State Schedule. Journal of Microcomputer Applications 7: 385–387

Kendell R E, Everitt B, Copper J E, Sartorius N, David M E 1968 The reliability of the Present State Examination. Social Psychiatry 3: 123–129

Roth M 1981 The diagnosis of dementia in late and middle life. In: Mortimer J A, Schuman L M (eds) The Epidemiology of Dementia. Oxford University Press, London, pp. 24–61

Simon R J, Gurland B J, Fleiss J L, Sharpe L 1971 Impact of a patient history interview on psychiatric diagnosis. Archives of General Psychiatry 24: 437–440

Spitzer R L, Endicott J, Fleiss J L, Cohen J 1970 Psychiatric Status Schedule: a technique for evaluating psychopathology and impairment in role functioning. Archives of General Psychiatry 23: 41–55

Spitzer R L, Endicott J 1968 Diagno: A computer programme for psychiatric diagnosis utilising the differential diagnostic procedure. Archives of General Psychiatry 18: 746–756

Wing J K, Cooper J E, Sartorius N 1974 The Description and Classification of Psychiatric Symptoms: An Instruction Manual for the P.S.E. and Catego System. Cambridge University Press, London

The relationship between depression and disability in the elderly — data from the comprehensive assessment and referral evaluation (CARE)

INTRODUCTION AND AIMS

Among the most frequent problems accompanying the advance of old age are depression and chronic disability. These two conditions have an important bearing on the quality of life of the elderly. There is a common belief that the advent of depression in chronic disability is almost inevitable and that increased rates of chronic disability in old age must make ageing a depressing experience. This belief if unchallenged could lead to a sense of fatalism on the part of ageing cohorts and therapeutic nihilism on the part of clinicians. Yet the evidence mentioned below conflicts with these assertions about age, depression and disability and suggests the need for further examination of these relationships.

The strength and direction of the association between depression and increasing age has been reviewed elsewhere (Gurland et al 1984a, Gurland, 1976). Cross-sectional data (albeit confounding the effects of age and generation) suggest that, at least in women, prevalence rates of depression of a clinical level of severity level out after 65 years and then decrease with ageing; and that the condition only affects a small minority of the elderly of either gender. Moreover, the relatively high suicide rate in elderly men appears to be an effect of membership of earlier generations rather than of age itself (Cross & Gurland 1984).

Thus there are inconsistencies in the rates of occurrence of depression (which does not show a linear rise with age) and chronic disability (which does). This introduces uncertainties about the role of age itself in influencing the relationship between depression and disability, and about other forces that determine this relationship. Clarifying these issues will help to set the record straight on the quality of life in old age, and whether the association between depression and disability is determined by factors that can be brought under clinical control. In this spirit, a detailed investigation of the relationship between depression and disability among the elderly is undertaken in this chapter.

A second purpose of this chapter is to demonstrate the usefulness of measures (such as appear in the CARE) of depression and disability in learning more about the quality of life of elderly persons.

DATA BASE

The original data to be analysed and discussed with reference to the relationship between depression and disability are taken mainly from the work of the US-UK Cross-National Project, a collaborative project between the Columbia University Center for Geriatrics and the Institute of Psychiatry in London. A brief description of the samples of subjects involved is given in *Table 8.1a*. The selection and demographic characteristics of the samples have been described elsewhere (Cross et al 1983, Gurland et al 1983); almost all are probability (representative) samples of those 65 years and older in the given setting.

The interview data are derived from the Comprehensive Assessment and Referral Evaluation (CARE) or one of its mutually compatible modified versions (Gurland & Wilder, 1984, Gurland, Golden et al 1984b, Gurland et al 1977). The CARE is a semistructured instrument with scripted probes, defined and coded responses and a multidimensional scoring system producing 22 homogeneous scales covering psychiatric, medical and social problems of the elderly (Teresi et al 1984, Golden et al 1984). Global ratings and operational criteria are also used to make assignments to classes of clinically relevant conditions. The psychometric properties of the CARE and its versions are given in the articles cited above.

Table 8.1a Examination of samples of the elderly using the CARE technique

Location	Type of sample	No. of respondents age 65 and over
Community-based		
New York City	Probability sample	445
London	Probability sample	396
Upper New York State	Probability sample	753
Los Angeles Hispanic	Probability sample	472
5 other regions in USA	Selected, systolic hypertension	551
Institutional-based		
New York City	Probability sample of all 65+ residents of long-stay institutions	162
London	Probability sample of all 65+ residents of long-stay institutions	159

MEASURES

The several indicators of depression and disability which were used in collecting the study data under discussion were incorporated in the CARE instrument but will be presented separately because of their special relevance to this chapter. Both conditions were analysed as continuous scale scores and categories defined either by a threshold score or by operational criteria for diagnosis. The reliability, validity and other psychometric properties of these measures have been published elsewhere.

Besides depression and disability, the CARE covers the dimensions shown in *Table 8.1b*. However these other dimensions are not crucial to an understanding of this paper and will not be detailed here.

Table 8.1b Content areas of the CARE

Physical problems
  Neurological
  Fits and faints
  Heart disease
  Coronary insufficiency
  Early cancer signs
  Bowel problems
  Skin problems
  Respiratory problems
  Fractures, operations
  Hearing problems
  Visual problems
  Dental problems
  Disfigurement
  Self-rating of health
  Arthritis
  Observation of above
  Overall physical illness

Psychological problems
  Orientation-memory
  Face-Hand test
  Subjective memory
  Depressed mood
  General anxiety
  Sleep disorder
  Phobic anxiety
  Elation
  Paranoid symptoms
  Anger
  Obsessional
  Delusions/hallucinations
  Hypochondriasis
  Insight

Social problems
  Retirement history
  Interests/organizations
  Social isolation
  Financial problems
  Family burden
  Housing/Neighborhood
  Crime
  Observation of above

Lifestyle problems
  Nutritional risk
  Excessive smoking
  Antisocial behavior
  Drug and alcohol abuse

Functional level
  Reduced energy levels
  Inadequate activities
  Impaired activities of daily living: basic and instrumental
  Immobility
  Impaired communication

Service utilizations
  Medical services
  Medications
  Formal social services
  Informal assistance

Global ratings
  100 global ratings, diagnostic criteria

Systematic summary

Depression

There are 29 items in a 'homogeneous' scale of depression (*see Table 8.2*) which is derived from a larger set of items by latent class analysis. The scale items include reference to mood, pessimism, suicidal ideation, diurnal variation and vegetative symptoms. Other items cover the duration of symptoms, their persistence, and change for the worse. Scores were based on addition of numbers of symptoms rated as present. Latent class analysis also produced a threshold score for membership of a statistically abnormal category; cases belonging to this category but not meeting the criteria for pervasive depression (see below) were called 'latent depression'.

Table 8.2 Homogeneous scale of depression

Admits to worrying
Worries about almost everything
In past month has been in depressed, sad, miserable mood
Has cried or felt like crying
Depression lasts longer than a few hours
There is a time of day that the depression is worst
Has felt that life was not worth living
Worried or pessimistic about the future
Future seems bleak or unbearable
Has felt suicidal or wished to be dead (ever)
Has suicidal thoughts or wished to be dead in the past month
Considered or tried suicide in the past month
Does not mention feeling happy in the past month
In comparison to other people his own age, dwells on his own physical shortcoming or handicap
Blames self for past or present behavior
Going out less than 7 days a week causes loneliness, boredom, frustration
Is bothered by current loneliness
Has been more irritable (than usual) lately
Not eating well due to poor appetite
Has sleep disorder due to altered mood
Subjectively slowed down in movements
Sits or lies around because of lack of energy, or is doing less than usual
Is especially slow in the morning
Describes headaches
Has enjoyed very little lately
Less interest in or enjoyment of activities previously enjoyed
Subject's loss of enjoyment or little or less interest in recreation due to depression or nervousness
Has been seriously depressed prior to the past month
Is not very happy

Criteria for diagnosis of 'pervasive depression' were applied to the CARE interview data in order to identify cases warranting clinical intervention to relieve depression. The key criteria are shown in bold face in Table 8.3; they emphasize the persistence of depression and its pervasive involvement of thought and attitude rather than the mere presence of negative mood. Specifically excluded were symptoms which were limited or circumscribed in their effect on the subject, such as depression lasting only a few hours (can snap out of it, occasional low days, worry only about specific problems, can turn mind to other things), crying only when a particular event or situation is discussed, or the future looking empty but not unbearable. Other criteria were used to subclassify pervasive depression.

Table 8.3 Criteria for diagnosis of pervasive depression

A. **Limited depression** (At least one item from two of the following groups)

Depression lasts only a few hours — can snap out of it
Occasional low days

Worried about specific problem — can turn mind to other things
Cries only when a particular event or situation is discussed

Future looks empty

Table 8.3 (*cont.*)

B. **Pervasive depression** (At least one item from two of the following groups)

Depression lasts whole day or longer
Cries or feels like crying, often

Depression is bothersome and not easily shaken off
Future looks bleak or unbearable

Can't stop worrying — worry is disproportionate to cause
Looks depressed through much of interview

C. **Vegetative symptoms** (At least one item from two of the following groups)

Palpitations
Trembling
Dizziness
Poor appetite
Constipation
Loss of weight
Sleep disturbance
Poor concentration

Early morning awakening
Lies awake with anxious or depressing thoughts
Depression worst in mornings

Weak or tired
Slow in speech or movement
Unexplained aches and pains
Subjective complaints of impaired memory

D. **Self-depreciation** (Any one item)

Self-conscious in public
Feels a failure
Feels guilty

E. **Suicidal or psychotic** (Any one item)

(not accounted for by non-depressive state)
Actively suicidal (strong impulse, preparations, or attempt)
Deluded or hallucinated with a depressive content
Mute or immobile
Serious injury or ill effect following suicidal attempt
Starvation or intercurrent infection
Homicidal behavior

F. **Other features**

Stress: a. Irrelevant ( )
      b. Necessary ( ) or sufficient ( )
      c. Concurrent ( ) or precedent ( )
Current or past excitement: Yes ( ) No ( )
Present episode: Yes ( ) No ( )
Past episode: Yes ( ) No ( )
Positive mood: Yes ( ) No ( )

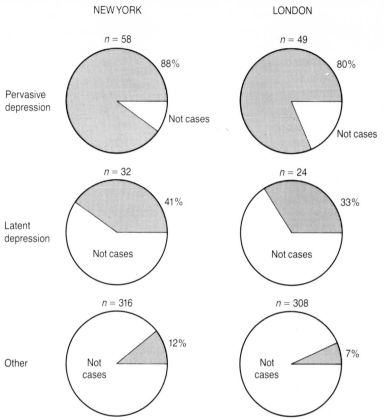

Fig. 8.1 Proportion of pervasive depressives and other subgroups judged to be cases. Representative samples of over-65s in the community in New York (*n* = 445) and London (*n* = 396), excluding cases of 'pervasive dementia'

Figure 8.1 shows that the great majority of pervasive depressives were independently judged in both New York and London (at face-to-face interview, by psychiatrists in all instances in London and in a random half in New York, with the remainder in New York being judged by social scientists) to be 'cases' requiring psychiatric intervention. The proportion of cases judged to be present in the latent class category was sharply lower than in the pervasive category; only a small proportion of the 'other' category were judged cases and these are not characterised by depressive symptoms. Thus the category of pervasive depression is not so broad that it contains many 'non-cases' nor so narrow that it excludes many cases of depression.

Disability

There are 39 items in the homogeneous scale of Activity Limitation, which measures disability through items regarding capacity for tasks of self-care, for carrying out household chores and for range of movement (*see Table 8.4*). Another aspect of disability was measured by a homogeneous scale which covered problems in ambulation. As in depression, scores and threshold levels for these scales were derived.

Table 8.4 Activity limitation

Going out less than 7 days a week causes essential tasks not to be done
Does not get out as often as needs
Has difficulty preparing own food
Impaired capacity to prepare own meals
Has difficulty shopping
Impaired capacity to do his own shopping
Physical difficulty getting to doctor's office
Difficulty cutting toe nails
Difficulty caring for feet
Difficulty getting shoes on/off
Difficulty reaching for toes
Can't reach toes
Difficulty reaching arms overhead
Can't reach dominant hand behind his back
Health trouble affects activities a little or a great deal
Health trouble limits leisure activities
Health trouble limits light chores
Health trouble limits heavy chores
Health trouble limits gainful occupation
Health trouble limits mobility
Health trouble limits carrying packages
Health trouble affects long distance travel
Health trouble limits social activities
Health trouble has other limiting effects
Health limitation is getting worse
Has problems handling personal business
Physical problems handling financial matters
Problems using toilet by himself
Physical problems using bath or shower
Difficulty bathing is a problem
Difficulty getting dressed by self
Difficulty grooming self
Physical difficulty grooming self
Does almost no chores by self
Difficulty doing chores by self
Chores are not always done and this creates a problem
Physical problem makes doing chores difficult
Has problems getting laundry done
Has a physical problem making laundry difficult to do

A diagnostic category of disability based upon someone having to give time to the subject for personal assistance (Personal Time Dependency: PTD) was defined by operational criteria, shown in *Table 8.5*. A specific decision tree was provided for determining that the need for donation of personal time by someone to the subject was related to the presence of a disability and that personal assistance was actually rendered. This category identified persons who were so disabled that they needed the personal time of others to enable them to survive in the community.

Table 8.5 Criteria for personal time dependency

Nature of disability	Related need for donation of personal time from another
Physiological disability Disturbance of automatic movements such as swallowing, protective reflexes, shifting movements, control of bladder and bowel, healing processes, etc.	Medical or nursing consultation Treatment or prevention of pressure sores. Nursing of wounds. Tube or intravenous feeding. Cleaning of incontinence. Toilet training. Care of catheter, diaper nursing.
Disability in activities of daily living Disturbance of coordinated movements such as feeding, standing, moving inside residence, managing stairs, moving about outside residence, bathing, dressing, grooming, effort intolerance, etc.	Assistance or supervision in bathing, grooming, walking, transferring, feeding, routine care of feet or fingernails.
Faulty or inconsistent awareness Disturbance of awareness, anticipation or orientation, with and inability to avoid simple dangers, remain aware of basic needs, find way around, be alert to or remember episodes of falling or illness, maintain consciousness, make plans for the future, etc.	Reminders and supervision to avoid dangers or find way around. Advice on business, finances, accounting, budgeting. Alerting and warnings of impending or actual illness, fainting or falling.
Limitation in instrumental activities of daily living Disturbance of complex tasks such as household cleaning chores, shopping, cooking and preparing meals, managing cash, writing and reading, following medication or nursing regimen, public transport, etc.	Substitution or assistance in shopping, planning meals, following diet plan, preparing food, cooking; housekeeping tasks, laundry; errands, correspondence, reading; escort for outside excursions; managing cash (not budget); using public transport, administering medications or nursing care.
Inadequate emotional autonomy Disturbance of self-regulation and self-sufficiency with an inability to tolerate being alone, maintain motivation, take needed exercise, maintain interests and activities, etc.	Encouragement or persuasion to take exercise, carry out tasks and engage in activities. Companionship, sitting services
Indequate social initiative Inability to take required or desired social action such as communicating, or obtaining medical help when needed, obtaining physical assistance when needed (e.g. chairs, walkers, rails), tolerating contact with the public, decorum and manners; making, breaking and maintaining interpersonal relationships.	Advocacy and intermediation for subject as an individual. Summoning medical or social help as needed. Sheltering from public contact. Protecting from repercussions of social behaviour, governing social relations, maintaining minimal relationships

The category of PTD could be predicted from specific item ratings, with high accuracy (correlation 0.94 in New York and 0.92 in London), showing the reliability of the category. The value of using the category rather than a scale based on item ratings is that the category is more readily understood in a discussion of utilisation of formal and informal personal assistance services.

PREVALENCE

About 13% of the elderly living in the community were found to be pervasively depressed. Major depressions are only a small subset of the pervasive category, while the latent class category is somewhat smaller than the pervasive category and, by definition, mutually exclusive to it.

About 30% of the community elderly in both New York and London were PTD, with roughly equal thirds needing occasional and minor personal assistance, frequent or substantial personal assistance and almost constant or intensive personal assistance housebound. The disabled (PTD) elderly tended to be over-represented among the widowed, females, and oldest age groups. There was a variable relationship with living alone and the quality of the neighborhood; and a low correlation with education, occupation or income.

Given these prevalence rates, at least 4% of the general elderly population would have both disability and pervasive depression even if the association between them was due to chance overlap only; however, as described below, the association is much higher than chance would dictate.

ASSOCIATION OF DEPRESSION AND DISABILITY

Community elderly

That the prevalence of pervasive depression is raised in the presence of PTD is shown in Figure 8.2. Furthermore, there is a statistically significant correlation between the scale of depression and both the presence and severity of PTD. The correlations between disability (as measured in this

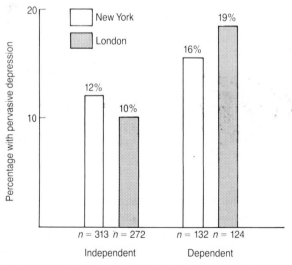

Fig. 8.2 The frequency of pervasive depression in the presence of personal time dependence. New York and London community elderly (as Fig. 8.1).

instance by the Activity Limitation Scale) and other homogeneous scales is shown in *Table 8.6*. The correlation with the depression scale is 0.50, among the highest.

Table 8.6 Correlation of disability (activity limitation scale) with other health and social problems*

Other indicators of disability	
Ambulation problems	0.78
Possible causes	
Physical illness	0.49
Cognitive impairment	0.34
Stroke	0.32
Arthritis	0.32
Leg swelling	0.38
Vision disorder	0.38
Heart disorder	0.25
Respiratory symptoms	0.22
Possible consequences	
Service utilization	0.60
Depression	0.50
Isolation problems	0.40
Sleep disorder	0.32
Financial hardship	0.28
Miscellaneous	
Complaints of memory	0.24
Retirement dissatisfaction	0.13
Cancer alert	0.12
Hearing disorder	0.15
Hypertension	0.16
Neighbourhood dissatisfaction	0.10
Fear of crime	0.06

* Combined New York and London community elderly ($n = 841$) at baseline

Conversely, the major correlates of depression, when a wide spectrum of health and social problems is scanned, are the two scales of disability (Activity Limitations and Ambulation Problems); also somatic symptoms and sleep disorder, but these latter two are probably symptoms of depression. The strengths of the associations between depression, disability and various social problems are compared in *Table 8.7*.

Table 8.7 Correlation of depression and various social problems*

Social problem	Correlation
Activity limitation	0.50
Ambulation problems	0.46
Retirement dissatisfaction	0.20
Total service utilization	0.27
Financial hardship	0.36
Neighbourhood dissatisfaction	0.21
Fear of crime	0.15
Social isolation	0.36

* Combined New York and London community elderly ($n = 841$) at baseline

A significant and substantial correlation between scales of disability and of depression was present not only on analysis of cross-sectional data but also on analysis of data collected one year apart, at base-line and one-year follow-up, on 292 community elderly in New York. Significant odds-ratios were obtained between the scales of depression and activity limitation at baseline, at follow-up, and with respect to change scores.

Depression in the companions of the disabled

The association between depression and disability is not confined to the disabled victim. Their elderly companions are also more likely to be depressed as shown in *Figure 8.3*. The result is that depression is particularly likely to be found in the households of those who are disabled, either in the index case or their companion.

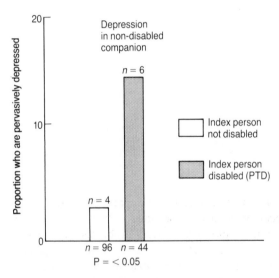

Fig. 8.3 Frequency of pervasive depression in the presence of disability (New York sample — $n = 445$)

Consistency of the association between disability and depression across populations

The extent to which the relationship between disability and depression is a consistent finding (i.e. constant across populations) can suggest the degree to which inquiry into this relationship should be directed at general principles or at local characteristics such as health services and cultural influences. Data on four representative samples of community-residing elderly were compared in order to examine this issue.

Table 8.8 shows that rates of depression and disability (as measured here by threshold scores on the scales of Depression and Activity Limitation or Ambulation Problems) vary between populations. Moreover, they do not necessarily vary together. Yet correlations between depression and disability are all high across the four populations.

Table 8.8 Percentage prevalence of depression and disability in the elderly of four populations

	LA Hispanic	NYC	London	N-E NYS
Depression	22.7	14.8	13.4	8.5
Activity limitations	26.9	17.5	14.0	18.2
Ambulation problems	24.8	27.0	29.0	23.8
	($n = 472$)	($n = 445$)	($n = 396$)	($n = 753$)

Intercorrelation of depression and disability in the elderly of four populations

	LA Hispanic	NYC	London	N-E NYS
Depression with:				
Activity limitations	0.50	0.50	0.32	0.44
Ambulation problems	0.49	0.46	0.29	0.43
	($n = 472$)	($n = 445$)	($n = 396$)	($n = 753$)

In order to determine whether the results on the cross-population comparisons might be influenced by culturally biased responses to the interview technique, the internal consistency (alpha) of the scales was tested on each sample separately. Alphas were high on all samples. For depression these were respectively 0.88, 0.87, 0.86 and 0.84 for Los Angeles (LA), New York City (NYC), London, and North-Eastern New York State (N-E NYC). The actual item frequencies in each sample for selected items from the depression scale are shown in *Figure 8.4*. The relative frequencies for individual items tend to mirror those for overall scores. Thus there is no evidence to suggest that relative rates of depression are a cultural artefact. A corresponding analysis of disability items produced similar results.

Exceptions to the rule of a high association between depression and disability

Variation in the association between depression and disability

Referring again to *Table 8.8*, it is noted that although correlations between depression and disability are all high across populations, the correlations in London are distinctly lower than in the other three samples. Another view of the same source of data is shown in *Figure 8.5*, which compares the degree to which depression is associated with disability (Personal Time Dependency) in London and in New York. The cumulative curve of the

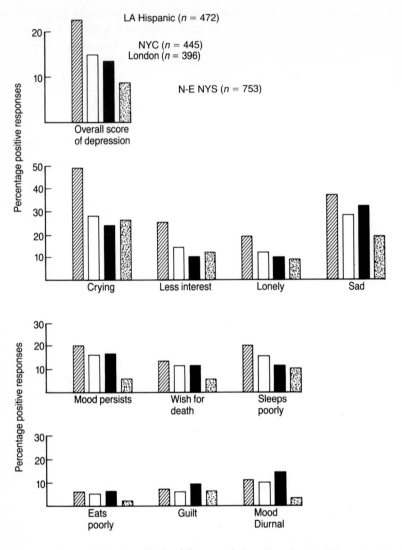

Fig. 8.4 Item frequencies in the elderly of four populations (Los Angeles Hispanic, New York City, London and North-East New York State) for selected items in the depression scale

frequency of depression shifts towards higher scores in the PTD groups compared with independent elderly in both cities, but this shift is less marked in London than in New York.

The exceptional result for London cannot readily be dismissed as a psychometric artefact. The alphas of the scales were consistent across populations and the rates of depression and ambulation problems were similar in New York and in London. This comparison between New York and

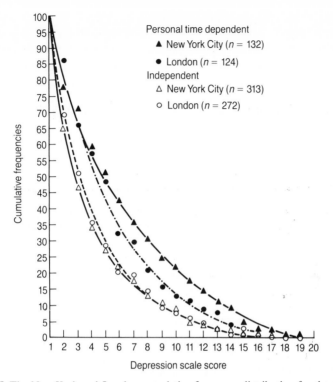

Fig. 8.5 The New York and London cumulative frequency distribution for the depression scale for dependent and independent elderly people living in the community

London is shown in greater detail in *Table 8.9*. When severity of disability is controlled, the means for depression scores are still lower in London than in New York for both moderate and severe disability. Furthermore, depression scores do not rise with increasing disability in London but do in New York.

One possible reason for disability being less depressing in the London than in the New York community elderly is that gaining access to long-term care services is easier and less stressful in London because in that city:
1. There are only two channels to explore for access (primary care and the

Table 8.9 Severity of disability and relationship to depresssion in New York and London

Scale scores (means)	Independent	Mildly dependent ('limited home care')	Moderately dependent ('equivalent to adult home')	Severely dependent ('equivalent to nursing home')
Depresssion				
New York	2.58	4.11	4.31	5.72
London	2.73	4.48	3.64	4.44

New York and London community elderly (n = 445 and 396 respectively).

social services) and these are interconnected and their offices and telephone numbers are known; in New York there are a myriad of changing ways to explore before the effective route to services is found; 2. The elderly have assigned doctors who are known to them prior to an urgent or complex need arising; and 3. Community formal and volunteer home care services are more active. It is consistent with this view that there was less expressed worry about health among the London than the New York elderly.

Another variation of the rule of a relationship between disability and depression was noted in a study of long-term care facilities in New York and London. Only subjects with a Mental Status Questionnaire Score of 7 or less were interviewed so as to eliminate those whose cognitive impairment might invalidate their responses to questions about depression. Classification of depression and disability was based respectively on threshold scores on scales of depression and activities of daily living. The correlation between depression and disability was stronger in London (0.32) than in New York (-0.08); the converse of the findings among the community elderly. *Figure 8.6* shows that there is an orderly increase of rates of depression with increasing disability in London, but not in New York; in the latter city the rate of depression in severe disability unexpectedly falls rather than rises. The rate of depression in severe disability is significantly lower in New York than in London; this difference was restricted to short-stay patients (less than one and a half years).

Cross-national variation in the internal consistency of the disability scale was examined to see if it accounted for the cross-national differences noted in the long-term care facilities. The item-whole correlations are shown in

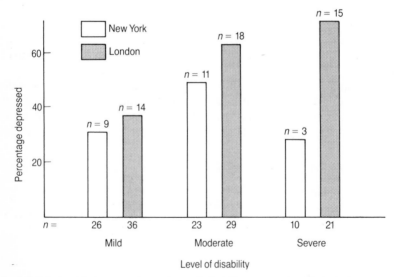

Fig. 8.6 Relationship between depression and disability among the elderly in long-term care facilities (New York: $n = 162$; London: $n = 159$)

Table 8.10. Some of the items do vary between the cities in their contribution to the scale score, for example bathing and stair climbing. However, elimination of the last-named items from the scale produced an alpha of 0.92 in New York and 0.89 in London; both satisfactorily high.

Possible reasons for disability being less depressing in the New York than in the London institutional elderly include the greater intensity of nursing care and activity programmes in New York than in London long-term care facilities. For the very disabled elderly this could have helped to relieve their immobility, pain, inactivity and hence depression. For the less disabled elderly, these services were probably not so crucial to their well-being.

Table 8.10 Comparison of item scores on elderly residents in long-term care facilities in New York and London

| | Proportions | | Item-total Correlations | |
Item content	US	UK	US	UK
Mobility level	0.73	0.74	0.71	0.51
Walking	0.58	0.60	0.60	0.54
*Bathing	0.81	0.91	0.63	0.37
Dressing	0.62	0.54	0.79	0.74
Toileting	0.56	0.47	0.74	0.79
Bowel	0.33	0.26	0.63	0.56
Bladder	0.39	0.42	0.66	0.58
Wheeling	0.38	0.33	0.68	0.63
Transferring	0.39	0.37	0.75	0.72
Eating/feeding	0.40	0.24	0.72	0.49
Communication	0.12	0.14	0.36	0.35
*Stair climbing	0.78	0.62	0.55	0.61

*Items which we found to lack invariance across subgroups (J. A. Teresi et al, 1981)

Recovery from depression associated with disability

Another set of departures from the rule of parallelism between the occurrence of depression and disability is found in longitudinal patterns of the relationship between these two conditions. This is brought out by the data from two longitudinal studies which are described below and show in particular that recovery from depression may occur even where recovery from disability does not take place.

In the first of these studies, 110 elderly subjects were interviewed in 1971 and again in 1975 (Wilder et al 1986). At the earlier point in time they were interviewed as part of a representative sample of community-residing elderly persons in New York City. They were seen again four years later if they had not relocated. In 1971, 18% were disabled (a threshold score of 3 or more on a scale of Activities of Daily Living) and the great majority (81%) of these were also disabled (Personal Time Dependent) at follow-up, i.e. most cases were chronically disabled. As expected, the initial depression (4 or above on an ad hoc scale) rates were four times as high among the disabled (60%) than among the non-disabled (15%). However, it was surprising to find that among the disabled group (who were mostly chronic), 6 out of 12 cases of depression recovered (6 or less on a 'rational' scale in 1975), while, among the non-disabled group, by the same token only 3 out of 13 cases of depression recovered.

These findings suggested that even though depression is increased in cases of disability, recovery from depression is not prevented by the presence of disability; recovery from depression occurred in a substantial proportion of those who were disabled and depressed and occured at least as frequently among the disabled as among the non-disabled elderly.

In the second of the studies on recovery from depression in disability, 292 elderly who completed a one-year follow-up were assessed for levels of depression and disability at initial and follow-up interviews. These subjects were part of a representative sample of 445 community-residing elderly. Classification of cases was based on threshold scores for the two conditions. Tables (*Tables 8.11a,b,c*) have been constructed from four defined outcomes; 'never' a case at either T_1 or T_2; a 'chronic' case with the condition present at T_1 and T_2; a 'new' case being present at T_2 but not T_1 and a 'recovered' case being present at T_1 but not T_2.

New cases of depression (31/292) are about equal to chronic cases of depression (39/292) and new cases of disability (38/292) are about equal to chronic cases of disability (33/292). New cases of depression occur in 33.3% of new cases of disability and 41.7% of chronic disability but only 7.7% of recovered disability and 9.7% of the never disabled (proportions refer to those not depressed at T_1). Recovery from depression occurs at the rate of 28.6% among the chronically disabled group and in 35.7% of the newly disabled, in contrast to recovery rates of 50% or more among those with recovered disability and those who were never disabled (proportions refer to those depressed at T_1). About 62% of chronic depressions occur in relation to chronic or new disability. Conversely, among those who were never disabled ($n = 202$) there were only 29 cases of new or chronic depression (less than 15%).

It might appear that the emergence of new depression could be minimised, and recovery from depression could be enhanced by: 1. preventing new disability; and 2. improving existing disability. Nevertheless, recovery from depression does take place in 28.6% of cases who are depressed at T_1 even when the disability is unremitting; and almost 40% of cases of chronic disability are free of depression at T_2.

The recovery rate of depression among the disabled in the first study is higher than in the second study. The extent to which this might be due to the longer interval of follow-up in the first study (4 years) than in the second (1 year) is not known. It may be that depression recovery rates continue to increase with the passage of time, even after several years.

Table 8.11a One-year course of depression and disability*

No. of cases Disability	Depression				
	Never	Recovered	New	Chronic	Total
Never	158	15	17	12	202
Recovered	12	3	1	3	19
New	16	5	8	9	38
Chronic	7	6	5	15	33
Total	139	29	31	39	292

Table 8.11b Percentages of depression in each disability group*

Disability groups	Depression groups				Depressed at T_2	Percentage of recovered depressions out of all T_1 depressives	Percentage of new depressions out of those *not* depressed at T_1
	Never	Recovered	New	Chronic			
Never	78.2	7.4	8.4	6	14.4	55.5	9.7
Recovered	63.1	15.8	5.3	15.8	21.0	50.0	7.7
New	42.1	13.1	21.1	23.7	44.7	35.7	33.3
Chronic	21.2	18.2	15.2	45.4	60.6	28.6	41.7

Table 8.11c Percentage proportions of disability in each depression group*

Disability group	Depression groups			
	Never	Recovered	New	Chronic
Never	81.7	51.7	54.8	30.8
Recovered	6.2	10.3	3.2	7.7
New	8.3	17.2	25.8	23.1
Chronic	3.6	20.7	16.1	38.5
% of recovered disability out of T_1 disabilities	63.1	33.3	16.7	16.7
% of new disability out of these not disabled at T_1	9.2	25.0	32.0	42.9

* NY community sample: n = 292 completed a 1-year follow-up
  T_1: initial interview
  T_2: follow-up

PATHWAYS BETWEEN DEPRESSION AND DISABILITY

Time sequencing of depression and disability

The analysis reported in the previous section was restricted to consideration of the extent to which the course of disability predicts the course of depression. Additional evidence on the causal direction of the association between depression and disability can be found by referring back to the tables (8.11a,b,c) for the New York City one-year follow-up study.

Only 12.6% (25/199) are depressed at T_2 if not depressed nor disabled at T_1; 24% (6/25) are depressed at T_2 if disabled but not depressed at T_1; 51.2% (21/41) are depressed at T_2 if depressed but not disabled at T_1; and 66.6% (18/27) are depressed at T_2 if both depressed and disabled at T_1. It appears that the predictive power of disability for depression at T_2 is at least in part due to its association with depression at T_1. Nevertheless, the presence of disability alone at T_1 almost doubles (24% vs. 12.6%) the chances of depression at T_2.

There is also evidence that depression might have a causal influence on the onset and persistence of disability. Disability at T_2 occurs in 12.1% (24/199) of those neither disabled nor depressed at T_1 and rises to 34.1% (14/41) at T_2 in those depressed but not disabled at T_1. The corresponding proportions at T_2 for those disabled but not depressed at T_1 is 48% (12/25) and for those disabled and depressed at T_1 is 77.8% (21/27). Thus, the risk of disability arising one year later is increased threefold in the presence of depression alone. Similarly, recovery from disability is less likely where there is associated depression at T_1 (22.2% or 6/27) than where there is none (52% or 13/25).

Age and sex in an explanatory model

Rates of disability rise with age consistently across studies and this was true also for the New York City and London community samples. The rise of rates of disability is especially regular among females. Yet rates of depression do not rise regularly with age in these same samples. This is surprising in view of the previously described strong association between disability and depression.

One possibility that would reconcile these conflicting data is that the strength of the relationship between disability and depression is most evident in the young-old age group and does not apply to the same degree to the old-old age group. Further analysis, by age, of the turnover tables previously presented for the community elderly in New York City indicates that there is a significant correlation between new disability and new depression in the young-old ($n = 175$) but not in the old-old ($n = 117$). Correspondingly, new depressions are uncommon in the old-old; the new-to-chronic depressions ratio is 5:4 in the young-old but 1:3 in the old-old.

The decline in rates of depression in disability with increasing age is shown in detail for North-Eastern New York. Both in males (Fig. 8.7a) and females (Fig. 8.7b), rates of depression are low in the non-disabled; these rates are dramatically raised in the young-old disabled females, modestly raised in the young-old disabled males and only slightly raised in the old-

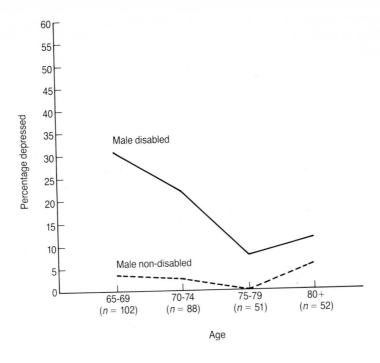

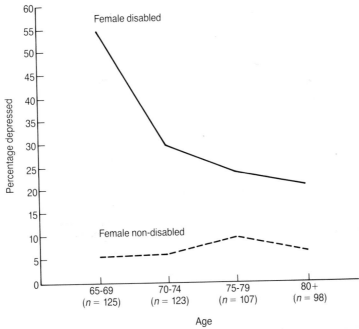

b

Fig. 8.7 Age variation in the relationship between disability and depression. In North-East New York State ($n = 746$) a) men b) women

old females and males. Age does not appear to affect rates of depression in the non-disabled.

These data are cross-sectional and confound cohort and ageing effects. Nevertheless, they suggest that disability is less depressing as age increases; at least in part because disability is more likely to be chronic than new with advancing age.

Gender has little effect on rates of depression among the non-disabled elderly, yet, among the disabled, females have much higher rates than men across the older age-span. Contrary to a widely held belief, older women seem to react to disability more severely than do older men.

These data, in addition to being confounded by cohort effects, represent only those subjects who have survived to this age and are still living in the community. It is possible that the survivors are selectively resistant to depression. In order to test this hypothesis, the power of predicting death one year after assessment in the sample of New York community elderly was calculated by odds ratios and using homogeneous scales. These were statistically significant for both depression (2.1) and disability (2.4). However, when interactions between the scales and with age, sex, cognitive impairment, stroke, and isolation were taken into account, disability but not depression retained its predictive power. This evidence weighs against the likelihood that resistance to depression is acting as a selective factor for survivors.

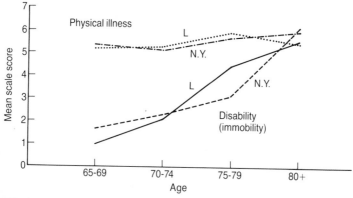

Fig. 8.8 Physical illness vs. disability (immobility) in elderly women, New York (*n* = 266) and London (*n* = 258)

The diminishing strength, as age increases, of the relationship between depression and disability could also be influenced by the degree to which physical illness accompanies disability in successive age groups. Figure 8.8 shows that whereas the mean score for disability increases with age, physical illness does not. One can infer that as age increases, disability tends to be less likely to be associated with active symptomatic physical illness.

CONCLUSIONS

This series of observations confirms that depression and disability are associated in important ways in older persons. Chronic disability is probably the main cause of chronic depression, outranking other situational causes of stress such as isolation, unsatisfactory retirement, financial hardship or a deteriorated environment. Nevertheless, the strength of the association varies in equally important ways, challenging the stereotype that ageing and its accompanying disabilities are inevitably depressing.

Table 8.12 Possible causal links between disability and depression

Vulnerability	Consequences
Family history	Pain–discomfort
Previous history	Altered self-image
Age (inverse)	Restricted movement
Female	Inactivity
Race and ethnicity	Isolation
Poor social support	Medications
Lack of roles	Life threatening
Social disadvantage	Dependence
Bad neighbourhood	Loss of control
Poor housing	Loss of roles
High crime	Loss of gratifications
Poverty	
Causes	**Caretaking**
Heart failure, angina	Reciprocal effects
Stroke	Formal supports
Fractures	Institutional location
Perceptual deficit	Environmental barriers
Early dementia	Expectations of recovery
Late dementia (inverse)	Expectations of roles
	Usurping initiatives
Course	**Treatment**
Recent onset	Health care system
Recent deterioration	Non-specific
Duration	General physical
Severity	Specific mental

We fully recognise the complexity of the possible causal pathways between disability and depression (see Table 8.12). The analyses we have undertaken have mostly skimmed the surface but also give some deeper insights. Disability appears to be less depressing when caregiving services are more active and reliable. This might explain the comparatively lower rates of depression among the disabled elderly living at home in London and in institutions in New York. Moreover, recovery takes place in a substantial proportion of cases of depression in disability: especially if the disability itself improves but even in chronic disability. Thus, a hopeful and therapeutically active view is justified.

The proportion of elderly who are free of depression despite being disabled increases with age, making therapeutic optimism and activism appropriate even with those who are very old. Men retain their advantage over women in resistance to depression throughout the lifespan.

The variety of ways in which depression is linked to disability in the elderly suggests a corresponding range of potentially effective interventions. There is every reason to improve the recognition and response to the presence of depression accompanying disability in the elderly. To assist this effort it is important to adopt a concept of depression, such as the one described here, which is inclusive of the majority of cases needing clinical intervention but not so broad as to present an overwhelming demand on the available services.

Treatment of depression can be directed primarily at the mood state or at the underlying disability. The intended outcome is to relieve the depression as the first concern. In addition, as these findings suggest, when the depression lifts the disability may follow suit.

It may be a comfort to some that age enhances the prospects of successfully coping with disability. By the same token, health care professionals may be encouraged to set positive goals for therapeutic interventions designed to reduce the strength of the relationship between depression and disability among the elderly.

REFERENCES

Cross P S, Gurland B J, Mann A H 1983 Long-term institutional care of demented elderly people in New York City and London. Bulletin of the New York Academy of Medicine 59: 267–275
Cross P S & Gurland B J 1984 Age, period and cohort views of suicide rates of the elderly. In: Pfeffer C, Richamn J (eds) Suicide and the life cycle. Proceedings of The American Association of Suicidology 15th annual meeting, New York, April 1982 p. 70–71
Golden R R, Teresi J A, Gurland B J 1984 Development of indicator-scales for the Comprehensive Assessment and Referral Evaluation interview schedule. Journal of Gerontology 39: 138–146
Gurland B J 1976 The comparative frequency and types of depression in various adult age groups. Journal of Gerontology 31: 283–292
Gurland B J, Wilder D E 1984 The CARE interview revisited: development of an efficient, systematic, clinical assessment. Journal of Gerontology 39: 129–137
Gurland B J, Kuriansky J B, Sharpe L, Simon R, Stiller P, Birkett P 1977 The Comprehensive Assessment and Referral Evaluation (CARE) — rationale, development and reliability. International Journal of Aging and Human Development 8: 9–42
Gurland B J, Copeland J R M, Kelleher M, Kuriansky J B, Sharpe L, Dean L 1983. The mind and mood of aging: the mental health problems of the community elderly in New York and London. Haworth Press, New York
Gurland B J, Golden R, Lantigua R, Dean L 1984a The overlap between physical conditions and depression in the elderly: a key to improvement in service delivery. In: Aronowitz E, Bromberg E M (eds) Mental health aspects of long term physical illness. Watson Publishers International Canton, Massachusetts p. 23–36
Gurland B J, Golden R, Teresi J, Challop J 1984b The SHORT-CARE: an efficient instrument for the assessment of depression, dementia and disability. Journal of Gerontology 39: 166–169

Teresi J A, Cross P, Gurland B J, Golden R R 1981 Measurement invariance. A method for detecting item bias in geriatric assessment scales. Annual Meeting, Gerontological Society, Toronto

Teresi J A, Golden R R, Gurland B J, Wilder D, Bennett R 1984 Construct validity of indicator-scales developed for the Comprehensive Assessment and Referral Evaluation interview schedule. Journal of Gerontology 39: 147–157

Wilder D, Gurland B J, Bennett R 1986 The chronicity of depression among the elderly. In: Erlemeyer L, Kimling N M (eds) Life span research on the prediction of psychopathology. Lawrence Erlbaum, New Jersey, p 205–222

Measuring mood

The management of affective disorders is broadly speaking the same for the elderly as for younger patients though with increasing age the incidence of affective disorders increases. The same criteria for diagnosis and the same measures of severity are used for both younger and for elderly patients. However the elderly present a somewhat more complicated clinical picture and standardised rating scales may therefore have to be applied with greater care and sensitivity of observation.

The measurement of depressive illness, whether it is specifically in the elderly or in the general age range, takes place in two stages. The first stage is to establish the presence of illness, taking great care to distinguish the symptoms from those of other illnesses. The measurement of severity of the illness, which is the second stage, cannot be made meaningfully unless accurate diagnosis has first been made.

This chapter will review briefly the scales commonly used for diagnosis of affective disorders and for the measurement of severity of illness. It will also review some of the particular problems the clinician may encounter in their application to the elderly.

DIAGNOSIS

The first task of the clinician in the management of depressive illness is to differentiate the syndrome of depression from a wide variety of conditions which may have a similar presentation. The same word 'depression' is in general use both to describe the normal transitory changes in mood which occur in response to adverse events in everyday life and to denote the profound hopelessness and gloom of the patients suffering from a severe depressive illness. A person may demonstrate features of depressive symptomatoloty but this does not necessarily mean he is suffering from a depressive illness. It is quite possible, for example, for a person to be unhappy and worried, to have loss of enjoyment of normal activities and for this to be a reasonable reaction in the circumstances. This reaction is normally short-lived and the duration of depressive symptoms is an important criterion for the diagnosis of depressive illness. Depressive illness may be precipitated by adverse events but its course and development will be independent of the events. A distinction is necessary between the unhappy and those with depressive illness in order to assess the need for treatment. Antidepressant treatment is clearly appropriate only for those suffering from depressive illness.

A further differentiation has to be made between the syndrome of depressive illness and depressive symptomatology which may occur in the context of a number of other psychiatric illnesses. Marked depressive symptomatology is seen for example in schizophrenia, and in obsessional neurosis, and these must be distinguished from depressive illness. Depressive symptoms may also appear secondary to physical illnesses. In such cases the primary illness is the first concern for treatment.

It may not always be easy to identify those patients suffering from depressive illness for whom antidepressant treatment would be appropriate, because of the similarity of depressive symptomatology across different conditions. If there were clear biological tests for the presence or absence of illness, as there are for some physical illnesses, selecting relevant treatment for patients would be relatively straightforward. There is much interest in the biochemical changes associated with the affective disorders but our understanding of their functional relevance is unfortunately very limited. In the absence of simple biochemical tests, diagnosis therefore continues to be made on the basis of clinical observation of symptomatology, on knowledge of past history, and of the course of the illness.

The difficulty with diagnosis based on clinical observation alone is that the decision to accord a diagnosis of depression is not standardised and may be affected by a number of factors. These include differing attitudes to the presence of depression and presentation found from one culture to another and also differing psychiatric perspectives which can be found even within the same culture. Attempts have been made to resolve this rather unsatisfactory state of affairs with the introduction of diagnostic schemata. The main purpose of these lists of diagnostic criteria is the more accurate and reliable characterisation of groups of patients under investigation.

The last decade or two have seen a concentration of effort into the development of new antidepressant treatments and a proliferation of research testing the efficacy of putative antidepressant compounds. One of the important contributions made by this research has been the steady improvement and refinement of the methodology used in clinical research. The improved definition of patient material to facilitate replicability of results has been one of the focuses of attention.

Because of the difficulty of establishing a valid and universally accepted classification of affective disorders, a number of different investigators have proposed sets of operationally-defined criteria which can be used to categorise patients. These are not, strictly speaking, rating scales in that they are designed to place patients in categories rather than to measure them on a continuum. Such systems also suffer from the shortcoming that they concentrate on assessment of psychopathology at a particular time and tend not to encompass other important factors such as history of the illness, family history, previous episodes, etc., all of which may be relevant. As with all kinds of rating scales they are more useful for standardising groups of patients than in assisting with the management of the individual patient. Examples of the diagnostic scales most commonly used are the Present State Examination (Wing et al 1974), its geriatric derivative (GMS) (see Ch. 7), the St Louis criteria (Feighner et al 1972) and DSMIII (American Psychiatric Association 1979). These systems vary from each other in the stringency with which the diagnosis of depression may be applied.

The Present State Examination has been used extensively for large-scale cross-cultural comparisons of diagnosis. Raters must be trained to use the scale which is lengthy and based on a structured interview. Patients' responses can be classified into psychiatric syndromes using computerised analysis of the interview information. Because of its size and structure its main use has been in survey research in schizophrenia. Its use in depression research has been limited by the relative paucity of the number of depressive items in the PSE.

The St Louis criteria (Feighner et al 1972) require that a patient has dysphoric mood plus five symptoms from a list of the symptoms most commonly and characteristically found in depressive illness. In accordance with clinical practice, the St Louis criteria also stipulate a list of exclusions from the diagnosis of primary affective disorder. Organic brain syndrome is obviously excluded, as well as depression in the context of other major psychiatric illness or secondary to other illness. All the diagnostic categorisations discussed make these exclusions. A further criterion which must be fulfilled concerns the duration of depressive symptoms. The St Louis criteria stipulate that the depressive symptomatology must have been present continuously for a period of four weeks.

More recently the DSMIII (American Psychiatric Association 1979) diagnostic criteria were developed. These attempt, with greater or lesser degrees of success, to categorise and give definitions to the complete range of psychiatric illnesses. They have now become widely adopted in research studies of psychiatric illness. A certain number of depressive symptoms as well as dysphoric mood must be present before the diagnosis of major depression can be given. However the definitions in the DSMIII tend to be rather broad, so that it may be easier for doubtful cases to fulfil the criterion for major depression. Another weakness is the requirement that the depressive symptoms should have been present for a period of only two weeks before the diagnosis of major depression is given. This somewhat limited duration is a less stringent criterion than the four weeks required by the St Louis criteria and it is possible that a number of personality disorders with transitory mood swings or anxiety states may be given the diagnosis of depression.

As a result of these less stringent requirements a wider spectrum of illness is likely to be gathered under the heading of DSMIII major depressive illness than might be the case in general psychiatric practice in Europe. In this context it is interesting to note that a comparison made between the St Louis diagnostic criteria, the DSMIII criteria and routine clinical diagnosis indicated that the St Louis criteria accorded most closely with clinical practice.

Categorisation by diagnostic instruments has as its main objective the delineation of homogenous groups of patients for research studies. However from the clinical point of view diagnostic categorisation is probably more concerned with prognosis and in identifying patients who will respond to treatment.

A further diagnostic categorisation which has been used extensively in depression research concerns the separation of endogenous and reactive or neurotic depression. This division has prognostic implications, the efficacy of standard antidepressants being shown most unequivocally in patients defined as suffering from endogenous depression. Some of the most thorough work on the classification of the affective disorders in this context has been carried out by the Newcastle group (Carney et al 1965, Gurney et al 1972) The inventory produced in 1965 to predict those patients likely to respond to ECT gives a positive weighting to the more 'biological' features associated with endogenous depression and a negative weighting to features associated with reactive depression. Cut-off scores for endogenous or reactive depression are given. This Newcastle diagnostic inventory provides a useful additional measure for describing groups of patients which is particularly important for research methodology. However the predictive power for response is not straightforward and it has been shown that patients scoring in the mid-range of 'endogeneity' have a better response to treatment than patients with very high scores or very low scores.

Diagnostic problems in the elderly

In principle the diagnostic scales for the elderly and for younger groups are the same. In practice it is likely that a good deal of depressive illness in the elderly is missed. Many elderly persons with depression may not reach the attention of the clinician and in those who do, the depression may not always be recognised. Difficulties in recognising depression in the elderly may arise from a number of factors. These include somewhat untypical clinical presentation, the confounding presence of physical illness, symptomatology produced by medication, the attribution of symptoms to organic causes, and confusion associated with dementia. The attitude that depression is a normal state in the elderly is unfortunately still to be found.

Community surveys of the prevalence of depressive illness in the elderly have varied in their estimates, but mostly agree that it is relatively common and frequently goes untreated. The percentage of the elderly in the community with untreated severe depression is probably relatively small.

In the community study of Kay et al (1964), for example, only 2% were found to be suffering from severe depression although a substantial number (8–12%) suffered from milder forms. Certainly in terms of incidence, depressive illness was more important than dementia, being responsible for twice the number of hospital admissions. In the study of Busse (1978), which examined a sample of people over the age of 65 in the community in Chicago, 20% of subjects reported significant depressive episodes in the previous three years. Broadly similar figures were found in a later, much larger, study (Blazer & Williams 1980) and in the US–UK geriatric study (Gurland et al 1983, see also Ch. 8).

Some elderly patients suffering from depression may remain untreated because of prevalent attitudes towards old age. Old age is inevitably a time of loss and mourning, loss of loved ones, loss of work role, loss of physical and mental abilities. But it is not uncommon to find the assumption that old age is also therefore a time of inevitable gloom and decline. This approach can lead to the perception of depressive symptomatology as being an understandable response in the circumstances by the patient and even by the unwary clinician. Depression which is amenable to treatment may be overlooked.

It is of course true that some changes in behaviour patterns may be determined by external factors. Loss of interest in activities that had previously been enjoyed may be an appropriate response to naturally dwindling energy levels. Eating and sleeping patterns may be affected in an elderly person who suddenly finds himself in a situation of unaccustomed social isolation. These 'symptoms' do not necessarily represent depressive illnes.

Clinical presentation

On superficial examination the clinical picture presented by the elderly can differ substantially from that of younger patients. Careful examination will, however, probably reveal that while the elderly suffer from the same symptoms as the younger patients, they do not necessarily complain of the same ones. The picture is frequently dominated by apathy, loss of interest, lassitude and memory disturbance. It is these symptoms which probably prevent the milder degrees of depression from reaching the clinician. The elderly depressed patient, who may in any case already have suffered a natural reduction in energy levels, loses interest, slows down and stays at home unaware that help might be available.

One obvious difficulty in applying research diagnostic criteria such as the St Louis criteria or the DSMIII criteria is that they both require primarily the presence of dysphoric mood. The elderly depressive, however, does not necessarily complain primarily of depressed mood. Prominent complaints are more likely to include tiredness, malaise, loss of appetite and inability to remember things. Establishing the presence of dysphoric mood in the elderly often needs more care than in younger patients.

A further complication is that the elderly patient is frequently preoccupied with somatic symptoms and complaints of specific or non-specific pains and these complaints can reach hypochondriacal levels. It is possible that elderly patients focus their depressive disorder onto physical symptoms since physical complaints may be culturally acceptable in old people where low spirits are not. This somatic overlay is quite likely to lead to the underlying depression being missed even where careful examination shows that criteria for depressive illness are well fulfilled. The risk of physical illness in the elderly is high and the presence of somatic complaints tends at first consideration to suggest physical rather than psychological illness. The hierarchical nature of medical diagnosis, by which physical illness is treated before psychological illness, can also contribute to the delay in recognising the presence of depressive illness. There is a further risk of misdiagnosis even when physical illness has been ruled out. A diagnosis of depression may not be given because the hypochondriacal features seem to accord more closely with anxiety. Where there is doubt it is probably better to take the problems of presentation into account and lean in the direction of depression rather than anxiety when diagnosing illness in the elderly. All but the most severe anxiety responds better to antidepressant treatment than to treatment with benzodiazepines.

Physical illness and concurrent medication

A further complication in diagnosing depression in the elderly is the fact that there may indeed be a coexisting physical illness which may mask or mimic depressive symptomatology. Malignant disease, for example, may manifest itself in the early stages with behavioural changes. Metabolic abnormalities, endocrine disturbances and infectious disease can all lead to apathy, reduction in activity, and loss of appetite. All the diagnostic criteria for primary depression which we have discussed exclude depression secondary to illness. The requirements in the younger or older age groups are not different but the influence of physical illness is likely to be more frequent in the elderly. The distinction between such depressive symptoms and the syndrome of depression is made more difficult because not enough is known about normal levels of activity in the elderly. Certainly the elderly have a wide inter-individual variation in activity levels.

Concurrent medication may also obscure the clinical picture. This can of course be a problem with all age groups, but is more likely to occur in the elderly since the number of medications a patient is prescribed increases with age. In a general practice survey, Shaw & Opit (1976) found that half of a randomly selected group of elderly patients were taking drugs regularly, and of these more than a third were taking three or more drugs.

Elderly patients with multiple physical problems are often given most complicated dosage regimens and there is the risk of polypharmacy escalating benign forgetfulness into confusion. It may be difficult to disentangle confusion associated with depression from that caused by medication or from the confusion associated with dementia in the elderly. Some of the drugs prescribed more frequently for the elderly (for example some antihypertensive drugs) can also produce the symptoms of depression, and these must also be distinguished from depressive illness.

Pseudodementia

Much depression is probably overlooked because of the bias towards expecting dementia in the elderly. Confusion and memory impairment are features common to many illnesses in the elderly, including depression. The depressed elderly patient may indeed show very marked cognitive impairment and be wrongly given the diagnosis of dementia. This is a likelihood even in milder levels of depression, where the patient loses interest and activity is too much effort. His failure to keep himself informed and his general slowness may be interpreted as signs of early dementia. The need which this book addresses for clear and reliable criteria for distinguishing dementia is obvious, since the cognitive disability seen with depression may easily be misdiagnosed as dementia. In many of these patients, if the depression is treated the 'dementia' disappears. The number of patients mistakenly receiving the diagnosis of dementia is high. Estimates vary but one report estimated a 30% error rate (Marsden & Harrison 1972). There is a comparative paucity of scales to differentiate pseudodementia, benign forgetfulness and early Alzheimer's disease. In this respect the diagnostic scales for depressive illness reviewed above are not particularly helpful. A further issue is of course depression in dementia. It is not clear whether the depression occurs as a response to cognitive loss or if it is directly associated with the brain changes. Depression is a treatable illness and should be aggressively treated even in the presence of dementia.

SCALES FOR MEASURING SEVERITY

The measurement of severity of illness has to be considered quite separately from diagnosis, and different scales must be used. This should be obvious, since the two functions are quite different. Diagnosis is concerned with categorisation of patients into 'yes/no' exclusive categories. The measurement of severity attempts to arrange patients on a continuum of greater and lesser degrees of illness. Scales developed for one purpose are unlikely to be very satisfactory if used for another. The diagnostic scales most commonly used require the presence of a minimum number of symptoms in order to fulfil the criterion for a diagnosis of an illness. However, the presence of a greater number of symptoms does not necessarily imply a greater severity of illness. Scales which have been designed to quantify severity of illness in defined groups of patients are equally unlikely to be the best measures to use for diagnostic purposes.

The object of rating scales for measuring severity of illness is to quantify severity and standardise measurement. Their main use is probably in clinical research, to achieve homogeneity of patient groups and replicability of results. Scales must be valid, that is, they must measure what they purport to measure. The results obtained with a scale must be reliable. The scales must also be sensitive to changes in severity with treatment if they are going to be useful in clinical research.

Many of the early rating scales intended to measure severity were constructed on the basis of an ad hoc collection of items thought to be relevant to the illness. As a result of this approach, some scales are weakened by the inclusion of irrelevant or rarely occurring items, diagnostic items or some which do not show marked changes with treatment. The best-known example is perhaps the Hamilton Rating Scale (Hamilton 1960). In its earliest form this scale contained four items which were subsequently dropped as being of diagnostic interest rather than of value in measuring severity.

There are a large number of rating scales for depression and they are still increasing, so only some of the most frequently used are reviewed here. The most obvious categorisation of the many scales available is into observer-rated and self-rated. The choice of which type to use will depend on what the scale is being used for, the setting in which it will be used and the type of patient who is to be rated. In addition to observer- and self-rated scales, there are visual analogue scales which can be rated either by an observer or by the patient.

Observer-rated scales in depression

With observer-rated scales, a skilled observer elicits and assesses the information from the patient on the basis of a structured or semistructured interview. The judgements as to the severity of different areas of symptomatology are recorded as ratings on the scale. The merit of a rating scale will depend on its validity and reliability but also on whether it is easy for the rater to use and assists him in making the judgements. It is clearly easier to rate some patients than others, and very depressed retarded patients can present a considerable problem. Nevertheless the skilled rater, with the help of observation from the care team, can usually make a valid rating even with the most difficult patient.

The observer-rating scale in most common use has been the Hamilton Rating Scale (Hamilton 1960) for depression. This scale comprises 21 items of which the first 17 are used to summarise severity. Many of the items in the scale relate to somatic symptoms and there is a rather heavy weighting on the anxiety component of depression. The scale is meant to be used to cover a rating period of the previous few days or a week, and minor fluctuations in mood are meant to be avoided. Several different versions of the scale with a number of additional items have been produced. A more radical development of the scale has been proposed by Beck & Rafaelson (1980) who produced a scale containing 11 items. Most of the items are the same as, or equivalent to, those in the original scale, with an increased emphasis on retardation and a reduction in the number of somatic items. These later versions have produced some confusion and have reduced the comparability of results from different studies, since results can only be compared if the studies have used the same measures.

The Montgomery & Asberg Depression Rating Scale (Montgomery & Asberg 1979) was developed in 1978 (Montgomery et al 1978a) and is now in wide use. The scale was designed to be sensitive to changes with treatment, and sensitivity and accuracy of change estimates were major criteria for inclusion of items. The ratings on this scale are made on the basis of a clinical interview. It has ten items, which cover the core symptomatology of depressive illness, including the anxiety component. As part of the construction of the scale, only those items were included which were shown to occur frequently, to be reliably rated and to be sensitive to treatment change. Each item is in effect an individual scale, with the grades of severity defined in order to improve the precision of measurement. It has been shown to be more sensitive to treatment change than the Hamilton Rating Scale and the Beck self-rating scale (Montgomery & Asberg 1979). It has also been found to be easy to use and reliable even in the hands of untrained raters and this broadens the scope for its use (Montgomery et al 1978b). The defined scale steps appear to improve its stability and to reduce systematic bias, which with many other scales requires frequent training to correct.

Self-rating scales

The self-rating scale is completed by the patient, typically by answering questions according to a limited choice of response categories. Self-rating scales are most useful where ratings must be made frequently. They require less time from a skilled and busy clinician, and they can be used with very large numbers of patients, for example in community surveys where individual interviews would be impractical. They are also used by some because they feel the patient's opinion is more valid than the observer's judgement. Self-rating scales, however, have considerable drawbacks which make their value in assessing depressed patients very doubtful. To fill in a self-rating questionnaire requires a cooperative, reasonably competent, literate patient. A severely depressed patient with retardation or agitation is unlikely to be able to fill in a questionnaire. Self-rating scales are clearly least useful in patients who have lost insight and in such cases only an observer can make a valid assessment of severity.

A further weakness is due to the considerable inter-individual variability in the way the patients respond in self-rating questionnaires. An observer makes the judgement of severity by comparing the patient's symptoms against his experience of other patients. The patient has no such frame of reference and extreme ratings are more likely and may be less often appropriate. This increased variability makes self-rating scales less useful in clinical research, since the increased variance is likely to obscure differences which exist. Behavioural items such as retardation are also not easily self-rated and the observer is in a better position to make a valid judgement. For reasons such as these the sensitivity of self-rating scales is generally found to be much less than that of observer scales. Studies commonly report that self-rating scales fail to demonstrate an effect which is clearly seen with observer scales.

Nevertheless a number of self-rating scales are used in depression research and these include the Beck Depression Inventory (Beck et al 1961), the Zung Self Rating Depression Scale (Zung 1965) and the Wakefield Self Assessment Depression Rating Inventory (Snaith et al 1971) All these scales are prone to measure changes in anxiety states as though they were changes in depression.

The Beck Depression Inventory (Beck et al 1961) which was originally designed to be an assisted self-rating scale, is now used almost invariably as a self-rating scale. It fails as a useful measure of severity of depression in several ways. It has been found to be less sensitive to change with treatment than observer-rating scales, and its discriminatory power between moderate and severe depression is poor. Agreement between the Beck and observer scales has been shown to be poor in a substantial number of patients.

The Zung Self Rating Depression Scale (1974) — the version most commonly used is a modification of an earlier version published in 1965. It has 20 items covering a range of depressive symptomatology which are rated for severity and frequency of occurrence. Ratings on this scale do not always correlate well with ratings on an observer scale such as the Hamilton Rating Scale particularly when assessing the more severely ill.

The Wakefield Scale (Snaith et al 1971) was an attempt to improve on the Zung Scale. The Zung Scale has 20 items rated on a 0–4 scale according to frequency of occurrence. The Wakefield Scale is shorter, having only 12 items each graded from 0 to 3. It was shown to correlate quite well with the Hamilton Scale, but its ability to differentiate between grades of severity is not impressive.

Visual analogue scales

This type of scale has a line with its two ends defined as the most and the least extreme of the particular variable of interest. The rater marks the point on the line which represents the level of severity. At first sight it would appear to be a very crude measure but it appears to be quite useful. It is easy to use and has been found to correlate well with measures of global judgement.

Use of general-purpose scales

General purpose scales which attempt to cover the whole range of psychiatric illness are sometimes used in assessing depression. One such is the Symptom Check List developed from the Hopkins Symptom Check List (Derogatis et al 1973). A major drawback to this kind of scale is its unwieldy length. Since the objective is to screen all psychiatric illness, it follows that a minimum number of questions covering the different kinds of symptomatology will be required. Factor analysis of the Symptom Check List has suggested clusters which correspond to different psychiatric illnesses, but the whole 90-item questionnaire is administered for rating purposes. This may be a possibility with very mildly ill patients but a severely depressed patient is unlikely to be able to concentrate for such a long time. Scales of this kind have little place in careful studies of depression in the elderly.

Severity rating scales in the elderly

The careful assessment of the severity of depression in the elderly using rating scales which permit quantification and replicability has tended to be overlooked until comparatively recently. Severity rating scales have come to be used most extensively in clinical trials to test the efficacy of treatments. Clinical investigations of antidepressant efficacy of new compounds have however tended to exclude the elderly because of a number of presumptions. Elderly patients have been thought by some to respond less well to standard antidepressants; indeed the dose of an antidepressant may need to be altered in the elderly because of age-related changes in metabolism. The elderly are thought by some to suffer from increased side-effects. There may be increased concomitant physical illness and consequently an increased risk of adverse drug interactions.

The proportion of elderly patients in the population is however increasing, and their care must take up greater resources than hitherto. Clinicians who are occupied with the psychiatric care of the elderly need information on the suitability of treatments for their patients. It is now recognised that the measurement of the response of the elderly to an antidepressant is an important factor in assessing the clinical usefulness of a drug.

The depression scales briefly reviewed here can all be used in elderly patients, although some will be easier to use than others and are likely to give more valid ratings. It would of course be unwise to generalise about the difficulties that may be encountered, since the range of physical or mental incapacity of elderly depressed patients is very wide.

There are likely to be more difficulties in the use of self-rated scales than with observer scales. Many of the criticisms levelled at self-rating scales apply particularly acutely in the elderly. The cognitive deficit frequently seen in the elderly depressed patient is likely to interfere with the capacity to understand or respond to the questionnaire. Lack of concentration, which is part of depression in all age groups, is likely to exacerbate this disability. Co-existing physical impairment is also likely to interfere with the patient's ability or willingness to respond. Many of the self-rating scales focus on symptoms which are not core symptoms of depression and this would reduce the validity of the assessment in the elderly.

The skilled observer can take these problems into account and make a judgement of severity based on clinical experience. He can also call on information provided by the people caring for the depressed patient either at home or in the hospital. However, the rating of depression in the elderly is often a more time-consuming process and raters may have to take even greater pains than they would with younger patients. Some scales are easier to apply than others and have been shown to be more robust when used for different groups of patients and by different mental health care workers. Effort has been made to improve the robustness of some of the scales (e.g. the Montgomery & Asberg scale) but not others. Care should be taken in training raters to the required level in order that the assessments should be valid.

The general experience of the use of observer rating scales in the elderly is that they are able to distinguish active treatments from placebo treatments with greater or lesser ease depending on their sensitivity. One of the features which does interfere with their sensitivity in the elderly could be an over-representation of items which may be confused with physical illness. Items involving hypochondriasis, somatic features of anxiety or somatic complaints often make for extra difficulties. These items, which are over-represented in the Hamilton Rating Scale, have been found to increase the difficulties of the assessment of severity of depression in an elderly patient if there are a lot of somatic complaints. The more recently developed scales, the Montgomery & Asberg Depression Rating Scale and the Beck-Rafaelson scale (1980), appear to have avoided this particular difficulty and may therefore be thought more useful for this group of patients.

The refinement in the methodology of categorising and measuring the severity of depressive illness has made it possible to undertake a higher quality of research than was possible previously. These instruments should enable important findings to emerge, using smaller numbers of patients, which has obvious ethical and practical advantages. It is hoped that these advances will enable us to achieve a better understanding of the underlying processes of depression in the elderly.

REFERENCES

American Psychiatric Association 1980 DSMIII Diagnostic and statistical manual of mental disorders. 3rd edn. American Psychiatric Association, Washington DC

Beck A T, Ward C H, Mendelson M, Mock J E, Erbaugh J 1961 An inventory for measuring depression. Archives of General Psychiatry 4: 561–571

Beck P, Rafaelsen O J 1980 The use of rating scales exemplified by a comparison of the Hamilton and the Beck Rafaelsen Melancholia Scale. Acta Psychiatrica Scandinavica Suppl 285: 128–131

Blazer D G, Williams C D 1980 The epidemiology of dysphonia and depression in an elderly population. American Journal of Psychiatry 137: 439–444

Busse F W, 1978 The Duke longitudinal study. 1. Senescence and senility. In: Katz R, Terry R, Bick K (eds), Alzheimer's disease, senile dementia and related disorders. Raven Press, New York

Carney M W P, Roth M, Garside R F, 1965 The diagnosis of depressive syndrome and the prediction of ECT response. British Journal of Psychiatry 111: 659–674

Derogatis L R, Lipman R S, Covi L 1973 SCL-90: an outpatient psychiatric rating scale — preliminary report. Psychopharmaceutical Bulletin 9: 13–28

Feighner J P, Robins E, Guze S B, Woodruff R A, Winokur G, Munoz R 1972 Diagnostic criteria for use in psychiatric research. Archives of General Psychiatry 26: 57–63

Gurland B, Copeland J, Kuriansky J, Kelleher M, Sharpe L, Dean L L, 1983 The mind and mood of ageing. Croom Helm, London

Gurney C, Roth M, Garside R F, Kerr T A, Schapira K 1972 Studies in classification of affective disorders. British Journal of Psychiatry 121: 162–166

Hamilton M 1960 A rating scale for depression. Journal of Neurology Neurosurgery and Psychiatry 23: 56

Kay D W K, Beamish P, Roth M 1964 Old age mental disorders in Newcastle upon Tyne: a study of prevalence. British Journal of Psychiatry 110: 146–668

Marsden C D, Harrison M J G 1972 Outcome of investigation of patients with presenile dementia. British Medical Journal 2: 249–252

Montgomery S A, Asberg M 1979 A new depression scale designed to be sensitive to change. British Journal of Psychiatry 134: 382–389

Montgomery S, McAuley R, Montgomery D B 1978a Relationship between mianserin plasma levels and antidepressant effect in a double-blind trial comparing a single night-time and divided daily dose regimens. British Journal of Clinical Pharmacology 5: 71S–76S

Montgomery S, Jornestedt L, Thoren P, Traskman L, McAuley R, Montogomery D, Shaw P, 1978b Reliability of the CPRS between the disciplines of psychiatry, general practice, nursing and psychology. Acta Psychiatrica Scandinavica Suppl 272: 29–32

Shaw S M, Opit L J 1976 Need for supervision in the elderly receiving long-term prescribed medication. British Medical Journal 1: 506–507

Snaith R P, Ahmed S N, Mehta S, Hamilton M 1971 The assessment of primary depressive illness: Wakefield Self-Assessment Inventory. Psychological Medicine 1: 143–149

Wing J K, Cooper J E, Sartorius N 1974 The measurement and classification of psychiatric symptoms. Cambridge University Press, London

Zung W W K 1965 Self-rating depression scale. Archives of General Psychiatry 12: 63–70

Zung W W K 1974 The measurement of affects: depression and anxiety. Modern Problems Pharmacopsychiatry 7: 170–188

Psychological approaches to the assessment and treatment of old people

INTRODUUCTION

A range of quantitative assessment procedures measuring psychological function and behaviour have been presented in this book. It is encouraging for the clinician to find such widespread interest in producing valid, reliable and practical scales which can be used with elderly people. Not before time, it has become accepted that traditional assessment measures, devised for use with younger people, usually have inadequate normative data for older age groups and provide information which is of limited value in planning effective interventions with elderly people. Of necessity the instruments described in previous chapters have been concerned with measuring the needs and characteristics of populations as well as individuals. This chapter redresses the balance by concentrating on the use of psychological assessment to help in managing the individual.

To meet the special needs of the elderly person, any assessment measure must be able to be carried out without causing undue distress and must address questions of relevance to psychological well-being and management. Quantitative assessment measures, however well devised, will never by themselves be able to fulfil these two basic aspects of assessment for every elderly person, on every occasion. The information gathered using quantitative measures will always need to be balanced, both with qualitative observation of the elderly person's behaviour during formal assessment and with information obtained by direct observation of behaviour in a 'natural' setting. Figure 10.1 shows the variety of evidence that may be used to decide on the neuropsychological assets and deficits of an elderly person.

Conclusions about neuropsychological status are not reached, as is sometimes supposed, by the administration of a test yielding a positive or negative result, but rather by a process which has been called the quasi-judicial method (Bromley 1977). This process is akin to the collection, examination and weighing up of evidence in a court of law and is, as Bromley suggests, a much neglected scientific method.

The importance of qualitative information and the direct observation of behaviour can be illustrated by considering their advantages over quantitative assessment procedures.

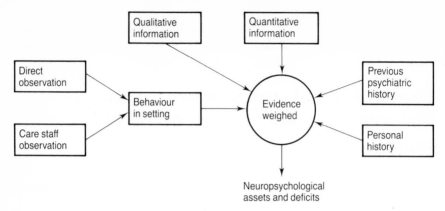

Fig. 10.1 Evidence used to decide on psychological function in an elderly person

1. *Neuropsychological test batteries can take a number of hours to administer*; for example, the Haltstead-Reitan Battery is inappropriately long and normal elderly people have been shown to perform poorly on some of its subtests (Klisz 1978). Extended periods of assessment are poorly tolerated by elderly people, especially the infirm and very elderly. Patient distress, fatigue and non-compliance are some of the problems which may arise.

Whilst these effects can to some extent be ameliorated by the test administrator being sensitive to each individual's different ability to tolerate the assessment procedure, many tests remain unsuitable for use with elderly people. Tests of learning and memory have commonly been used to distinguish between dementia and other diagnoses. Unfortunately, tests such as the Modified Word Learning Test (MWLT) (Walton 1958) and the Inglis Paired Associate Test (IPAT) (Inglis 1959) have been constructed in such a way that their administration to someone who performs badly is likely to provoke a catastrophic reaction. To subject elderly people to such indignity is inexcusable and may reduce compliance to further testing. Irving et al (1970) and Williams (1961, 1968) have shown that it is possible to devise tests of memory and learning which are useful and relatively non-threatening. It should be noted, however, that even well-constructed tests can be administered in an insensitive and threatening way. Pragmatically, tests such as the MWLT and IPAT have been shown to misclassify appreciable numbers of elderly people.

2. *Generally it is most difficult, if not impossible, to administer quantitative tests of neuropsychological function when the elderly person's cognitive state is most in doubt.* In such cases, the qualitative features of the individual's behaviour in direct contact and/or through observation may be the only evidence upon which diagnostic and management decisions can be made.

3. Whilst the identification of small changes in cognitive function is important diagnostically, *the psychological management, particularly of more impaired elderly people, rests upon a much coarser analysis of neuropsychological*

state. For example, an appreciable change in a good score on a sensitive test of receptive language, the Token Test (De Renzi & Vignolo 1962), would have little implication for management, whereas a change from being able to understand three-stage commands (for example, please get dressed, then have a wash and come to breakfast), to finding a simple short command difficult to follow, undoubtedly would. Only a change in neuropsychological state large enough to affect the elderly person's ability to function in the environment is relevant to psychological management.

4. *Particular neuropsychological impairments can cause a wide range of behavioural consequences, many of which are subtle and not easily quantified.* As will be seen later, these behavioural consequences may be mistakenly seen as indicating other psychiatric diagnoses. In such cases, the qualitative aspects of behaviour can provide important discriminatory evidence.

5. *The tendency of an individual's behaviour to be situation-specific, and the related problem of the generalisation of behavioural change to other environments, are well recognised issues in psychological therapy* (Rimm & Masters 1967). The increased dependency of the elderly person's behaviour on the environment, arising from the process of ageing, is likely to exaggerate these effects. An illustrative example in the area of self-help behaviour is a study by Andrews & Stewart (1978), who found, in a consecutive sample of stroke patients, that each activity of daily living was performed less well in the home situation in 25–45% of cases, and that in 52% of cases the main carer reported that the stroke patient did not do two or more activities at home of which she was capable in hospital.

Clearly then, the assessment and observations on which management should be based must focus on the elderly person in her natural familiar environment.

QUALITATIVE ASPECTS OF NEUROPSYCHOLOGICAL ASSESSMENT AND DIAGNOSIS

In this section, the use of a more qualitative approach to neuropsychological assessment in the elderly in clarifying diagnostic questions will be explored.

Short term memory

Deficits in short term memory (STM) (sometimes called secondary memory — see Wilson & Moffat (1984) for a more detailed discussion) and learning are recognised as being early and common indicators of senile dementia of the Alzheimer's type (SDAT) and multi-infarct dementia (MID) in elderly people. As we have indicated, many early tests developed must be regarded as unsuitable for use with older people. Even newer tests such as the Revised Kendrick Battery, which showed near perfect discrimination in its validation sample (Kendrick et al 1979), has been shown to misclassify nearly half of a sample of elderly long-stay psychiatric patients (Gibson et al 1980). Indeed any diagnostic test will vary in its accuracy of classification according to the composition of the sample of patients being tested. This is known as the base-rate problem. Ley (1976) provides an excellent introduction to this problem and notes that in some instances the use of a diagnostic test will result in more errors than the use of no test at all.

Brief orientation/information scales are available which provide immediate and valuable information about STM function in the elderly person: for example, the Clifton Assessment Procedures for the Elderly Orientation/Information Scale (CAPE O/I) (Pattie & Gilleard 1979, and see Ch. 5), and the Hodkinson Scale, (Hodkinson 1972, Qureshi & Hodkinson 1974). Such tests can be administered in a completely unthreatening manner (though sometimes they are not) and performance has been related to outcome (Pattie & Gilleard 1979), pathological changes (Blessed et al 1968) and degree of atrophy on Computerised Axial Tomography (Jacoby & Levy 1980). They have proved more effective in this respect than standard tests of intellectual function and verbal learning, (Whitehead & Hunt 1982).

Although score on an orientation test does often provide accurate diagnostic information when the diagnosis is in doubt, the pattern of scoring can provide a more useful indication of STM function. Consider a severe depressive illness presenting as a pseudodementia. Despite being disorientated, the elderly person is probably not suffering from any absolute impairment of STM. Rather, the individual's disorientation arises from internal preoccupations and disengagement from the environment and the reduced ability of the ageing body to cope with a serious illness. This is in contrast to individuals with dementia, who have a permanent, acquired reduction in absolute STM function. The questions on a typical orientation scale are likely to highlight this difference. For example, the CAPE O/I scale can be divided into items which are overlearnt and relatively resistant to the effects of an acquired permanent impairment of STM (list A), and those which have been learnt more recently, or must be relearnt regularly (list B) (see Table 10.1).

When someone presents as disorientated but can give correct responses to items such as those on list B, doubt must be raised as to whether this person is suffering from a dementia. This may be confirmed or refuted through further tests or observations. Although it is beyond the scope of

Table 10.1   Items from CAPE O/I scale (Pattie & Gilleard 1979)

List A	List B
Name	Prime Minister
Date of birth	President, USA
Town	Month
Colours of the British flag	Year

this chapter, it should be noted that markedly variable orientation scores may reflect dysphasia, frontal dysfunction or acute medical illness.

In a few cases it is impossible to even assess orientation, as the patient may refuse to answer or respond with 'don't know'. Allowing a patient the opportunity to learn information, for example presenting your name on two or three occasions during interview (provided it is easy to learn), and 're-assessing' her a few hours or a day later, sometimes provides evidence that the patient has more capacity to learn new information than is apparent.

It is impossible to provide a detailed account of memory in this chapter, but it should be noted that memory is not a unitary function, and organic pathology affects different aspects of memory function selectively. For example, in SDAT it is short-term memory for facts and information (declarative memory) which is impaired, whereas facial recognition memory is generally preserved even with a moderate degree of dementia (Ferris et al 1980). Diagnostically such distinctions can be useful. Thus it would be expected that someone with dementia would recognise ward staff as familiar after a period on the ward, but would have great difficulty in remembering and using their names appropriately. Careful questioning of ward staff will usually elicit such distinctions and highlights the important role of staff observation in a qualitative approach to assessment. Such information should be gathered from more than one staff member so that its reliability may be gauged.

In clinical practice it is not uncommon to find different staff giving contradictory accounts of an elderly patient's functional ability. All disciplines should be trained in careful observation and reporting of behaviour.

Case study 1

Mrs I O was a 69-year-old married woman with a two-year history of depressive illness. After a failure to respond to anti-depressants, ECT was commenced but stopped after two applications as she had become confused. A psychologist's opinion at the time was that it was unlikely that there was an organic memory deficit, but no test results were recorded.

ECT was recommended, her mood improved, she started to eat again and it was agreed to send her home with regular nursing support. She appeared to do reasonably well for some weeks but eventually had to be readmitted as she had stopped eating and drinking. On this admission she was disorientated, repeatedly stated that a van was coming to take dead bodies away from the ward and repeatedly asked for help to do things such as go to the toilet.

In the assessment Mrs I O was preoccupied with depressive thoughts. She tended to be apathetic and uncooperative except when discussing her family. Table 10.2 shows evidence gathered about her orientation and memory. The inconsistency in her responses and unreliability of her direct report gave some strong clues about the presence or not of an organic STM impairment. Thus her failure to learn one of the author's names (Mr Church) on repeated occasions, under varied conditions (a few seconds to some minutes), was in stark contrast to her level of orientation. Her knowledge of the names of the Prime Minister and of the President of the USA and the rapid nature of her responses also indicated that her 'disorientation' was probably not organic in nature.

Table 10.2 Qualitative assessment of Mrs I O's memory and orientation

Test	Score	Qualitative features
CAPE O/I Scale	8/12	Correctly names PM and President USA: response is rapid and angry. Incorrect responses characterised by apathy.
Asked to remember interviewer's name on ten occasions using varying delay intervals.	'Incorrect'	No effort made, responds repeatedly with 'I don't know'.
Apparently unable to find toilet for self. Interviewer asks for help to find male toilet.	'Correct'	Inconsistent verbal behaviour. Able to give accurate directions to male toilets.

The unreliability of her verbal report was noted by the fact that she denied knowing where the female toilets were and requested help to find them at the end of the interview, yet was able to give accurate directions to the male toilets (in the vicinity of the female toilets). Discussion with the staff indicated that this pattern of dependent behaviour was reinforced at home by her husband, and her CAPE Behaviour Rating Score (BRS) confirmed that her level of behavioural function was much worse than would be expected from her level of orientation. The absence of any other qualitative indicators of dementia, for example nominal aphasia (see later), led to a conclusion that this was a depressive illness in which there was a dependent pattern of behaviour.

Language

Problems in the use of language are commoner than is often supposed in those with dementia. This is because early changes are often subtle and may not be apparent in free speech.

Nominal aphasia

Nominal skills are impaired in frontal and parietal lesions, but are more impaired in parietal lobe lesions. It seems that word-retrieval processes are subserved mainly by structures in the left temporal lobe (Coughlan & Warrington 1978).

Although Rochford (1971) concluded that errors in naming shown by patients with senile dementia were largely attributable to a failure in recognition (visual agnosia), Bayles (1982) failed to find such agnostic type errors in naming tasks. Skelton-Robinson and Jones' (1984) detailed study of naming in SDAT patients confirmed Bayles' finding and indicated that the degree of naming difficulty may be a reliable indicator of severity of dementia.

Naming depends on intellectual ability, educational level, familiarity with the language and word frequency. McKenna and Warrington (1980) have produced a graded test for nominal aphasia which adjusts for intellectual and educational ability. This test is particularly useful for detecting minimal changes in naming ability amongst well-preserved elderly people with possible or early organic pathology, if formal testing can be carried out. However, some of the picture drawings used in this test are unclear and it would also be difficult to administer such a test to a more disturbed elderly person. In such cases simple, familiar everyday objects can be used to test for the presence of a nominal aphasia. An old-style watch and fountain pen can provide up to ten items for a relatively unthreatening assessment (see Table 10.3). When testing for a nominal aphasia it is important to determine whether the elderly person recognises what she is seeing. Asking 'What is it for?' or 'What does it do?' will elicit this information; examples of responses confirming recognition are shown in Table 10.4. The firm identification of nominal aphasia rests on the presence of dysphasic errors rather than lack of response (see Case study 2). Despite the lack of appropriate research in this area, clinical observation confirms that in severe depressive illness dysphasic errors do not occur, although the patient may be unable or unwilling to provide even simple naming responses.

Table 10.3 Parts of watch and pen used for testing for nominal aphasia

Watch	Pen
Hands (or fingers*)	Nib
Face (dial or front)	Cap (top cover)
Winder	Clip
Strap	
Buckle (fastener)	

* Common colloquial use

Table 10.4 Examples of responses which exclude failure of recognition as a cause of naming difficulty

Strap	'Binds the container, the watch mechanism to opposite points'
Cap	'Screws over the pen'
Clip	'Spring that fixes it out to your clothes'
Hands	'Handles, showing the time'

Case study 2

Mrs N V was a 71-year-old widow admitted with complex visual hallucinations and disorientation. As the visual hallucination subsided, Mrs N V's disorientation continued and she was referred for psychological assessment. Her CAPE O/I score of 8/12, her William's Memory Test error score of 31, and her failure to learn my name on repeated presentations (although she always recognised me at follow-up as being from the hospital) were strongly indicative of an organic memory impairment. She additionally had a finger agnosia. Table 10.5 presents the results of a test of forced naming.

Mrs N V showed clear naming difficulties with objects and their parts, and this was also apparent in free conversation. For example, on one occasion she heard an ambulance in the distance and commented 'That's a white thing, with a light that flashes on top', but was unable to name it. The psychiatric history, taken with these findings, indicated a SDAT. Computed Tomography (CT) scan results which were available subsequently indicated non-specific brain atrophy.

Table 10.5 Mrs N V's responses on testing for a nominal aphasia

Test object/part	Response
Watch	Watch
Hands/fingers	*Digitals*
Face/dial/front	Front
Winder	*Controller*
Strap	Straps
Buckle	No response (NR)
Pen	Pen
Nib	NR
Top/cap	*Digital*
Clip	*Capsule*
Television aerial	*A spiral*
Eyebrows	*Whiskers*

Dysphasic errors in italics

Receptive aphasia

Although less common, particularly amongst those with a milder degree of dementia, the recognition of an impairment in the ability to understand language — receptive dysphasia — is important for diagnosis and management. For younger adults the Token Test (De Renzi & Vignolo 1962) has been the test of choice for assessing receptive function. Although a short form of the test has been produced (Spellacy & Spreen 1969), no norms are available for those over 65 years of age.

In general, the receptive function of an elderly person can be simply and efficiently screened by the use of three or four easily recognisable everyday objects. These can be used to give 'commands' of gradually increasing complexity, for example 'Pick up the matchbox', 'Put the coin beside the matchbox', 'Put the key inside the matchbox and the coin on top of the matchbox', etc. When assessing receptive language in this manner, care should be taken to take account of any deficit in STM which will confound the results.

When even such a simple unthreatening test cannot be administered, an impairment in understanding can be readily identified by careful observation of the elderly person's response to verbal questions or conversation. The responses will be increasingly inconsistent as the quantity of non-verbal and contextual information decreases.

Case study 3
Mrs C S was a 53-year-old woman who was referred for psychological assessment two months after admission onto an acute psychiatric ward. She had a ten-year history of personality disorder with neurological problems diagnosed as 'hysterical' and having a 'functional overlay'. The referral stated '. . . rather "odd" picture, loses her way on the ward, undresses in front of other patients, drinking hot water, repetitive mannerisms . . . however, remembers mealtimes, GP's address etc, fluctuating picture'. The formal assessment lasted less than ten minutes, during which attempts to engage her in conversation and administer the CAPE O/I scale failed, and she insisted on leaving the room. Her failure to respond appropriately to questions, and the repeated giving of 'correct' answers to the wrong questions, indicated a gross deficit in receptive language function. Further informal interaction with her and observation on the ward confirmed that her stock responses ('yes', 'no' and 'don't know') varied according to her observation of social cues; she would shift her response when the interviewer indicated non-verbally that response was inappropriate. This tended to give an observer the impression she understood what was being said. Her ability to respond to non-verbal cues was further evidenced by a report that she had comforted another patient who had been in tears. The fact that her verbal responses were always short (the longest noted was a five-word sentence) with nouns and verbs predominating suggested an impairment of expressive as well as receptive function indicative of diffuse pathology. A neurological opinion supported the conclusion of an organic state of uncertain origin, but because of her refusal to cooperate in having a CT scan, no conclusive diagnosis has been reached.

This case shows that the presence of even a severe language impairment is not always identified in an acute psychiatric setting. It also highlights the fact that someone can be misconstrued as being inconsistently orientated, when in fact the primary deficit is one of language.

Constructional apraxia

Free drawing and copying have frequently been used as measures of constructional apraxia. It has been demonstrated that patients with right-sided lesions, usually of the parietal-occipital area, produce free drawings of objects which are scattered and fragmented in nature, showing a loss of spatial relationships. Those with left-side lesions produce free drawings in which accurate spatial relationships are preserved, but which are grossly over-simplified. The provision of a drawing to copy markedly improves the performance of patients with left-sided lesions, but makes little difference to those with right-sided lesions. Warrington (1976) summarises this finding and gives illustrative examples.

Although free drawing and copying has, for some years now, been suggested for routine clinical use (Institute of Psychiatry 1973), until recently little information was available about what tasks might be appropriate and what results might be expected from elderly people with organic pathology as compared to normal elderly people. Moore (1981) and Moore and Wyke (1984) have provided detailed information about drawing disability in senile dementia, and, for example, identified one aspect of performance — labelling of a feature — as peculiar to those with dementia. Table 10.6 summarises these findings. Interestingly, it was found that normal elderly (as well as younger) people showed a poor performance when drawing a cube. This confirmed that simpler tasks such as drawing and copying a house, clock, or face were of more diagnostic value.

One area of caution which should be noted is the lack of available evidence about the variation in drawing ability in elderly people with severe depressive illness. Clinical observation suggests there may appear to be gross impairment, which is reversed when the depressive illness is successfully treated.

Table 10.6 Characteristics of drawings of patients with senile dementia (Moore 1981)

Spontaneous drawings

Grossly impoverished with essential features omitted
Written labels added
Perseveration across items
Small and cramped appearance

Copies

Improved performance with increased number of essential details
Details wrongly positioned
Larger than spontaneous drawings

Frontal function

The most recently developed parts of the brain, the frontal lobes, far from being silent areas, play a basic role in human behaviour. Presented in Table 10.7 is a list of some of the consequences of pathology in the frontal lobes. The ill-defined and varied nature of these consequences shows that the identification of frontal pathology rests heavily upon direct behavioural observation, the report of relatives or care staff, and the qualitative performance of the elderly person on assessment.

Diagnostically, the identification of behaviour arising from frontal pathology is important because it can sometimes be mistakenly seen as a sign of other psychiatric disorder; for example, emotional lability may be misconstrued as indicating depressive illness, or disinhibition as hypomania. It is also important because impairment in this area can arise in the absence of any other gross indications of organic pathology. One longitudinal study (Snowden 1983) indicated that four out of 20 subjects with dementia showed a primary deficit in frontal function, possible indicating a separate disease process (i.e. Pick's disease versus SDAT)

Table 10.7   Effects of frontal lobe dysfunction

Personality change
Planning problems
Poor monitoring of behaviour
Apathy
Disinhibition
Euphoria
Perseveration
Motor problems
Lack of initiative
Poor reasoning
Childishness
Poor memory
Reduced verbal fluency
Inability to change set
Concrete thinking

Luria et al (1964) give a detailed account of some simple clinical tests of frontal function. Care must be taken when interpreting findings from such tests, as some 'frontal' abilities (for example, the ability to change set as measured by the Weigl Colour Form Test) have been shown to deteriorate rapidly in the more aged (Walker 1982). Any test of frontal function should therefore be used circumspectly.

Case study 4

Mrs N I was a 66-year-old German woman who had a history of sexual and marital difficulties. She had been admitted six months earlier after 'amputating' her toe on the instruction of 'voices'. Her state remitted spontaneously (although she was left with a voice which said 'one') and a psychological assessment had indicated average intellectual ability (she was a classical piano teacher) with a drop in her Wechsler Adult Intelligence Scale (WAIS) performance scale score which was not significant.

On her re-admission six months later, she reported that the voices telling her to harm herself had not re-emerged, but that she heard thoughts coming from her 'subconscious mind' in the form of a commentary, and also repetitious musical songs referring, for example, to her smoking. The results of her psychological assessment are shown in Table 10.8. It can be seen that routine assessment of her orientation and verbal learning alone would not have identified any difficulties (testing for nominal aphasia was impossible as her first language was German). However, there were clear signs of organic pathology on tests of frontal function, and strong indications of general intellectual decline with dominant parietal/temporal involvement indicated by her marked constructional apraxia and finger agnosia.

A CT scan carried out two months later was apparently normal, with some question of reduced density around the dominant temporo-parietal region. However, she continued to decline and some six months later a memory impairment was becoming apparent in everyday life.

Table 10.8 Mrs N I's test results

Assessment Measure	Performance
CAPE O/I scale	Fully orientated
Names learning test (Irving et al 1970)	Within normal range
Drawing and copying	Performance indicative of constructional apraxia (possibly dominant hemisphere)
In between test (see Kingsbourne & Warrington 1962)	Finger agnosia confirmed
Wechsler Adult Intelligence Test (WAIS) (Short form)	i) Loss of 21 IQ points in 6 months ii) Confirmation of constructional apraxia on Block Design
Predictive sequence using coloured blocks e.g. RWRWRW Then RWWRWWRWW (R = red W = white)	Frontal function problem
Recoding of verbal instructions e.g. 'tap once when I tap twice' 'tap twice when I tap once'	Failure on this task, including disconnection between verbal and motor behaviour, indicative of frontal dysfunction

As well as being indicative of a dementia, frontal dysfunction can indicate the presence of a congenital disorder or space-occupying lesion. A 67-year-old woman exhibited disinhibited sexual behaviour with her husband (out of character) and verbal abuse. She showed no evidence of generalised intellectual deterioration and no specific neuropsychological deficits except in frontal function. Subsequent CT scanning confirmed the presence of a congenital frontal malformation, the effects of which were unmasked by ageing (Wattis & Church 1986).

It can be seen from these examples that knowledge of qualitative signs of frontal dysfunction and some simple confirmatory tests may be essential in clarifying diagnosis. Simple screening measures for frontal dysfunction should be a routine part of all psychiatric assessments in elderly people. A minimum set of tests would include motor coordination, prediction of a logical sequence and ability to recode information (see Luria et al 1964).

Other neuropsychological deficits

It is not possible in this chapter to cover the full range of neuropsychological impairments: aphasias, apraxias, agnosias, frontal and subcortical function and loss of acquired knowledge. Rather, in this next section we will demonstrate how a simple qualitative approach to assessment can be used to identify unusual neuropsychological presentations.

Holden and Woods (1982) have described how a pictorial magazine can be used as a quick, simple and unthreatening screening test, to assess such abilities as reading, recognition of pictures, objects and colours, and object naming. Adopting such measures when faced with an unusual presentation can provide valuable information, which a more traditional screening interview might miss. One example of this is the identification of an occipital stroke: although rare, this often results in unusual neuropsychological impairment, which can go unrecognised. The resulting behaviour problems (sometimes exacerbated by inappropriate management) may lead the elderly person to present as a psychiatric problem. Case study 5 is an illustration of this.

Case study 5

Mr K M was a 69-year-old man who had been admitted to a psychogeriatric ward in a distressed state with vivid hallucinations, after being sent home from the casualty department. The vivid hallucinations had persisted despite no evidence of alcohol abuse (suspected because of his frequent patronage of the hospital social club). Psychological assessment indicated lack of insight, mild disorientation (CAPE O/I scale = 9/12), some problems in verbal learning, with gross misrecognition of objects and pictures. Table 10.9 presents some examples of his responses during assessment. As can be seen, he was unable to correctly identify objects or what they were used for, confirming the presence of a visual agnosia (as opposed to a nominal aphasia). Interestingly, the use of vision and touch still resulted in the misidentification of objects. However, the use of touch alone (eyes closed) allowed the accurate

Table 10.9 Examples of Mr K M's test results indicating a visual agnosia

Test	Use of vision	Vision and touch	Touch/eyes closed
Watch	'It's a triangle' 'It's used in buildings' 'It's Y-shaped'	'It's like an octopus'	Correct response
Key	'Like a building that has fallen down'	'Baccy knife for cutting me baccy'	Correct response
Rubber	'It's a lorry'. Asked if a toy lorry, 'Yes'	'Don't know. I felt this yesterday' (He was assessed twice)	Correct response

identification of objects. It seemed in this case that Mr K M's visual 'interpretation' was prepotent (overriding other sensory information).

Observation of his everyday behaviour suggested that Mr K M was actively putting meaning into what he was seeing. For example, he showed staff a baby on the floor (pointing to a small vacuum cleaner). The 'distorted' nature of the information perceived visually was also indicated by his drawings. His free drawing of a house was recognisable and relatively coherent, whilst his copy was totally fragmented (see Figs. 10.2 and 10.3). It may be noted that his ability to recognise faces (he recognised a magazine parody of Hitler, as Charlie Chaplin) was not grossly impaired.

Further examination showed the presence of an agnosic alexia, which meant he could write normally (with a few errors) but was unable to read

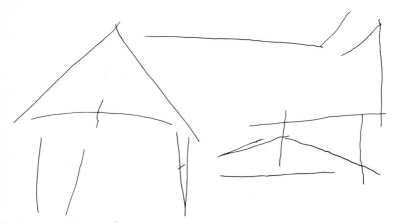

Fig. 10.2 Mr K M: free drawing of a house

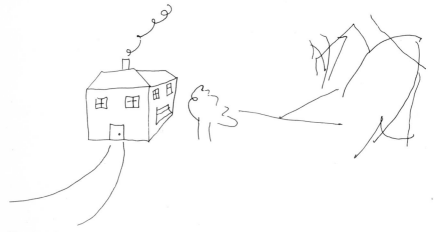

Fig. 10.3 Drawing of house by psychologist and Mr K M's copy

or recognise letters. This finding confirmed the involvement of the region supplied by the posterior cerebral artery (Walsh 1978). CT scanning suggested an anoxic or ischaemic progressive encephalopathy.

At six-months follow-up, he was slightly more disorientated (CAPE O/I score = 6/12) (possibly as a result of being placed on a long-stay ward), his general level of function as measured by the CAPE BRS was unchanged, and his ability to interpret visually had improved. He now recognised letters presented individually and read some words correctly. His 'hallucinations' were apparently much less frequent. However, his occasional aggressive outbursts have prevented him being rehabilitated to residential care.

MANAGEMENT

The provision of specialist services for elderly people is based on the premise that elderly people have special needs arising from the process of ageing, which cannot be met generically. This can be most clearly seen in relation to elderly people with dementia. Traditional services often provide too little and the wrong kind of help. Yet appropriate management with this group of people is particularly important because of the dispro-portionate amount of time and resources which they can demand if not managed well. In this section it will be argued that, in dementia, an understanding of the elderly person's neuropsychological assets and deficits will lead to more appropriate interventions. The implications for basic good practice and the use of behavioural interventions will be discussed. We will conclude by altering the focus from that of changing the individual through individual intervention to improving services to elderly people through organisational change, a much neglected area in psychiatry.

Preserved abilities in dementia

As people age they become increasingly more dependent on the environment. Whilst medicine and medical services have readily adopted a model based on prosthesis, when there is obvious physical handicap (e.g. hearing aid to reduce deafness), they have largely ignored the necessity of extending this model to other less obvious effects of ageing on the individual, notably its effects on psychological wellbeing. Rather than attempt a comprehensive definition of psychological wellbeing, we will try to identify some important aspects of it and the implications that dementia has for the elderly person.

The basis of good practice with any client group is the ability of the supporter involved (whether doctor, nurse, relative, etc.) to develop and/or maintain a trusting relationship with the client, which enhances her feelings of control and self-esteem. Such a relationship will improve compliance with any intervention whether medical, psychological or social. In a person with dementia not only will a failure to achieve this prevent any opportunity of helping the individual make the best use of her remaining abilities, but it may also contribute directly to the development of behaviour problems.

Two areas of ability which are commonly preserved in dementia allow for the development of a trusting client/supporter relationship.

Visual recognition memory

Ferris et al (1980) have shown that visual recognition memory is relatively well preserved, even with moderate degrees of dementia. Thus, although the elderly person will have great difficulty in learning any supporters' names, even with repeated reminders, she will soon come to recognise someone as familiar. If the contacts are warm, friendly and helpful, the supporter's face will be associated with pleasant events and they are likely to be recognised as a friend; a trusting relationship develops. However, if these contacts are unfriendly and distressing (for whatever reason), the supporter will be recognised as someone to be afraid of, or an enemy; the relationship will deteriorate. In the former case compliance with any help will be maximised and in the latter case minimised.

Social and non-verbal skills

Although there have been no reports of any detailed research concerning the preservation of social skills in those with dementia, clinical observation indicates that interactional skills are generally well preserved (see Hussain 1984). It should not be surprising to find this because the use of eye contact, gaze shift, turn taking, responsiveness to tone of voice and facial expression are all skills which develop at an early age (prior to formal language) and are greatly overlearnt throughout the life span.

One of the authors has observed two elderly women (both scoring less than three on the CAPE O/I scale), holding a 'perfect', unprompted conversation including turn taking, hand touch, eye contact, attentiveness and laughter, for 20 minutes. One was speaking dysphasic Latvian (her language of origin), the other fluently dysphasic English.

When language is preserved in dementia, it is possible to use humour to develop and maintain a relationship. However, this will require a sensitive awareness of the individual's sense of humour. The difference between laughing with someone and laughing at them is marginal. Once humour has become an established part of a relationship, it can be used as a specific technique, for example to defuse an aggressive outburst.

In summary, then, it is the ability of the individual with dementia to respond to cues, which allows the use of skilled interaction to promote a cooperative relationship between the elderly person and the supporter. As was mentioned earlier, socially skilled behaviour by the supporter is basic good practice with all clients. However, there are a number of aspects of ageing and dementia which make the use of such skills indispensable in work with elderly people suffering from dementia.

1. As people age they become more vulnerable to the effects of everyday institutional practices, not least because they have little spare physical capacity for use. As a consequence they are less likely to protest when subjected to public toileting, being talked about in the third person during a ward round, or when their future is being decided for them without proper consultation. When they do protest, or try to meet their needs, they are more likely to be labelled in ageist terms, as a 'dirty old man', or a 'silly old woman'. Twining (1981) pointed out that, rather than teach older people assertive skills so as to be able to survive the rigours of institutional life, as one study suggested, the emphasis should be on teaching the staff in these settings more appropriate skills.

2. When the elderly person does not recognise the supporter, either because visual recognition is not preserved or because it is a first contact, the appropriate use of verbal and non-verbal skills is the *only* means with which to gain trust and increase the probability of cooperation.

3. With a more marked degree of dementia, the understanding of language is often impaired. The verbal content of supporters' conversation will convey little to the elderly person; the majority of information taken in will come from the tone of voice and a variety of non-verbal cues such as facial expression and body posture.

4. The correct use of any compensatory technique to ameliorate the effects of particular neuropsychological deficit is itself a complex skill. One example of this is the use of first sound cueing to aid word retrieval (Myers-Pease et al 1978). The timing with which the cue is provided to someone who is searching for a word is crucial. Repeatedly presenting the cue too soon will reduce the recipient's experience of success and may precipitate depressed mood, whilst presenting the cue too late may lead to anger and frustration. Indeed the optimum timing is likely to vary considerably from individual to individual and situation to situation (Church 1986).

Although the authors believe that the implementation of such good practices as a rule rather than the exception (as is currently the case in medical settings) will dramatically improve the effectiveness of care for elderly people with dementia, there will always be individuals who will need more specialised interventions.

The reasons for this may include the inadequacy of the present provision of services, poor staffing levels in residential and long-stay care, difficult pre-morbid personality and the effects of certain neuropsychological deficits, notably frontal lobe dysfunction.

Neuropsychology and management

The everyday and longer-term management of patients with organic pathology will depend on their ability to function in the setting they are in and will return to. The more such settings are able to compensate for the neuropsychological deficits present, both through changes in supporter behaviour and modification of the physical environment, the more likely the elderly person will be able to function adequately.

The patient's neuropsychological assets and deficits provide much more useful information than psychiatric diagnosis with this client group. Thus even when two individuals have the same diagnosis, for example senile dementia of the Alzheimer type, they may have quite different patterns of deficit. One might have little impairment in short-term memory but great difficulty in understanding speech, whereas the other may have a severe impairment in short-term memory, but a relatively well preserved ability to understand speech. In the former case the correct approach would be to provide information, guidance and help using short sentences containing single ideas. In the latter, the individual would probably benefit from being orientated regularly to time, person and place, in a relaxed and unthreatening way.

Lack of space prevents a detailed account of the range of interventions that arise from a consideration of the results of the neuropsychological assessment. Instead, an illustrative case is presented next. A more detailed account of the implications of neuropsychological deficits for management is provided elsewhere (Wattis & Church 1986).

Case study 6

Mr D N, a 66-year-old man, was admitted for assessment following increasing self-neglect. A summary of his neuropsychological deficits is presented in Table 10.10. One important aspect of his functioning identified was the subcortical component of his dementia (Albert et al 1974). Thus he showed a marked slowness in carrying out tasks during the assessment. Removing the timing element of the task produced a very marked improvement in performance and he was now able to complete many tasks. This was confirmed by behavioural observations made on the assessment ward. When, with his agreement, he was placed in a residential home, this information allowed staff to respond appropriately to maintain his abilities. If this slowness had been interpreted as an inability to carry out or complete the task, the staff might have intervened and effectively 'untrained' him.

Table 10.10 Case study 6: Mr D N (adapted from Wattis & Church 1986)

Neuropsychological deficits	Management and implications
Nominal aphasia	Staff to use cueing, e.g. to say first letter or syllable of word he cannot find
Receptive dysphasia	Requests, commands, and conversations to include only short simple sentences with one idea at a time
Sub-cortical involvement (slowness, occasional irritable outbursts)	Allow him time to complete tasks

The danger of this happening in institutional care is illustrated by Ferm (1974). In four psychogeriatric wards, in which some three-quarters of the patients had dementia, she found that these patients showed a bimodal distribution on various self-care skills: they either had the skill, or did not. One interpretation of these results is that as soon as a patient developed a degree of difficulty with a skill such as dressing, the staff took over and began dressing the patient, who then lost her remaining ability. Whilst all psychiatric patients are at risk from over-zealous caring, those with subcortical slowness are especially so.

The behavioural approach

As well as considering the implications of possible neuropsychological deficits for the management of individuals, situational factors of another kind should be considered. The behavioural approach emphasises that maladaptive behaviour is learned. Unfortunately, this potentially important tool for intervention for the clinician has failed to fulfil its promise because much research in this area has ignored the value of neuropsychological assessment prior to behavioural intervention (Hodge 1984). Two reasons for carrying out such an assessment prior to behavioural intervention will be presented next.

Deciding on appropriate intervention

Elderly people with severe and debilitating behavioural problems vary from those with minimal or questionable organic impairment to those who are grossly demented. The nature and aims of any intervention made are likely to be completely different depending on the degree of dementia present. A neuropsychological assessment will provide information about what level of behavioural function might be reasonably expected of any elderly person in a particular environment. An example of a severely behaviourally disturbed woman is presented next.

Case study 7

Mrs F S was a 71-year-old woman who, after her husband's death ten years previously, had drunk heavily, gradually suffered reduced social contact and had made a move to a bungalow (which she later regretted). She had had one psychiatric admission two years previously with confusion, neglect and poor motivation. Her decline had continued after discharge and she had received gradually increasing levels of domiciliary support until the present level of seven days a week was reached. She was regarded as the most difficult case in that Social Services division. When she was referred for psychological help her present problem behaviours included immobility (no physical cause), refusal to help lift herself, double incontinence, day and night, refusal to use the commode, and throwing faeces around the room. Her intransigent behaviour had reduced several home helps to tears. The assessment confirmed the domiciliary staff's view that she was, in fact, a relatively cognitively unimpaired woman. She scored 7/12 on the CAPE O/I scale, was easily able to learn the psychologist's name in the interview, showed no evidence of nominal aphasia or language deficits. No evidence of depressive illness was found. The home help who had established a working relationship with her, achieved this by giving as good as she got and using a sharp sense of humour. Mrs F S's behaviour was not explainable in terms of a severe organic state, or a depressive illness. However, it was clear from a behavioural viewpoint that there was little incentive for her to produce more adaptive behaviour. Her 'helplessness' had resulted in gradually increasing input, reinforcing her maladaptive behaviour. A hierarchy of problems to be tackled was drawn up, the first being her refusal to help with transfer from bed to chair during the day. Table 10.11 shows how this was broken down into four steps and the technique of 'backward chaining' (moving from d to a) was adopted, with clear rewards for successful completion of each stage, and reduced reinforcement for failure to comply. (It should be noted that a behavioural intervention such as this must be tailored to fit the existing level and pattern of care). Within two weeks she was able to move from bed to chair with verbal prompting and a light guiding hand only. During the same period a similar approach was successfully used to initiate basic self-help skills such as cleaning and filing nails (which were filthy). Also, prior to the returning of a commode, (which was removed when Mrs F S refused to use it), she stopped throwing faeces, instead wrapping them up in paper and putting them beside her chair. At the time of writing, Mrs F S is now being regularly walked around the room using a frame, has achieved her first two days and nights of continence, using a bedtime commode (never achieved during hospital admissions) and writes shopping lists for the home help.

Table 10.11 Mrs F S: stages in transfer from bed to chair

---

a) Moving self from bed to chair once hands are on chair
b) Moving to take up position as in (a)
c) Moving legs from bed to floor
d) Moving bed clothes back

This case is only in its early stages, but illustrates how the neuropsychological findings suggested that this woman could be managed successfully in her own home, with less domiciliary support, given the appropriate behavioural intervention. Had the assessment indicated a severe dementia, the most appropriate action would have been to find her some more appropriate long-term residential care, as the potential for change, given the level of domiciliary services already being provided, would have been limited.

Cause of problem behaviour

In an elderly person, a particular problem behaviour will have many different possible causes, only some of which are amenable to a behavioural approach. This is illustrated in Table 10.12 for the problem of urinary incontinence. It should be noted that once a neuropsychological deficit has been implicated as a possible cause of the problem behaviour, then a behavioural approach may be used as part of the intervention. For example, if there is difficulty in remembering where the toilet is, this problem may be reduced by changing the physical environment, providing signposting and a colour-coded door, as well as having regular behavioural rehearsal.

Table 10.12 Problem behaviour — urinary incontinence in an elderly confused person (adapted from Wattis & Church 1986)

Reason	Solution
1 Medical (UTI)	Treat medical condition
2 *Incontinence being reinforced by staff*	*Rewarding periods of dryness*
3 *Cannot find toilet (short-term memory) impairment)*	*Practise, use of a variety of cues, and signposting*
4 Cannot recognise toilet (visual agnosia)	Use a colour code, e.g. only red in unit is toilet door
5 Cannot get to toilet in time (mobility)	Increase availability of toilet
6 Stress incontinence	Perineal muscle exercises, possible surgery
7 *Cannot dress or undress*	*Practise dressing/undressing skills*
8 Toilet uncomfortable (e.g. commode seat-top missing)	Make more comfortable
9 *Lack of motivation*	*Encourage and reinforce successful toileting and dryness*
10 Cannot understand verbal instructions to toilet (receptive aphasia)	Use alternative cue, e.g. visual
11 Cannot express need for toilet (expressive aphasia)	Staff sensitive to individual's attempt to communicate needs. Knowledge of individual's routine
12 Toilet area too cold	Provide heating
13 Toilet area lacks privacy (i.e. commode in middle of room)	Find suitable small enclosed area

Italics indicate that a contingency management approach should be used

It can be seen from this example that a problem-solving approach is the most appropriate framework in which to view the elderly person's behaviour. Any number of factors — neuropsychological, behavioural, medical and environmental (physical) — may be involved in 'causing' the problem behaviour.

Case study 8

Mrs M R was an 80-year-old woman suffering from Parkinson's disease and a valve abnormality of the heart, who had been discharged from a geriatric ward, mobile with a frame, with good domiciliary support. However, she apparently 'gave up' and had to be admitted to a geriatric rehabilitation unit until she was again mobile, continent and able to prepare food.

Again, she did not cope on discharge and was eventually admitted into residential care after further rehabilitation. Within two weeks of entry to the home, she was again fully dependent. Despite repeated 'successful' hospital rehabilitation, she 'relapsed' on every return to residential care. Psychological help was eventually requested by the hospital social worker. The psychological assessment indicated that despite a CAPE O/I score of 6/12, the pattern of her score, her ability to retain new information, and lack of nominal aphasia suggested that she did not have a significant degree of dementia. A number of observations were made regarding her situation, specifically her mobility problem (see Table 10.13). The low staffing level (and morale) and consequences of the poor physical design of the residential home led to a decision not to attempt to implement a behavioural programme. Instead, a case was made to try her in a more modern, purpose-built home, where she could be with intellectually intact residents, have closer and easier access to toilets, and where the doorways were much wider. When an alternative place became available, staff were carefully prepared to meet any problem behaviours. Within a week of entering the home, she was again walking with a Zimmer frame, was continent, had made a friend in the lounge area and was a different woman. Six months later, the social worker reported that Mrs M S had maintained her progress.

Table 10.13   Observations regarding Mrs M S's mobility problem

1 Low level of staffing with high-dependency resident group
2 Dependency reinforced
3 Physical design of home (an old stately building) inappropriate, i.e.
  a) Corridors very long with few support rails
  b) Doorways too narrow so she became fearful as confused residents pushed past her, e.g. at meal-times
  c) She was kept downstairs with residents suffering from dementia as no lift facilities available. (The four or five non-confused residents lived upstairs)

To summarise, then: to be effective, the behavioural approach must be utilised in a broader framework, which emphasises a wide range of factors influencing an elderly person's behaviour. Holden and Woods (1982), and more recently Wisocki (1984) and Hussain (1984), have presented reviews of this area.

The development of behaviour problems in dementia

The importance of the behavioural approach can be illustrated by considering a simple model of how an elderly confused person may develop behaviour problems (see Fig. 10.4). As the elderly person becomes more confused, supporters find it less easy to converse with her and spend more time elsewhere. Browne (1984) reported some of his preliminary findings,

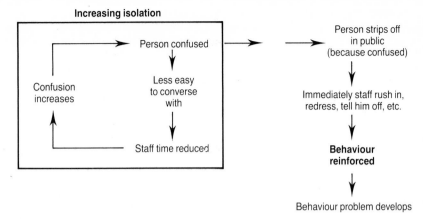

Fig. 10.4 Model of the development of a behaviour problem in confused elderly people

which showed that nurses interacted with more oriented individuals for 15% of the time, but with more disorientated individuals for an average of only 5.6% of the time. This reduction in input is likely to lead to increased confusion and the patient may, for example, strip off in public as a result. The immediate consequence is increased attention from supporters, involving redressing and often, reprimands. In the context of lack of interaction at other times, this reaction to the person's inappropriate behaviour is positively reinforcing and hence the behaviour is more likely to recur.

On the other hand, when an elderly confused person behaves appropriately, for example using dinner utensils rather than fingers, sitting quietly or occupied in the corner of the room, or urinating in the toilet, there is often an immediate withdrawal of interaction. Thus, appropriate behaviours result in supporters leaving immediately and getting on with other work, while inappropriate behaviours tend to be followed by increased attention. In institutional settings with a shortage of staff and lack of structured activities during the day, this can be the basis for an elderly confused person developing a wide range of behaviour problems to the point of becoming unmanageable. Even when the disruptive behaviour arises primarily from a central deficit such as frontal lobe dysfunction, there is no reason to suppose that environmental contingencies are irrelevant. The modification of behaviour arising from frontal damage has been demonstrated in patients with closed head injury (Wisocki 1984). Further empirical research is urgently needed with patients suffering from dementia.

Behavioural techniques, such as physical prompting, behavioural rehearsal, reinforcement and shaping, show particular promise for use with elderly people with moderate to severe degrees of dementia (Hanley 1981). Even small improvements in self-care abilities, for example continence, can have marked effects in improving the quality of life of both elderly sufferers and their supporters.

ORGANISATIONAL CHANGE AND IMPROVING SERVICES

The current low levels of service provision for elderly people with dementia mean that the focus for intervention for most psychogeriatric teams is the management of the elderly individual and her family and supporters *in crisis*. The danger is that crisis management becomes prepotent and the introduction of organisational changes which improve the quality of life more widely and foster a preventative approach to care, become submerged by an ever-growing tide of 'emergencies'. To conclude this chapter, we will explore some aspects of how psychogeriatric services might be improved through organisational change.

Staff selection and training

As we suggested earlier, the effective management of elderly people rests on the supporter being able to develop a trusting relationship with each individual. The preserved abilities of visual recognition and responsiveness to verbal and non-verbal cues allow the supporter to do this. However, whether or not the supporter utilises their skill to relate to the elderly person in a constructive and therapeutic way depends on the supporter's attitudes, values and principles. Table 10.14 shows examples of key principles which should facilitate appropriately caring responses, (King Edward's Hospital Fund for London 1985). Unfortunately the myth of professionalism still dominates thinking within the Health Service. This is based on the assumption that once the health service professional has completed their training, they have somehow developed the appropriate beliefs, principles and skills with which to meet the needs of all groups of clients, including those with dementia. This is sadly not the case. An overemphasis on professional status may hide a lack of appropriate skills and may result in misuse of scarce resources.

Table 10.14 Examples of principles of good practice in services for the elderly severely mentally infirm (King Edward's Hospital Fund for London, 1985)

Elderly people with mental disabilities have the same human value as anyone else irrespective of their degree of disability or dependence

Elderly people with mental disabilities have the same varied human needs as anyone else

Elderly people with mental disabilities have the same rights as other citizens

Every elderly person with mental disabilities is an individual

Elderly people with mental disabilities have the right to forms of support which don't involve exploitation of family or friends

---

Although it may be possible to train professionals to show more appropriate social and caring skills, the costs involved in this would be enormous. It would be much more cost-effective to change the basis of selection into various professions. Given that many people are competing for few places in a variety of professions, it is now possible to move beyond academic criteria, and select on the basis of those who show the appropriate level of social skills, and the ability to relate to people in a warm, supportive way. As part of this, training should develop away from the purely didactic and incorporate experiential techniques. Those who work with elderly people must have the opportunity to experience what it is like to be old and be able to look closely at the false and prejudiced values and principles that many people have in relation to ageing and dementia.

One recently developed community care programme in Sheffield, the Elderly Persons' Support Unit,* which selected support workers carefully on their ability to be 'caring' and relate to elderly people as equals, has adopted such an approach to training. For those involved in the training programme there has been no doubt about the dramatic change in views some of the prospective workers undergo. They come to have quite different expectations of the elderly person, and their approach changes accordingly.

Physical environment and psychological well-being

The importance of physical design on the psychological well-being of elderly people with or without dementia is still largely unrecognised in psychiatry. The provision of apppropriately designed physical environments may cost less and be more effective in raising quality of care than carrying out individual intervention. Finlay et al (1983) looked at 39 residents in three old people's homes, who were unable to rise unaided out of the chairs provided for them. However, with DHSS recommended chairs, 30 (77%) could get up themselves. It was estimated that nearly £2000 had been spent on unsuitable chairs and that the staff would have been saved a minimum of 300 lifts a day with the provision of appropriate chairs. The human cost of enforced dependency could not be measured.

A simple change in physical design can be highly effective in enforcing the right of the more disabled elderly to privacy in a toilet area (Wattis & Church 1986, p 162). Such measures do not rely on the compliance of staff, a problem with most psychological interventions.

New models of community care

Traditional community support for elderly people with a range of disabilities consists of the elderly person being 'assessed' for one or more of a limited range of existing services (such as home help, meals on wheels, warden, incontinence, laundry, etc). There is often little match between the client's problems and needs and the service being offered. One clear gap

* Elderly Persons Support Unit, Family and Community Services, Wordsworth Avenue, Ecclesfield, Sheffield. Telephone 454897

in most current service provision for the elderly with dementia and their relatives is the opportunity for help with night-time disturbance, one of the commonest and most disturbing behavioural problems (Church & Middleton 1981, Gilleard et al 1981).

A number of projects providing alternatives to traditional community support have been developed. The Kent community project showed how organisational change can lead to a more effective, flexible support service for elderly people (Challis & Davies 1980, 1984). They looked at elderly people 'on the edge' of community care but who wished to remain in their own homes. Specialist social workers with reduced case loads were enabled to use up to two-thirds of the money which would have been used in institutional care, in any way they wished, in order to support the elderly person at home. The results of this study showed a dramatic reduction in admissions to residential care, as compared to a service organised in the traditional way. They suggested that this kind of care would be cost-effective for the extremely dependent person with mental and physical frailty who receives a considerable degree of informal support and for the elderly person with only a moderate degree of dependency, suffering from non-psychotic psychiatric disorder.

Such studies emphasise the importance of good organisational practices such as the use of a key worker and a problem-oriented approach. Through the use of such good practices, it is possible to devise a pattern of care which fits closely to the problems and needs of each individual.

The importance of being aware and responsive to routine and habitual behaviour is even greater in the care of elderly people with dementia. Once routine and habitual behaviour are lost they are difficult, if not impossible, to re-establish because of the memory and other difficulties; disorganised and problem behaviours fill the void.

Organisation and the evaluation of psychiatric services

It is unfortunate that there are no formal guidelines encouraging the adoption of good organisational practice by psychiatric teams in the National Health Service, and the quality of services vary accordingly. The implementation of the Griffith Report, with new management structure and the notion of clinical budgeting, allows the possibility of a change in the organisational structure of the services. Although of all medical specialities, psychiatry is the most difficult to quantify and measure cost-effectiveness, there are simple organisational changes which would improve the accountability of psychiatric teams and make it easier to measure their effectiveness. One example would be the gradual ending of the practice of different consultants and psychiatric teams sharing admission ward facilities. Not only does the sharing of admission wards tend to prevent the development of coherent treatment policies on that ward, but it makes it impossible to relate measures of outcome to the effectiveness of a particular team. If it were possible to make psychiatric teams more accountable in this way, it might facilitate changes in organisational deficiencies which are less easy to identify. For example, although the importance of psychological intervention has been recognised in psychiatry, in practice it is still rare to find psychological interventions used as an integral part of the psychiatric treatment plan. Usually psychological intervention is an afterthought when physical intervention has failed.

CONCLUSION

In this chapter we have underlined the importance of the qualitative approach to assessment in elderly people with dementia. The qualitative aspects of behaviour shown during formal assessment and the observation of elderly people in their everyday environment have too often been neglected in clinical practice because they lack the rigour of formal tests. However, we have demonstrated that qualitative information about neuropsychological state is not only an adjunct to formal test results, but may provide answers to diagnostic questions and management problems, which formal tests cannot.

In our final section we saw how an understanding of the neuropsychological assets and deficits of elderly people with dementia can lead to conclusions about the development of psychogeriatric services and how organisational changes can be more effective than individual intervention.

We hope that readers will be encouraged to look further and find an effective balance between individual management and longer term organisational change in their area of clinical practice.

REFERENCES

Albert M L, Feldman R G, Willis A L 1974 The 'subcortical dementia' of progressive supranuclear palsy. Journal of Neurology, Neurosurgery and Psychiatry 37: 121–130
Andrews K, Stewart J 1979 Stroke recovery: he can but does he? Rheumatology and Rehabilitation 18: 43–48
Bayles K A 1982 Language function and senile dementia. Brain and Language 16: 265–280
Blessed G, Tomlinson B E, Roth M 1968 The association between quantitative measures of dementia and senile change in the cerebral grey matter of elderly subjects. British Journal of Psychiatry 114: 797–811
Bromley D B 1977 Personality description in ordinary language. John Wiley, London
Browne K 1984 Confusion in the elderly. Nursing 2: 698–705.
Challis D, Davies B 1980 A new approach to community care for the elderly. British Journal of Social Work: 10
Challis D, Davies B 1984 Community care schemes: a development in the home care of the frail elderly. In: Grimley Evans J, Caird F I (eds) Advanced geriatric medicine 4. Pitman, Bath, pp 35–45
Church M A 1985 Submission to Health Service Suggestion Competition. Journal of Health and Social Services
Church M A 1986 Issues in psychological therapy with elderly people. In: Hanley I G, Gilhooly M L M (eds) Psychological therapies for the elderly. Croom Helm/Methuen, London

Church M A, Middleton C 1981 An assessment of a psychogeriatric service. British Society of Gerontology Annual Conference, Hull

Coughlan A K, Warrington E K 1978 Word comprehension and word retrieval in patients with localised cerebral lesions. Brain 101: 163–185

De Renzi E, Vignolo L A 1962 The Token Test: a sensitive test to detect receptive disturbances in aphasics. Brain 85: 665–678

Ferm L 1974 Behavioural activities in the demented elderly. Gerontological Clinic 16: 185–194

Ferris S H, Crook T, Clarke E, McCartney M, Roe D 1980 Facial recognition memory deficits in normal ageing and senile dementia. Journal of Gerontology 35: 707–714

Finlay O E, Bayles T B, Rosen C, Milling J 1983 Effects of chair design, age and cognitive status on mobility. Age and Ageing 12: 328–331

Gibson J A, Moyes I C A, Kendrick D A 1980 Cognitive assessment of the elderly long-stay patient. British Journal of Psychiatry 137: 551–557

Gilleard C J, Wath G, Boyd W D 1981 Problems of caring for the elderly mentally infirm at home. 12th International Congress of Gerontology, Hamburg

Hanley I G 1981 The use of sign posts and active training to modify ward disorientation in elderly patients. Journal of Behaviour and Experimental Psychiatry 12: 241–247

Hodge J 1984 Towards a behavioural analysis of dementia. In: Handley I G, Hodge J (eds) Psychological approaches to the care of the elderly. Croom Helm, London

Hodkinson H M 1972 Evaluation of a mental test score for assessment of mental impairment in the elderly. Age and Ageing 1: 233–238

Holden U P, Woods R T 1982 Reality orientation: psychological approaches to the 'confused' elderly. Churchill Livingstone, New York

Hussain R A 1984 Behavioural geriatrics. In: Herien M, Eiser R M, Miller P M (eds) Progress in behaviour modification 16. Academic Press, London

Inglis J 1959 A paired associate learning test for use with elderly psychiatric patients. Journal of Mental Science 105: 440–8

Institute of Psychiatry, Psychiatric Teaching Committee 1973. Notes on eliciting and recording clinical information. Institute of Psychiatry, London

Irving G, Robinson R A, McAdams W 1970 The validity of some cognitive tests in the diagnosis of dementia. British Journal of Psychiatry 117: 148–156

Jacoby R J, Levy R 1980 Computed tomography in the elderly. 2. Senile dementia: diagnosis and functional impairment. British Journal of Psychiatry 136: 256–259

Kendrick D C, Gibson A J, Moyes I C A 1979 The Revised Kendrick Battery: clinical studies. British Journal of Psychiatry 18: 329–339

King Edward's Hospital Fund for London 1985 Living well into old age. Applying the principles of good practice to services for elderly people with severe mental disabilities (draft paper) Kings Edwards Hospital Fund for London, London

Kingsbourne M, Warrington E K 1962 A study of finger agnosia. Brain 85: 47–66

Klisz D 1978 Neuropsychological evaluation in older persons. In: Storandt M, Siegler I C, Elias M F, (eds) The clinical psychology of ageing Plenum Press, New York, p 71–96

Ley P 1976 Acute psychiatric patients. In: Mittler P (ed) The psychological assessment of physical and mental handicap. Tavistock Methuen, London

Luria A R, Pribram K H, Homskays E D 1964 An experimental analysis of the behavioural disturbances produced by a left frontal arachnoidal endothelioma (meningioma). Neuropsychologia 2: 257–280

McKenna P, Warrington E K 1980 Testing for nominal dysphasia. Journal of Neurology, Neurosurgery and Psychiatry 43: 781–788

Moore V R 1981 Analysis of drawing ability in adults with dementia. M Phil Thesis, University of London

Moore V, Wyke M A 1984 Drawing disability in patients with senile dementia. Psychological Medicine 14: 97–105

Myers-Pease G D, Goodglass H 1978 The effects of cueing on picture naming in aphasia. Cortex 14: 178–189

Pattie A H, Gilleard C J 1979 Manual of the Clifton Assessment Procedures for the Elderly (CAPE) Hodder and Stoughton, Sevenoaks

Qureshi K N, Hodkinson H M 1974 Evaluation of a ten question mental test in the institutionalised elderly. Age and Ageing 3: 152–157

Rimm D C, Masters J C 1967 Behaviour Therapy: Techniques and Empirical Findings. Academic Press, New York

Rochford G 1971 A study of naming errors in dysphasia and demented patients. Neuropsychologia 9: 437–43

Skelton-Robinson M, Jones S 1984. Nominal dysphasia and the severity of senile dementia. British Journal of Psychiatry 145: 168–171

Snowden J 1983 Frontal function in dementia. Special Interest Group in Neuropsychology, Coventry

Spellacy F J, Spreen O 1969 A short form of the Token Test. Cortex 5: 390–397

Twining T C 1981 Social skill, psychology disorder and ageing. XII International Congress of Gerontology, Hamburg

Walker S 1982 An investigation of the communication of elderly subjects. M Phil Thesis, University of Sheffield

Walsh K W 1978 Neuropsychology: a clinical approach. Churchill Livingstone, Edinburgh

Walton D 1958 The diagnostic and predictive accuracy of the Modified Word Learning Test in psychiatric patients over 65. Journal of Mental Science 104: 1119–1122

Warrington 1976 Neurological deficits. In: Mittler P (ed) The psychological assessment of mental and physical handicaps Tavistock/Methuen, London

Wattis J P, Church M A 1986 Practical psychiatry of old age. Croom Helm, London

Whitehead A, Hunt A 1982 Elderly psychiatric patients. A five-year prospective study. Psychological Medicine 12: 149–157

Williams M 1961 The measurement of mental performance in older people. Nuffield Foundation, London

Williams M 1968 The measurement of memory in clinical practice. British Journal of Social and Clinical Psychology 7: 19–34

Wilson B A, Moffat N 1984 Clinical management of memory problems. Croom Helm, London

Wisocki P A 1984 Behavioural approaches to gerontology. In: Hersen M, Eiser R M, Miller P M (eds) Progress in behaviour modification 16. Academic Press, London

Measuring effects of psychoactive drugs

Elderly patients are more frequent users of psychoactive drugs than their younger counterparts, are more likely to be sensitive to the unwanted side-effects of drug administration and are liable to have a different, more difficult and lengthier metabolism of psychoactive agents. There are notorious difficulties in trying to assess the impact of psychoactive drugs in the older patient for the reasons given above and because the measures used to assess the patient are often insensitive to the great inter- and intra-subject variability in intellectual and psychomotor abilities and cognitive functions. Recent evidence would suggest that there now exist techniques and systems by which an adequate assessment of the effects of psychoactive drugs in the elderly patient can be made. It is these issues which are the concern of this chapter.

THE INCREASED FREQUENCY OF PSYCHOACTIVE DRUG USE IN THE ELDERLY

The main reason for a more frequent use of medicines by elderly patients is that they have more physical and psychological diseases than their younger counterparts. A general practitioner survey (Hamdy & Zakaria 1977) found that even the fit elderly person living at home had at least one illness whilst hospitalised patients had, on average, six diseases.

The increase with age in the number of pathological conditions requiring pharmacotherapy leads inexorably to the state of polypharmacy which characterises the drug treatment regimens of many elderly patients. This is especially true of patients receiving psychotropic agents, as psychological disorders and diseases affecting thinking, memory and reasoning are much more prevalent in elderly patients than in any other age group. The increased frequency of 'life events' such as retirement and bereavement, and poor physical health contribute to the increase of psychological illness, particularly anxiety states, in elderly patients (Bergman 1971). Age-related biochemical changes, such as a decrease in the formation of aminobutyric acid (McGeer & McGeer 1976) could also explain the higher incidence of anxiety in the elderly, while loss of noradrenergic function has been associated with Korsakoff-type psychosis (McEntee & Mair 1978) and a progressive failure of cholinergic transmission has been shown (Perry et al 1978) to correlate with the severity of mental impairment, in patients with dementia of the Alzheimer type. There has also been speculation that age-related neuroendocrine changes may initiate many of the physical and psychological disorders associated with old age (Denckla 1978; Finch et al 1980).

Most who complain of insomnia and sleep-related disorders such as excessive daytime drowsiness are older people. Increased age brings a steady increase in interruptions to sleep, a steady fall in the amount of slow-wave sleep (Oswald 1981) and a progressive reduction in the number of hours of sleep at night.

Although only a small proportion of depressive illness first comes to notice after the age of 70 (Post 1968), this does not prevent a substantial number of elderly patients receiving treatment for affective disorders. Even though psychological, social, developmental and genetic factors play a role in the genesis of affective illness there is still a predominant argument that depression and mania have a biological origin in the functional deficiencies, or excesses, of brain amines (Mendels et al 1976).

It is generally believed that psychological disorders, sleep disturbance and cognitive deficits in the elderly are the end-product of underlying physiological, neurochemical or neuroendocrine changes. This has led to the popular practice of treating 'psychogeriatric disorders' with psychoactive drugs intended to adjust the levels of brain amines, or to effect a change in the basic biological and physiological equilibrium of the nervous system. This has resulted in elderly patients (over 60 years) being the highest users of prescribed medications of any age group (Whittington & Petersen 1979). Elderly patients are also notorious for their use of 'over-the-counter' medicines (Petrie 1983), although no statistics exist to indicate the extent to which non-prescription psychoactive substances, particularly the antihistamines, are used. Sangiorgi (1979) has also emphasised the toxic, metabolic and synergistic action of ethanol when taken in conjunction with psychotropic medicines.

THE UNWANTED EFFECTS OF PSYCHOACTIVE DRUGS

A survey of 209 people aged over 65 (Busse 1978) indicated that some 20% had received treatment for depressive illness at sometime during the previous three years. As many as 33% of patients hospitalised for medical, non-psychological, reasons were administered anti-anxiety agents (Shaw & Opit 1976) and 45% of patients in general practice over 70 years old were found to be regularly taking nocturnal hypnotics (McGhie & Russell 1962).

Psychomotor effects

The fact that elderly patients are, in general, frequent users of psycho-tropics is reason enough to wish to measure the clinical effects and unwanted 'side-effects' of such drugs on patients' psychomotor performance and intellectual functions. Another reason is the concern for the patients' safety, in that many accidents in the home (especially injury resulting from falling), on the road (either as a pedestrian or a car driver), or at work are felt to be the direct result of taking certain psychoactive drugs. Femoral fractures following nocturnal falls have been shown to be as high as 90% in elderly patients taking barbiturates (Macdonald & Macdonald, 1977) while Macdonald (1985) concluded that the use of phenothiazines, tricyclic antidepressants and sedative benzodiazepines was a contributing agent to falls in the elderly. Impairment of sensorimotor coordination has been detected for up to 36 hours after a single nocturnal dose of nitrazepam in elderly subjects (Castleden et al 1977) and Macdonald (1985) reported an association between hospital referrals for falls and clinical use of nitrazepam in a population of 1622 geriatric patients.

It is equally important to determine which psychoactive drugs have no effect on psychomotor ability and which are, therefore, potentially safer. An estimate of the 'safety' of a drug in clinical use can be made by reference to large-scale epidemiological surveys where accidents and drug treatment regimens are correlated. Such studies often pose problems at a statistical and/or methodological level and it is not always possible to isolate the effect of a particular drug from that of the underlying disease and that of other drugs, or to correlate a particular drug with particular accident character-istics.

A more direct way of measuring the liability of a drug to disrupt sensori-motor activity is to use a battery of specific psychomotor assessments in a controlled study of that particular drug in a population of patients. Macdonald (1985) recognises the sparsity of objective information from such test systems and feels that the lack of direct evidence (relating particular drug use to falling accidents) is a substantial defect in present knowledge of the role of drugs in accidents in the elderly.

Intellectual and cognitive effects

The unwanted effects of psychotropics not only show up on measures of psychomotor co-ordination but also on information processing, memory and higher mental processes. Furthermore, assessment of drug action on cognitive functions is necessary to identify those substances with side-effects which in clinical use could produce a 'pseudodementia' syndrome of confusion, blunting of faculties, restlessness, apathy, drowsiness and/or excitement and disorientation (Rudd 1972). For example: Evans and Jarvis (1972) reported confusion, disorientation and dysarthria in elderly patients taking nocturnal doses of nitrazepam; a 50% reduction in immediate memory capacity was found in elderly anxious patients (Paes de Sousa et al 1981) during treatment with lorazepam and an overall reduction in information processing ability was demonstrated (Hanks 1984) in a group of elderly patients during treatment with amitriptyline for 7 weeks. Such findings suggest that the most important reason for measuring the activity of psychotropic drugs in the elderly is to establish the duration of unwanted psychoactivity and side-effects of the various substances in clinical use.

Duration and measurement of drug activity

The duration of the psychotherapeutic activity of psychoactive drugs needs also to be assessed specifically in the elderly; especially as the dose and treatment regimens for psychotropics are usually decided early in the clinical development of a drug on the basis of information from populations of young, healthy, psychologically normal volunteers and clearly defined groups of patients — excluding the elderly. It is generally accepted (Seide et al 1966, Hurwitz 1969, Learoyd 1972, Caranosos et al 1974) that elderly patients are more likely to suffer from adverse reactions to psychotropic drugs than younger ones, and likely to be more sensitive to the pharmaceutical agents. The increase in drug sensitivity and adverse reactions in elderly patients is due, in the main, to pharmacokinetic (drug absorption, distribution and elimination variables) and pharmacodynamic (drug-receptor site) changes which occur as part of the ageing process. It is difficult to isolate the purely pharmacokinetic factors which give rise to the great inter-patient variability in response and sensitivity to psychotropic agents in the elderly (Braithwaite 1982). It is, however, important to assess the duration and intensity of the pharmacotherapeutic effect of psychoactive drugs in elderly populations in order to decide an appropriate drug regimen for patient treatment. The use of batteries of psychomotor and cognitive tests can be used to provide such information.

Measurement of the psychological activity of psychotropics used in the elderly is evidently important: for assaying the 'safety' of drugs in clinical use; for determining the duration of therapeutic drug activity; and for identifying those drugs which can be counter-therapeutic by causing unwanted side-effects which could lead to a syndrome of 'pseudodementia'. Furthermore, proper psychometric assessments and psychopharmacological profiling of drugs can assist in the development of new psychopharmacological agents and in determining the extent to which different medicines and/or alcohol interact.

THE IMPORTANCE OF PHARMACODYNAMICS

The elderly suffer an increased incidence of adverse reactions compared with younger patients taking identical drug formulation and treatment regimens (Braithwaite 1982). While the apparent sensitivity to side-effects can be explained in part by physiological changes influencing the pharmaco-kinetics of drug absorption, distribution and both renal and hepatic elimination, such pharmacophysiological variables do not fully account for the severity, duration and nature of the side-effects reported by older patients following the use of a psychotropic drug.

It has been well established that some benzodiazepines (notably diazepam, flurazepam and chlordiazepoxide) have different pharmaco-kinetic profiles when studied in groups of elderly and groups of younger patients (Greenblatt & Shader 1980). Differences between old and young patients have also been shown when the pharmacokinetics of some tricyclic antidepressants (amitriptyline, imipramine, nortriptyline, desimipramine) have been investigated (Braithwaite 1982). However, the clinical implications of these differences are not fully understood as no clear correlations between, for example, blood levels, elimination half-lives, distribution volume, clearance times and clinical therapeutic activity have been unequivocally demonstrated. As there is no consistent pattern of age-related change of pharmacokinetic characteristics following psychoactive drugs, it is better to rely on empirical measures of the pharmacodynamic profile of drugs taken by elderly patients. Pharmacodynamic changes can be used to illustrate the extent, severity and nature of side-effects (and often the duration of desired clinical activity). The techniques used to measure the pharmacodynamic effects of psychotropic drugs are the basic concern of the rest of this chapter.

Methodological considerations

It is not proposed to discuss the general theoretical framework for measuring the effects of psychoactive drugs in man, as that would be outside the aims of this present chapter and has already been well covered in published texts (Spriet & Simon 1985). However, no evaluation of a psychoactive drug can be made without due regard to the usual methodological controls and the use of reliable and valid tests. A proper experimental control of relevant sources of variability must be made and appropriate statistical analysis employed with due regard to the nature and form of the data obtained.

Certain specific considerations have to be made when making any form of assessment in elderly patients and it is worth while remembering that psychological test performance will be influenced by several factors (Vingoe 1981) including:-
1. Overall level of patient's general intelligence.
2. Degree of rapport between tester and patient.
3. Patient's attitude to, and interest in, the test situation.
4. Patient's level of motivation, arousal and physical energy.
5. Patient's trait anxiety and/or emotional state.

6. Possible speech or visual hearing deficits.

7. Level of psychomotor function and eye–hand coordination.

In order to ensure that any clinical or volunteer experiment measures only drug effects, the above sources of variability must be excluded by pre-experimental screening or controlled by using placebo and/or verum treatments along with the investigational compound. However, the limiting factor of all psychopharmacological research in elderly populations is the appropriateness of the assessment measures used to determine the drug effects. As well as the usual criterion of test reliability, it is important for all psychometric procedures used in elderly populations to be well within the intellectual, sensory and memory capacities of the subjects. Elderly subjects have a slower rate of visual information processing than young adults (Walsh 1976, Walsh et al 1978); a poorer short-term memory capacity (Craik 1979, Taub 1972, Anders et al 1972, Fleischman 1982) a lengthened motor reaction time to a critical stimulus (Botwinik & Storandt 1974), a decreased learning ability (Botwinik 1973), poorer temporal resolution (Axelrod et al 1968) and lower attention and concentration (Broadbent & Heron 1962, McGhie et al 1965). Furthermore, the short-term retention of visual and acoustic information in the sensory register is greatly shortened in the elderly (Inglis & Caird 1963, Kline & Szafran 1975, Walsh & Thompson 1978) and Schaie and Zelinski (1979), reviewing the relationship of long-term memory and age, showed that the elderly had deficits in retrieval of information from memory and had difficulties in the encoding, especially in 'paced' tasks, of unfamiliar information. These overall deficits in cognitive function, perceptual processes, psychomotor ability and scanning of short-term memory information in elderly populations pose almost insurmountable problems for the experimenter wishing to test elderly populations on measures whose reliability and validity have been established in young adults with intact cognitive and perceptual abilities. It is also worth noting that elderly patients do not form homogenous groups with respect to scores on psychological test systems. As well as the great inter-patient variability in cognitive functions there is also a great intra-patient change in test scores as circadian variability in mood, drive, attention, arousal and affect act to modify psychomotor performance. Much of the inter- and intra-patient variability is due to the multimorbid nature of the clinical picture presented by most older patients. Cognitive disturbance is the predominant feature of Alzheimer-type dementias but, although not the dominant aspect, cognitive dysfunction is also associated with late-life depression and other psychological illnesses (Siegfried 1985).

THE PSYCHOPHARMACOLOGICAL APPROACH

Psychopharmacologists assume that the effects of psychoactive substances can be observed from the changes produced in the cognitive and psychological behaviour of individuals to whom the drugs are administered. The problem with elderly subjects is that the cognitive and psychological behaviours used as the basis for controlled measurement are constantly changing and variable. The age-related disturbances of many psychological functions, illustrated above, are often outside the usual experimental controls and the first task of the psychopharmacologist who wishes to investigate drug activity is to develop and verify measures which can be reliably and validly used. Test systems which are developed in isolation from an appropriate theoretical framework are not, generally speaking, meaningful as they lack psychological relevance. A review of the literature (Hindmarch 1980) shows that many tests purporting to measure the CNS activity of psychoactive drugs are little more than carefree inventiveness on behalf of the experimenter. Tests which have demonstrable sensitivity in specific populations cannot be assumed to have the same utility in elderly patient populations. For example; while proof-reading ability (Adams 1974), the speed of placing caps on ball-point pens (Lahtinen et al 1978) and the duration of visual after-images (Malpas & Joyce 1969) might discriminate between drug and placebo conditions in specific groups of young healthy volunteers, the inter- and intra-elderly patient variability in the measure would be probably far greater than any drug/placebo differences observed, even in a repeated measures design where subjects acted as their own control.

Thus if experimental psychopharmacology in elderly patients is to have any psychological relevance, the effects of drugs must be studied within a well-defined model of behaviour. The relationship between the overt behavioural activity of an individual subject (test performance) and the stimuli impinging on that individual at that time is an extremely complex one. The effects of a psychoactive drug are assumed to be ascertainable from the changes observed on overt behaviour. An information-processing model (Fig. 11.1) is a useful and parsimonious way of representing the major variables which govern test performance and which go towards determining the psychological response to the administration of a psychoactive drug. Such a model also serves a pragmatic cause, showing that a battery of tests

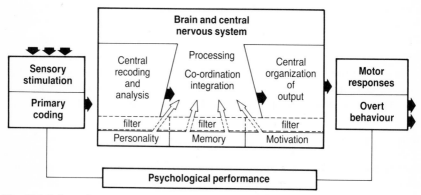

Fig. 11.1 Information processing model of behaviour and psychological response

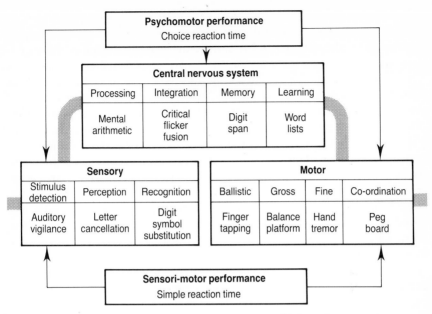

Fig. 11.2 How various tests can measure different aspects of information processing

examining the three distinct aspects of the flow of information — sensory encoding, CNS processing and motor output — is probably the best way to measure the overall impact of a psychoactive drug on the CNS. A realisation of the model in terms of the tests (Hindmarch 1980) which can be used to measure the different aspects of information processing is shown in Figure 11.2. The model should not, however, imply that the activity of the CNS in processing information is strictly or discretely compartmentalised. In reality there is much interaction between sensory, central and motor systems, but the complexity of these feedback and adaptive mechanisms precludes representation in this simple pragmatic model.

ASSESSMENT OF COGNITIVE AND PSYCHOMOTOR FUNCTION IN THE ELDERLY

The essential requirements of any test system for use with elderly patients have already been described. The task requirements have to be simple, placing little load on memory, comprehension and span of attention; free from learning effects, especially sensory motor skills, and without undue emphasis on verbal, numerical or auditory capacities. It is also essential that the test is drug-sensitive as well as age-sensitive. This implies that there is a definite drug dose–response sensitivity and age-related change manifest on the test measure and not simply an all–or–none indication of impaired function. It is also useful for any test system used in psychopharmacological studies to be robust upon repeated administration, as such measures are often required by experimental protocols. At the same time, tests have to account for sensory, central and motor components of information processing in terms of the theoretical framework underpinning the experimentation.

Auditory vigilance, cancellation tests and digit symbol substitution tasks have been shown (see Fig. 11.2) to be among the most sensitive indices of drug activity on the sensory aspects of information processing. Similarly, finger tapping, hand steadiness measures, peg-board performance and stabilometer scores were among the most drug-sensitive and discriminating measures of motor ability. The overall activity of the CNS was found to be best assessed using mental arithmetic, digit span, verbal learning or critical flicker fusion thresholds (CFFT). Interaction between sensory, central and motor components of the information processing model was found to be best assessed using a choice reaction time task. The review (Hindmarch 1980) did not identify tests which had a particular sensitivity in elderly patients. However, the considerations mentioned earlier would militate against those tests dependent upon learning new information, complex sensorimotor coordination and large-capacity short-term memory storage.

Tests for drug-produced changes

Few attempts have been made to identify those tests which can detect drug-produced changes in elderly patients. It has recently been shown (Siegfried 1985, Siegfried et al 1984) that certain tests are more discriminating than others of drug-produced changes in older patients treated with antidepressants. Siegfried and his co-workers, using factor analytic techniques, demonstrated that significant differences exist between clinically depressed and non-depressed elderly patients in their scores on a variety of psychomotor tests. Elderly depressed patients were characterised by significantly lower peformance levels on tests of attention (d^2 cancellation test); speed of perceptual patterning (block design test); learning of verbal material (paired-associative learning test); speed of information processing and general CNS arousal (critical flicker fusion test) and sensorimotor coordination (choice reaction time test). As well as demonstrating the importance of cognitive symptoms in late-life depression, Siegfried's work has identified some psychological test systems which are sensitive to drug-induced change in elderly patients, and also provided an excellent example for future research in this area.

A test battery which would offer a sensitive, reliable and robust discrimination between demented and non-demented patients while being sensitive to the action of anti-dementia drugs, has yet to be developed along the lines proposed by Siegfried (1985). Perhaps it should be made clear at this point that the needs of a psychopharmacologist wishing to measure the changes in patient behaviour brought about by the administration of a putative psychoactive substance are very different to the needs of a physician who wishes to assess the patient's clinical profile and response to the use of a therapeutic agent. The previous chapters bear witness to the numerous assessment modalities and scales for use in evaluating the severity and extent of a patient's clinical condition and many have proved useful in assaying a patient's response to various drug treatment regimens. However, none of those assessment techniques has a proven reliability in repeated measures designs where the methodology of an experiment requires multiple testing on the same rating instrument at frequent intervals over a short period of time.

Rating scales

Observer-rating scales are little more than recording, in a convenient manner, the opinion or judgement of an investigator concerning a patient's clinical or psychological state. Such scales must, therefore, be regarded as subjective measures and their value is dependent entirely on the quality of the data and the skill of the observer. Rating scales can be sensitive and of value in measuring the effects of psychoactive drugs if the raters are adequately trained and aware of the pitfalls of halo effects, constant error bias, proximity effects and the influence of their own personality and attitudes.

Self-rating scales are useful under certain circumstances but they have the obvious limitation that the rater must not be so ill or mentally incompetent as to be incapable of completing the requirements of the scale and reading and understanding the instructions. The elderly patient might have deficiencies in general intellectual skills and insight, reducing the usefulness of self-rating scales in such populations. If, however, the patient is seen to be capable of fulfilling the scale requirements then the self-assessment technique is most useful for monitoring the effects of treatment, although Paykel and Prusoff (1973) have shown the elderly to be persistent underraters compared to younger patients.

Should scales be needed for repeated measurement of short-term effects of treatment, then the 100 cm-line *visual-analogue rating technique* has much to offer both for observer- and self-rating. Aitken (1969) validated the visual analogue techniques of Freyd (1923) and Hayes and Patterson (1921). Bond and Lader (1974) demonstrated the utility of line analogue scales in drug evaluation studies, while Luria (1975) reported the validity and reliability of visual analogue ratings of mood in psychiatric populations. Subjects' responses to administration of hypnotics have been reliably assessed using self-completed line analogue scales (Oswald et al 1971, Hindmarch 1975, 1976, 1977) and using nurse ratings of sleep in populations of hospitalised geriatric patients (Murphy et al 1982). The clinically significant differences which exist between a sedative anti-anxiety agent (lorazepam) and a non-sedative one (clobazam) have been demonstrated (Hindmarch & Gudgeon 1980) on analogue ratings of alertness. Knox et al (1981) were able to distinguish between two anti-dementia treatments, hydergine and naftido-furyl, in a population of hospitalised geriatric patients using nurses' ratings of patients' ward behaviour on visual analogue scales. The sensitivity of line analogue rating scales is demonstrated by their ability to detect the 'stim-ulant' activity of 300 mg caffeine in late-middle-aged patients (Brezinova 1974) and the psychotropic action of hydergine in both volunteers and geriatric patients (Parrott & Hindmarch 1981). Scores on visual analogue rating scales for alertness and arousal were highly correlated with objective measures of CNS arousal (Parrott 1982) and Hamilton (1986) indicated a high correlation between analogue scales and standard psychopathological rating scales.

The great advantage of visual analogue rating scales is that with suitable design considerations they can be used to measure the changes in patient behaviour brought about both by pharmacotherapy and by non-drug treat-ments. Although such measures are eagerly sought by experimental psycho-pharmcologists it must be remembered that while being sensitive to rapid and large changes the scales are not as sensitive for the monitoring of slow and small alterations in behaviour, although weekly ratings over three to six months have been successfully made. Finally, some statisticians believe that all visual analogue scale scores should undergo some mathematical transformation to account for their grossly non-normal distribution. Other statisticians do, of course, doubt the value of this procedure.

Conventional rating scales for assessment of symptoms of illness and psychological function have been shown (Hamilton 1986) to be both valid, in doing what is required of them and reliable, in performing in a trust-worthy fashion but only when used for measuring the severity of a clinical condition. There is great inter-patient variability in the specific and indi-vidual nature of the presenting psychopathology and this produces great variability when scale ratings of individual patients are combined — an essential requirement of most clinical and scientific research. Furthermore, the factorial nature of most conventional rating scales implies that the same global score can be obtained by different patients with completely different symptom severity profiles. Such considerations cause the experimental psychopharmacologist to look elsewhere for more objective drug-sensitive measures of behavioural change.

Objective measures of drug response in the elderly

The fundamental problem associated with the use of objective assessments of drug effects is the validity of the measure used. The relationship between scores on a psychometric test of digit substitution and a patient's psycho-pathology is not at all obvious. In many instances and for many tests, it has to be admitted that there is little correlation between psychological test scores and clinical response to medication, or manifestations and severity of a psychological state or illness, or drug action. The task of psycho-pharmacology over the next few years will be to upgrade the correlation between psychometric test scores and observed clinical responses to drug treatment.

At present there are few objective assessments that warrant a status greater than being of use as an indirect measure of drug action. For a measure to have significance and be useful it must satisfy the criterion of simplicity in use mentioned earlier, it must be a valid measure of the underlying condition to be assessed, it must be consistently free from providing ambiguous results, test scores should be reliably age-related and the measure should be drug-sensitive.

There are few measures which satisfy many of these requirements but the measurement of critical flicker fusion thresholds (CFFT) seems to fulfil all the test criteria given above. The rest of this chapter reviews the evidence for such an assertion.

CRITICAL FLICKER FUSION THRESHOLD (CFFT)

The neurobiological basis of CFFT and the neuroanatomical localisation of the 'mechanism' are still the subject of much debate and experimental research (Ott & Kranda 1982). However, providing adequate experimental controls are imposed, then the measure serves as a sensitive index of the CNS activity of psychotropic drugs (Smith & Misiak 1976). As well as identifying those drugs which produce either a depression or elevation of the CFFT, Hindmarch (1982b) was able to show that the CFFT was both a reliable (from inter-study comparisons of the measured effects of a range of doses of the same drug) and a valid (from comparisons of CFFT scores with those obtained on other indices of psychomotor function) measure of the CNS effects of psychotropic agents. Measures of CFFT can not only discriminate between different antidepressants (Hindmarch 1982a), different benzodiazepine anti-anxiety agents (Hindmarch 1985), different antihistamines and neuroleptics (Hindmarch 1981) and different benzodiazepine hypnotics (Hindmarch 1984), but they have demonstrated the effects of nootropic agents such as hydergine (Hindmarch et al 1979, Parrott & Hindmarch, 1981) and dimethylxanthine (Parrott & Hindmarch 1975b). The increase of CFFT following the use of CNS stimulants has also been recorded (Parrott & Hindmarch 1975b, Hindmarch 1980).

Perhaps the most interesting development is the introduction of anti-dementia ('nootropic') drugs which can improve information-processing skills as measured on a variety of psychomotor functions without showing any increase in CFFT (Hindmarch & Subhan, 1985, Subhan & Hindmarch 1984, 1985). Such results would indicate that CFFT might be an important measure of the speed or rate of information processing but that other cognitive factors relating to the short-term storage, input and retrieval of information might be of greater importance in identifying potential anti-dementia drugs. However, the foregoing examples serve to illustrate the sensitivity of the CFFT to psychotropic drug effects.

The Leeds Psychomotor Tester and Leeds Flicker Fusion Tester* have been especially designed to facilitate the measurement of CFFT. The task requires the subject to press a button when a set of four flickering light-emitting diodes appear to stop flickering. The CFF threshold is measured using binocular vision and foveal fixation, to preclude the problems of changes in pupil size affecting the CFFT.

Using the psychophysical method of limits (Woodworth & Schlosberg 1958) the 'fusion' threshold can be found with descending frequencies and a 'flicker' threshold when the lights are seen to stop flickering and appear as a continuous light source. The CFFT is usually taken as the arithmetic mean of the 'fusion' and 'flicker' threshold scores and is calculated from at least three separate ascending and three descending scales. Small micro-processors control all aspects of the process and both the subject and experimenter tasks are simple and require no learning or complex training. There is little load placed on short-term memory capacity; all the subject is required to do is to press the hand-held button when the lights appear to flicker (descending scales) or become stable (ascending scales). Reliable CFFT readings in both patient and volunteer populations have been made over a wide age range from 20 to 90 years (Hindmarch 1981).

Variation of CFFT with age

Perhaps of greatest interest to the experimenter is the age-related regression and lowering of CFFT. This age-related decrease in CFFT was first reported in the 1940s (Brozek & Keys 1945, Weekers & Roussel 1946, Misiak 1947) using, collectively, subjects aged between 18 and 80 years. Colgan (1954), using 42 subjects aged between 65 and 95, demonstrated a linear age-related decline in CFFT and Coppinger (1955), with 120 subjects aged between 20 and 80 years, found a significant decline in CFFT after the seventh decade. More recent confirmation (Hindmarch 1981, Bobon et al 1982, Porter 1986) of the significant age-related decline in CFFT has been established for the age range 20–90 years. There are two studies (Miles 1950, Mackie & Beck 1965) which fail to show significant age-related changes in CFFT. They can, however, be ignored as contrary evidence, since one study used six glaucoma and six volunteer patients, and the other 29 voluteers with a mean age of 41 years and 29 brain-damaged patients with a mean age of 39 years: nor were the experimental designs adequate for measuring age-related CFFT changes.

Recent clinical studies of anxiolytics (Ponciano et al 1981, Hill et al 1981, Gringrass & Beaumont 1985) have shown that changes in CFFT have correlated with the clinical ratings of response to treatment in anxious patient populations and Khan et al (1984) and Hanks (1984) have shown CFFT scores to relate to the side-effects experienced by patients treated

* Leeds Psychomotor Services, 2 Acomb Court, Front Street, Acomb, York YO2 3BJ

with a variety of antidepressants. Siegfried (1985) has reported that the improvement of cognitive symptoms following treatment with nomifensine in late-life depression was evidenced, following a factor analysis of results, by the global improvement factor having its highest saturation with CFFT scores. Furthermore, Parrott and Hindmarch (1981) have shown the clinical response of patients to treatment with co-dergocrine mesylate to be related to their pre-treatment baseline CFFT levels.

The use of CFFT for measuring the effects of psychoactive drugs, especially in the elderly, has only recently received the attention it deserves. The evidence presented above shows that CFFT measures are simple to perform, reliably age-related, valid indicators of underlying clinical states and sensitive to the wide range of psychoactive substances currently used in the clinical management of elderly patients.

FUTURE PROSPECTS AND DIRECTION

A proper and appropriate assessment of psychoactive drugs in elderly patients is needed if the plethora of new substances for use in geriatric populations is to be properly evaluated and sorted to provide useful and safe drugs for clinical use. The current state of knowledge is not good. Too many studies employ tests insensitive to the drugs under consideration; others have test requirements which would task even the intellectually intact younger patient; many scales, developed for rating the severity of a clinical condition, are used quite wrongly to monitor the often transient effects of a particular medication, and most investigations do not use tests which have a proven age-related sensitivity.

It is not until pertinent clinical and experimental studies are performed using proper methodologies and controls that any real advance in the assessment of drug effects in the elderly patient will be made. However, the task of the psychopharmacologist is to develop the means of measuring drug effects and the role of the clinician is to assess the clinical impact of such drugs and treatment regimens in patient populations. The next few years promise to be exciting as the established clinical assessments are combined with the tests emerging from the psychological laboratory to properly assess the action of widely used drugs in an important and growing patient population.

REFERENCES

Adams R G 1974 Pre-sleep ingestion of two hypnotic drugs and subsequent performance. Psychopharmacologia 40: 185–190
Aitken R C B 1969 Measurement of feelings using visual analogue rating scales. Proceedings of the Royal Society of Medicine 62: 989–997
Anders T R, Fozard J L, Lillequist T D 1972 Effects of age on retrieval from short term memory. Developmental Psychology 6: 214–217
Axelrod S, Thompson L W, Cohen L D 1968 Effects of senescence on the temporal

resolution of somaesthetic stimuli presented to one hand or both. Journal of Gerontology 23: 191–195

Bergman K 1971 The neuroses of old age. In: Kay D W, Walk S (eds) 'Recent developments in geropsychiatrics'. British Journal of Psychiatry, Suppl. 6: 39–49

Bobon D P, Lecoq A, Mormont I 1982 Possible sensitivity to ageing of an overlooked (critical flicker fusion) variable. Pharmacopsychiatria 15: 57–60

Bond A, Lader M H 1974 The use of analogue scales in rating subjective feelings. British Journal of Medical Psychology 47: 211–218

Botwinik J 1973 Cognitive processes in maturity and old age. Springer, New York

Botwinik J, Storandt M, 1974 Cardiovascular status, depressive affect and other factors in reaction time. Journal of Gerontology 29: 343–348

Braithwaite R 1982 The pharmacokinetics of psychotropic drugs in the elderly. In: Wheatley, D (ed) Psychopharmacology of old age. Oxford University Press, Oxford, p: 46–54

Brezinova V 1974 Effect of caffeine on sleep: EEG study in late middle age people. British Journal of Clinical Pharmacology 1: 203–208

Broadbent D E, Heron A 1962 Effect of a subsidiary text on performance involving immediate memory by younger and older subjects. British Journal of Psychology 53: 189–198

Brozek J, Keys A 1945 Changes in flicker fusion frequency with age. Journal of Consulting Psychology 9: 87–90

Busse F W 1978 Duke longitudinal study: senescence and senility. In: Katz R, Terry R, Bick K (eds) Alzheimer's disease, senile dementia and related disorders. Raven Press, New York

Caranosos G J, Steward R B, Cluff L E 1974 Drug induced illness leading to hospitalisation. Journal of the American Medical Association 228: 713–717

Castleden C M, George C F, Marcer D, Hallett C 1977 Increased sensitivity to nitrazepam in old age. British Medical Journal 1: 10–12

Colgan C M 1954 Critical flicker fusion, age and intelligence. American Journal of Psychology 67: 711–713

Coppinger W W 1955 The relationship between critical flicker fusion and chronological age for varying levels of stimulus brightness. Journal of Gerontology 10: 48–53

Craik F I M 1979 Human memory. Annual Review of Psychology 30: 63–102

Denckla W D 1978 Interactions between age and the neuroendocrine and immune systems. Proceedings of the American Society of Experimental Biology 37: 1263–1267

Evans J G, Jarvis E H 1972 Nitrazepam and the elderly. British Medical Journal 4: 487

Finch C E, Felicio L S, Flurkey K et al 1980 Studies on ovarian–hypothalamic–pituitary interactions during reproductive ageing in C57/BL/6J mice. Peptides 1: 163–175

Fleischmann U M 1982 Zur Gauultigkeit des Zahlennachsprechens im hohen Lebensalter. Gerontology 15: 15–21

Freyd M 1923 The graphic rating scale. Journal of Educational Psychology 14: 83

Greenblatt D J, Shader R I, 1980 Effect of age and other drugs on benzodiazepine kinetics. Arzneimittel-Forschung 30: 886–890

Gringrass M, Beaumont G 1985 The effectiveness of repeated nocturnal doses of clobazam and dipotassium clorazepate on clinical measures of anxiety, patient ratings of mood and sleep and objective assessments of CNS activity. Royal Society of Medicine International Congress and Symposium Series 74: 73–79

Hamdy R, Zakaria G 1977 A special clinic for the over 65's in a G.P. surgery. Practitioner 219: 365–375

Hamilton M 1986 Assessment of Psychopathology. In: Hindmarch I, Stonier P D (eds.) Human psychopharmacology Wiley, London, p 1–17

Hanks G W 1984 The effects of amitriptyline and nomifensine on critical flicker fusion threshold in an elderly patient population. Royal Society of Medicine International Congress and Symposium Series 70: 95–97

Hayes M H, Patterson D G 1921 Experimental development of the graphic rating method. Psychological Bulletin 18: 98

Hill A J, Walsh R D, Hindmarch I 1981 Tolerability of nocturnal doses of clobazam in anxious patients in general practice. Royal Society of Medicine International Congress and Symposium Series 43: 133–140

Hindmarch I 1975 A 1,4 benzodiazepine, temazepam: its effect on some psychological aspects of sleep and behaviour. Arzneimittel-Forschung (Drug Research) 25: 1836–1839

Hindmarch I 1976 A sub-chronic study of the subjective quality of sleep and psychological measures of performance on the morning following night time medication with temazepam. Arzneimittel-Forschung (Drug Research) 26: 2113–2116

Hindmarch I 1977 A repeated dose comparison of three benzodiazepine derivatives (nitrazepam, flurazepam and flunitrazepam) on subjective appraisals of sleep and measures of psychomotor performance the morning following night-time medication. Acta Psychiatrica Scandinavica 56: 373–381

Hindmarch I 1980 Psychomotor function and psychoactive drugs. British Journal of Clinical Pharmacology 10: 189–209

Hindmarch I 1981 Measuring the effect of psychoactive drugs on higher brain function. In: Burrows G D, Werry J S (eds.) Advances in Human Psychopharmacology 2: 99–127

Hindmarch I 1982a Antidepressant drugs and performance. British Journal of Clinical Practice 19: 73–77

Hindmarch I 1982b Critical flicker fusion frequency (CFFF): The effects of psychotropic compounds. Pharmacopsychiatria 15, Suppl. 1: 44–48

Hindmarch I 1984 Psychological performance models as indicators of the effects of hypnotic drugs on sleep. In: Hindmarch I, Ott H, Roth T (eds) Sleep, benzodiazepines and performance. Springer, Heidelberg, p 58–69

Hindmarch I 1985 Anxiety, performance and anti-anxiety drugs. Journal of Clinical Practice 39 (5): 53–57

Hindmarch I, Gudgeon A C 1980 The effects of clobazam and lorazepam on aspects of psychomotor performance and car handling ability. British Journal of Clinical Pharmacology 10: 145–150

Hindmarch I, Subhan Z 1985 A preliminary investigation of (HWA 285) on psychomotor performance, mood and memory. Drug Development Research 5: 379–386

Hindmarch I, Parrott A C, Lanza M 1979 The effects of an ergot alkaloid derivative (Hydergine) on aspects of psychomotor performance, arousal and cognitive processing ability. Journal of Clinical Pharmacology 19: 726–731

Hurwitz N 1969 Predisposing factors in adverse reactions to drugs. British Medical Journal 1: 536–540

Inglis J, Caird W K 1963 Modified digit span and memory disorder. Disorders of the Nervous System 24: 46–50

Khan M C, Mahapatra S N, Stonier P D 1984 Nomifensine and mianserin: non-tricyclic antidepressants with distinct clinical profiles: a randomized double-blind study. Royal Society of Medicine International Congress and Symposium Series 70: 71–76

Kline D W, Szafran J 1975 Age differences in visual masking. Journal of Gerontology 30: 307–311

Knox J, Hindmarch I, Wallace M G 1981 Visual analogue scales in assessment of severe mental impairment. British Journal of Clinical Practice 16: 12–15

Lahtinen V, Lahtinen A, Pekkola P 1978 The effect of nitrazepam on grip strength, reaction time and subjective evaluation of sleep. Acta Pharmaceutica Toxicologia 42: 130–134

Learoyd B M 1972 Psychotropic drugs and the elderly patient. Medical Journal of Australia 1: 1131

Luria R E 1975 The validity and reliability of the visual analogue mood scale. Journal of Psychiatric Research 12: 51–57

MacDonald J B 1985 The role of drugs in falls in the elderly. Clinics in Geriatric Medicine 1: 621–636

MacDonald J B, MacDonald E T 1977 Nocturnal femoral fracture and use of barbiturate hypnotics. British Medical Journal 2: 483–485

McEntee W J, Mair R G 1978 Memory impairment in Korsakoff's psychosis: a comparison with brain noradrenergic activity. Science 202: 905–907

McGeer R, McGeer P L 1976 Generic treatment of psychologic disorders in the elderly. In: Terry R D, Gershon S (eds.) Ageing, Vol. 3 Raven Press, New York

McGhie A, Russell S M 1962 The subjective assessment of normal sleep patterns. Journal of Mental Science 108: 642–654

McGhie A, Chapman J, Lawson J S 1965 Changes in immediate memory with age. British Journal of Psychology 56: 69–75

Mackie J B, Beck C B 1965 Relations between age, I.Q. and critical flicker fusion. Perceptual Motor Skills 21: 875–878

Malpas A Joyce C R B 1969 Effect of nitrazepam, amylobarbitone and placebo on perceptual motor skills in normals. Psychopharmacologia 14: 167–177

Mendels J, Stern S, Frazer A 1976 Biological concepts of depression. In: Gallant D M, Simpson G M (eds) Depression: behavioural, biochemical, diagnostic and treatment concepts. Spectrum Publications, New York, p 19–74

Miles P W 1950 Flicker fusion fields: the effects of age and pupil size. American Journal of Opthalmology 33: 769–772

Misiak H 1947 Age and sex differences in critical flicker fusion thresholds. Journal of Experimental Psychology 37: 318–322

Murphy P, Hindmarch I, Hyland C M 1982 Aspects of short-term use of two benzodiazepine hypnotics in the elderly. Age and Ageing 1: 222–228

Oswald I 1981 Assessment of insomnia. British Medical Journal 283: 874–875

Oswald I, Lewis S A, Dunleavy D L F, Brezinova V, Briggs M 1971 Drugs of dependence though not of abuse: fenfluramine and imipramine. British Medical Journal 3: 70–73

Ott H, Kranda K 1982 Flicker techniques in psychopharmacology. Beltz, Basel

Paes De Sousa M, Fuguiera M L, Loureiro F, Hindmarch I 1981 Lorazepam and clobazam in anxious elderly patients. Royal Society of Medicine International Congress and Symposium Series 43: 12–123

Parrott A C 1982 Critical flicker fusion thresholds and their relationship to other measures of alertness. Pharmacopsychiatria 15: 39–43

Parrott A C, Hindmarch I 1975 Arousal and performance — the ubiquitous inverted U relationship. Comparison of changes in response latency and arousal levels with tranquillisers. IRCS Medical Science 3: 176

Parrott A C, Hindmarch I 1975b Clobazam, a 1,5 benzodiazepine derivative: Effects on anxiety, arousal and performance compared with those of CNS stimulants, sedatives and tranquillisers. IRCS Medical Science 3: 177

Parrott A C, Hindmarch I 1981 The effects of hydergine upon psychomotor performance, indices of alertness and behavioural ratings in studies involving normal and geriatric subjects. British Journal of Clinical Practice 61: 18–20

Paykel E S, Prusoff B A 1973 Response set and observer set in the assessment of depressed patients. Psychological Medicine 3: 209–216

Perry E K, Tomlinson B E, Blessed G, Bergman K, Gibson R H 1978 Correlation of cholinergic abnormalities with senile plaques and mental test scores in senile dementia. British Medical Journal 2: 1457–1459

Petrie W M 1983 Drug treatment of anxiety and agitation in the aged. Psychopharmacology Bulletin 19: 238–246

Ponciano E, Relvas J, Mendes F, Lameiras A, Vaz Serra A, Hindmarch I 1981 Clinical effects and sedative activity of bromazepam and clobazam in the treatment of anxious out-patients. Royal Society of Medicine International Congress and Symposium Series 43: 125–131

Porter L 1986 Age, personality and circadian effects on critical flicker fusion thresholds. PhD Thesis, University of Leeds

Post F 1968 The factor of ageing in affective illness. In: Coppen A, Walk A (eds.) Recent developments in affective disorders. Birtish Journal of Psychiatry 2: 105–116

Rudd T N 1972 Prescribing methods and iatrogenic situations in old age. Clinical Gerontology 14: 123–128

Sangiorgi G B 1979 Alcohol and drugs: interactions and iatrogenic injuries. In: Orimo H, Shimada K, Iriki M, Maeda D (eds) Recent advances in gerontology. Excerpta Medica, Amsterdam p 626–628

Schaie K W, Zelinski E 1979 Psychometric assessment of dysfunction in learning and memory. In: Hoffmeister F, Muller C (eds.) Age, learning ability and intelligence. Van Nostrand Reinhold, New York p 41–77

Seide L G, Thornton G F, Smith J W, Cluff L E 1966 Studies on the epidemiology of adverse drug reactions. Bulletin of the Johns Hopkins Hospital 119: 299–315

Shaw S M, Opit L J 1976 Need for supervision in the elderly receiving long-term prescribed medication. British Medical Journal 1: 505–507

Siegfried K 1985 Cognitive symptoms in late-life depression and their treatment. Journal of Affective Disorders, Suppl. 1: S33–S40

Siegfried K, Jansen W, Pahnke K 1984 Cognitive dysfunction in depression. Drug Development Research 4: 533–553

Smith J M, Misiak H 1976 Critical flicker frequency (CFF) and psychotropic drugs in normal human subjects — a review. Psychopharmacology 47: 175–182

Spriet A, Simon P 1985 Methodology of clinical drug trials. Karger, Basel

Subhan Z, Hindmarch I 1984 The psychopharmacological effects of Ginkgo biloba extract in normal healthy volunteers. International Journal of Clinical Pharmacology Research 4: 89–93

Subhan Z, Hindmarch I 1985 Psychopharmacological effects of vinpocetine in normal healthy volunteers. European Journal of Clinical Pharmacology 28: 567–571

Taub H A 1972 A comparison of young and old groups on various digit span tasks. Developmental Psychology 6: 60–65

Vingoe F J 1981 Clinical psychology and medicine: an interdisciplinary approach. Oxford University Press, Oxford

Walsh D A 1976 Age differences in central perceptual processing: a dichoptic backward masking investigation. Journal of Gerontology 31: 178–185

Walsh D A, Thompson L W 1978 Age differences in visual sensory memory. Journal of Gerontology 33: 383–387

Walsh D A, Till R C, Williams M V 1978 Age differences in peripheral perceptual processing. Journal of Experimental Psychology, Human Perception and Performance 4: 232–243

Weekers R, Roussel F 1946 Introduction a l'étude de la fréquence de fusion en clinique. Opthalmologia (Basel) 112: 305–319

Whittington F J, Petersen M 1979 Drug use and misuse among the elderly. In: Orimo H, Shimada K, Iriki M, Maeda D (eds.) Recent advances in gerontology. Excerpta Medica, Amsterdam p 629–630

Woodworth R S, Schlosberg H 1958 Experimental psychology. Methuen, London

Index